JOURNEY OF THE
ADOPTED SELF

Journey
of the
Adopted Self

A Quest for Wholeness

BETTY JEAN LIFTON

Fr Elizabeth —
who helps so many
on the journey —
B. J. Lifton

BasicBooks
A Division of HarperCollinsPublishers

Names of individuals interviewed by the author have been changed to protect their privacy.

Grateful acknowledgment is made for permission to reprint from the following:

Matsuo Basho by Makoto Ueda published by Kodansha International Ltd. Copyright © 1983 by Kodansha International Ltd. Reprinted by permission. All rights reserved.

"The Irish Cliffs of Moher," from COLLECTED POEMS by Wallace Stevens copyright 1952 by Wallace Stevens. Reprinted by permission of Alfred A. Knopf, Inc.

Library of Congress Cataloging-in-Publication Data

Lifton, Betty Jean.
Journey of the adopted self : a quest for wholeness / Betty Jean Lifton.
   p.   cm.
Includes bibliographical references and index.
ISBN 0-465-00811-9
1. Adoptees—United States—Psychology—Case studies. 2. Birthparents—United States—Case studies.   3. Parent and child—United States—Case studies. I. Title.
HV875.55.L53 1994
362.82'98'0973—dc20
   93–45482
   CIP

94 95 96 97 ❖/HC 9 8 7 6 5 4 3 2 1

To the memory of
my adoptive mother
Hilda
and my birth mother
Rae
who might have known
and even liked each other
in another life
and another adoption system.

CONTENTS

Part III
THE SELF IN TRANSFORMATION

PART I

The Self in Crisis

Was it you who came
Or was it I who went—
I do not remember.
Was that dream or reality?
Was I asleep or awake?
—BASHO

1

Betwixt and Between

"Then I shan't be exactly human?" Peter asked.
"No."
"What shall I be?"
"You will be Betwixt-and-Between," Solomon said, and
certainly he was a wise old fellow, for that is exactly how
it turned out.
—JAMES BARRIE, *PETER PAN IN KENSINGTON GARDENS*

MANY PEOPLE IDENTIFY WITH THE FAMILIAR condition of being Betwixt and Between, just as they identify with Peter Pan, the boy who did not want to grow up and face the responsibilities of the real world.

Peter, James Barrie tells us, is "ever so old," but really always the same age: one week. Though he was born "so long ago," he never had a birthday, nor is there the slightest chance of his having one. He escaped from his home when he was seven days old by flying out the window to Kensington Gardens.

Barrie doesn't tell us what was going on in Peter's family that after only seven days he knew he had to take off. But adoptees recognize Peter Pan as a brother. They, too, became lost children when they separated as babies from their natural families and disappeared into a place very much like never-never land. Like Peter, they are fantasy people. Denied the right to see their real birth certificates and the names of those who brought them into the world, they can't be sure they ever had a real *birth* day. They can never grow up because they are always referred to as an "adopted child."

I didn't realize that, like Peter, I wasn't "exactly human" until I was seven *years* old. It was the moment my mother told me I was adopted. Like most adoptive parents faced with breaking such bleak news, she tried to make adoption sound special, but I could feel the penetrating chill of its message. I was not really her child. I had come from somewhere else, a place shrouded in mystery, a place that, like myself, was Betwixt and Between.

As I listened, I could feel a part of myself being pulled into the darkness of that mystery—a place already carved out by Peter and the lost children. I would never be the same again.

This was to be our secret, my mother said. Hers and mine. I was not to share it with anyone—not even my father. It would break his heart if he suspected I knew. In this way I learned that secrecy and adoption were inextricably mixed, as in a witch's brew. By becoming a keeper of the secret, I was to collaborate in the family conspiracy of silence.

I didn't know then that our little family secret was connected to the *big* secret in the closed adoption system, just as our little conspiracy was connected to the larger social conspiracy around adoption. My mother and father had been assured that my birth records would be sealed forever, that I would never be able to learn the identity of my original family. Secrecy was the magic ingredient that would give our adoptive family the aura of a blood-related one. Secrecy was the magic broom that would sweep away all feelings of grief and loss on the part of any of the parties involved.

As I played my role of the good daughter—repressing a natural need to know where I came from—I was unaware that the secrecy inherent in the adoption system was shaping and constricting the self through which I organized my perception of reality. By denying my natural curiosity about where I came from, and my grief for my lost birth parents and for the child I might have been, I was shrinking my emotional space to the size permitted by that system. So, too, were my adoptive parents forced by the secrecy to shrink their emotional space as they denied their need to grieve for the natural child they might have had.

We were trapped in a closed family system where secrecy cut off real communication. We were not unlike those families who keep secrets around alcoholism, divorce, incest, and all the other things that family members are prone to hide from their neighbors and from one another.

I had no idea of this as a child. Having repressed my real feelings, I was not consciously aware of my pain. And as a consequence, I was not consciously aware of myself, except as someone unreal pretending to be real. I did things that my human friends did, even looked real in my high school and college graduation pictures, and in the photographs taken at my wedding, before I flew off with my husband to the Far East.

Perhaps I might have never been in touch with my feelings if, shortly after my return from Japan, a relative, recently married into my adoptive family, had not remarked about something she heard—that my natural parents had been killed in a car accident. Her statement was like a Zen slap, knocking me into another state of consciousness. I had been told my parents were dead, but I had not been told this story. When I tried to clear up the mystery of how they died, I was shocked to learn that they had been very much alive at the time of my adoption—and might still be.

Much that had lain repressed in me now began stirring. I started to wonder how my mind had been able to cut off the primal subject of who my parents were. Even if it were true that they were dead, why had I not asked any questions about them? After all, dead people have names; they have relatives they have left behind; they have graves. Why had I behaved as if death had wiped out all traces of their existence? It was my first conscious brush with the psychological mystery that forms the core of this book: How does a child's mind close down when it senses danger, and stay closed until some life event or crisis inadvertently jars it open? And what traumatic effects does this have on the child's growing sense of self?

As a writer, I set out to explore the psychological complexities of being adopted in my book *Twice Born: Memoirs of an Adopted Daughter*.[1] I was amazed, even alarmed, at what surfaced. The compliant adopted child within, as elusive as ever, was in many ways a stranger to the adult I had become. The anger, barely contained under what passed as irony and wit, could no longer be disguised as I dredged up memories of that child's helplessness in the face of mysteries too dark to comprehend. Even as I wrote about my search and reunion, I felt burdened with guilt, as if it were a disloyalty to my deceased adoptive parents. Nor had I fully absorbed the depths of what I had been through. I found a birth mother who had tried to hold on to me but, as an unmarried seventeen-year-old with no emotional or financial support, finally had to let go. Once she was defeated, she put on the scarlet letter—S for secrecy and shame—and did not tell either of her two husbands or her son about me. We met secretly twice before I had to leave for a summer in Japan. The psychic chaos I felt during those two months in Tokyo—as if I had fallen into a black hole—was so great that when I returned to the States I did not call her for fear of falling back into that dark place: a place, as we will see, that is not unfamiliar to many adoptees who have internalized the taboos of the closed adoption system. At the time of my reunion, there were no books to sanction my search for my mother or to prepare me for what I might experience.

My next book, *Lost and Found, the Adoption Experience*, was an attempt to write such a book and, in so doing, to illuminate the existential condition of being adopted.[2] I explored the psychological pitfalls that await adoptees all through the life cycle when they are forced to close off their real feelings and live *as if* their families of origin were not an inherent part of their identity. I laid out the difficult stages of awakening that adoptees experience before they dare to set out in search of the missing pieces in their lives.

As the search phenomenon was still relatively new at that time, the last part of the book gave an overview of the varieties of reunion experience and the psychological growth and accommodation that everyone—adoptee, adoptive parents, and birth parents—has to make.

Perhaps it was no accident that I chose to spend the next few years traveling back and forth to Poland and Israel for research on a children's-rights advocate named Janusz Korczak. Already renowned as a Polish-Jewish children's writer, doctor, and educator, Korczak became a legendary figure in Europe when he chose to accompany the orphans of the Warsaw Ghetto to Treblinka rather than save his own life. I realize now that I was drawn to Korczak as the idealized parent that all people, not just adoptees, seek—a parent who does not abandon his or her children, even in the face of death.

I was also drawn to the deep passion that Korczak had for defending the rights of the child, all children, regardless of race or creed. Children have a right to be treated by adults with tenderness and respect, as equals, not as masters and slaves, he wrote in *How to Love a Child*.[3] They have a right to grow into whoever they were meant to be, rather than who their parents want them to be. We can discern his fierce anger about how parents use children to fill their own egoistic needs in the writings of Alice Miller, who has been influenced by Korczak's work. And we can recognize the empathy they share for what we now call our "inner child," when she asks "whether it will ever be possible for us to grasp the extent of the loneliness and desertion to which we were exposed as children."[4]

With the publication of my Korczak biography, *The King of Children*,[5] I was released from his life to return to my own. I found an adopted woman waiting there, one who was more sensitive than ever to the lack of respect for the rights of adopted children to know who they are, and who was still absorbed with the psychological mysteries inherent in adoption. Once again I was faced with the same questions I had been grappling with earlier: Why do adopted people feel so alienated? Why do they feel unreal, invisible to themselves and others? Why do they feel unborn? Now, however, I had a new question that I felt would shed light on the others: How do adopted people form a sense of self in the closed adoption system?

The psychoanalyst Karen Horney defined the real self as the alive, unique, personal center of ourselves that wants to grow. When the real self is prevented from free, healthy growth because of abandoning its needs to others, one can become alienated from it. She quotes Kierkegaard on the alienation and loss of self as "sickness unto death."[6] Adoptees, who often say they feel they have no self, can be seen as expressing this despair. Having abandoned their need to know their origins for the sake of their adoptive parents, they are left with a hole in the center of their being. They feel they don't exist.

Of course, everyone has some kind of self. The adoptee born psychologically into the closed adoption system and shaped by its myths, secrets, and taboos from first conscious memory, and even before, has a unique self, an adopted self. But this fragile self has a basic inner division brought about by the need for denial that is built into the closed adoption system.

When I began research for this book, I was primarily interested in how secrecy affects the formation of the adopted self. I saw it as emotional abuse (of which adoptive parents are unaware) because it distorts the child's psychic reality. In the course of interviewing adoptees, however, I realized that it is not just secrecy that affects their sense of self but rather a series of traumas. This "cumulative adoption trauma" begins when they are separated from the mother at birth; builds when they learn that they were not born to the people they call mother and father; and is further compounded when they are denied knowledge of the mother and father to whom they were born.

I was not unfamiliar with the literature on trauma. My husband, Robert Jay Lifton, has been preoccupied with trauma on a massive scale.[7] As a journalist, I have reported on the war-wounded, orphaned, and traumatized children of Hiroshima, Korea, Vietnam, and the Holocaust. Still, as an adopted person, loyal to my adoptive parents, I didn't allow myself to see that closed adoption is also a form of trauma—an invisible and subtle one—until years later when I began noticing parallels between adopted children and children of alcoholics, children of survivors (even survivors themselves), and children who have been abused.

There has already been some misunderstanding about the linking of adoption to trauma. Far from being regarded as traumatic, adoption is still widely viewed as fortunate for the child who is rescued from homelessness, and for the adoptive parents who are rescued from childlessness. And in most cases it is. Yet the word *trauma* has been slipping into the psychological literature on adoption with increasing frequency in the last decade as clinicians come to realize the high psychic cost that both parent and child pay when they repress their grief and loss.

I have come to believe in the course of my research that it is unnatural for members of the human species to grow up separated from and without knowledge of their natural clan, that such a lack has a negative influence on a child's psychic reality and relationship with the adoptive parents. By enveloping their origins with secrecy, the closed adoption system asks children to disavow reality, to live *as if* they were born to the parents who raise them. They grow up feeling like anonymous people cut off from the genetic and social heritage that gives everyone else roots.

As I write this, we are Betwixt and Between change and stasis in the adoption field. We are between two systems: the traditional closed one that for almost half a century has cut adopted children off from their heritage, and an open one in which birth mothers choose the adoptive parents of their baby and maintain some contact with the family. It is a time when the best interests of the child, for which the adoption system was originally created, have become subordinate to the best interests of the adults, as fierce custody battles are waged over the few available healthy white infants.

Meanwhile, adoption records remain sealed in all but two states due to the influence of a conservative lobby group, the National Council for Adoption, that has managed to polarize the field by labeling those who seek reform as "anti-adoption."[8] Reformers who are working to open the system, as well as the records, however, are not anti-adoption but rather anti–closed adoption and pro–adopted children.[9]

While no amount of openness can take away the child's trauma of being separated from his mother, or save the child from the trauma of learning she was not born into the adoptive family, we can remove the secrecy that compounds those two traumas. We can begin to demystify the adoptive family and to see it with much of the strengths and weaknesses of other families. The conservatives argue for the myth of the happy adoptive family that has no problems because love conquers all. But we will see that something more is expected of the adopted family: an excess of happiness that is meant to make up for the excess of loss that everyone in the triad experiences, and an excess of denial to cover that loss. Exposing the myths of the adoptive family while still holding on to the very real need and love that parents and child have for each other has been the challenge facing me.

My previous work was deeply influenced by Erik Erikson's identity theory, which stresses the importance of continuity with one's past in the service of one's future.[10] Now I am also making use of theories of the self and concepts of psychological trauma to explore how adoptees put together a sense of self without that continuity.

Over the past few decades, I have been in touch in one way or another with hundreds of adopted men and women through my rap groups, my research interviews, and my part-time counseling practice with both adolescents and adults. For this book, I have drawn upon fifty in-depth interviews conducted with men and women adopted before six months of age, and over two hundred essay-style questionnaires that cover the adoptee's life cycle. I wanted to know how adoptees think that the separation from their birth mother and the secrecy in the adoption system have affected their sense of identity as well as their attachment to their adoptive parents. How they perceived themselves as children and adolescents, and how they perceive themselves now. What fantasies they had as children and adults. And, if they searched and had reunion, what the impact of that experience was on their sense of self.

I also sent questionnaires to fifty birth mothers about their experience in relinquishing their children and the quality of their reunions. And I interviewed twenty-five adoptive mothers about their reactions to their child's reunion with the birth parents. While the parental material threw light on the hopes, fears, and complexity of what both sets of mothers experienced, my main focus was on how it affected the adoptee's inner landscape.

The adoptees you will meet in this book are mostly successful people in that they are productive in their work and their private lives. But, as we will see, much of their psychic energy has been taken up with adjusting to the mystery of their origins by disavowing their need to have some knowledge of and contact with their blood kin.

In an attempt to understand what is unique about the adoption experience, I interviewed men and women who were children of survivors, alcoholics, divorce, and abuse. During the research, I was struck by how many feelings adoptees share with them—feelings of abandonment, powerlessness, low self-esteem, shame, depression, loss of trust, numbing, unreality, and rage. There is often the same attempt to mask one's true feelings, the same retreat into fantasy, the same difficulty with intimate relations, the same loneliness, and the same quest for an authentic identity.

And yet, it is not the same.

While it may be true that all families have secret motors under their hoods, there is a difference: the engine that propels the adoptive family system is the only one both created for and maintained by society. The only one to authorize, even promote, the separation of children from their birth families. The only one to build secrecy into the relationship between parent and child. The only one to make it taboo to know one's heritage.

The adoptive family has managed to "pass" until now; it remains, for the most part, an unexplored constellation that has escaped psychological detection. Many professionals regard its psychodynamics as being the same as that of other families, overlooking the trauma that the parents as well as the child experience due to the conspiracy of silence built into the closed system.

Because it is a social rather than a natural construct, we can see the strengths and malfunctions of the adoptive family as a laboratory to illuminate some of the most fundamental issues around mothering and mother loss, attachment and bonding, separation and loss, denial and dissociation, and the human need for origins. We can see the deep need that parents and child fill for each other, but we can also see the problems that occur between parents and child when secrets prevent open communication between them.

In *Lost and Found* I spoke of what I called the Adoption Game, a family system that operates by unspoken rules that require everyone in it to live a double life. While seeming to exist in the real world with their adoptive family, the children are at the same time inhabiting an underground world of fantasies and fears which they can share with no one. The adoptive parents also live a double life. Believing themselves to be doing everything for their children, they withhold from them the very knowledge they need to develop into healthy adults. This double role of savior/withholder eventually works against the adoptive parents, estranging them from their children. So, too, the birth mother is forced to live a double life from the moment she surrenders her baby. Advised to go on as if nothing has happened, she keeps secret what is probably the most important and traumatic event of her life.

In this book, I speak not of adoption games but of adoption ghosts. In many ways this book is a ghost story, for it tells of the ghosts that haunt the dark crevices of the unconscious and trail each member of the adoption triangle (parents and child alike) wherever they go. Unless one is aware of these ghosts, one will never be able to understand or to help the child who is adopted, the parents who adopt, or the parents who give up a child to adoption.

Who are these ghosts?

The adopted child is always accompanied by the ghost of the child he might have been had he stayed with his birth mother and by the ghost of the fantasy child his adoptive parents might have had. He is also accompanied by the ghost of the birth mother, from whom he has never completely disconnected, and the ghost of the birth father, hidden behind her.

The adoptive mother and father are accompanied by the ghost of the perfect biological child they might have had, who walks beside the adopted child who is taking its place.

The birth mother (and father, to a lesser extent) is accompanied by a retinue of ghosts. The ghost of the baby she gave up. The ghost of her lost lover, whom she connects with the baby. The ghost of the mother she might have been. And the ghosts of the baby's adoptive parents.

All of these ghosts are members of the extended adoptive family, which includes the birth family. In the search and reunion section of this book, I attempt to bring them out of the shadows and into the open, where they will materialize and mingle with one another in the real world. We are dealing with exorcism here; with placating hungry ghosts; with making the unconscious conscious.

We will see how adoptees cope with these ghosts as they struggle to put together an authentic adopted self. We will watch as they strive to get beyond Betwixt and Between—between their two mothers, between their two families, between their two selves, between hope and despair, and, at times, even between life and death.

This book, then, is about the search for the adopted self. It is not about the literal search in the material world, where one sifts through records and archives for real people with real names and addresses; but rather about the internal search, in which one sifts through the pieces of the psyche in an attempt to understand who one was so that one can have some sense of who one is and who one can become. It is the quest for all the missing pieces of the self so that one can become whole.

It is the search for the answer to that universal question—Who am I?—behind which, for the adoptee, lurks: Who is the mother who brought me into this mysterious world?

We will unravel these mysteries as we follow the adopted on their hero's journey through the dark woods and out into the high peaks of healing and transformation.

2

The Mothered /
Motherless Self

Our mothers
ancient
given to us for life
forever
standing in the windows
forehead glued to the pane
send forth their absence
watch out for us
who go away
who come back
who do not come back
—JERZY FICOWSKI, "OUR MOTHERS"

No ONE IS MORE ROMANTIC ABOUT MOTHERS AND
mothering than the adopted. They are like a blind person who tries to
envision the radiance that nature has bestowed upon a flower he will
never see. Those who know their mothers cannot imagine what it is like
not to know the woman who brought you into the world. What it is like
to be forbidden by law to see her face, hear her voice, know her name.
No one can imagine it because it is unimaginable.

The adoptive mother who feels threatened when the child she is raising asks quite naturally about his own mother—the "other mother," who
gave birth to him—does not stop to consider that she knows her own
mother, just as the legislator who approves sealing the identity of the
adopted child's mother knows his own mother, and the lobbyists who
work to keep adoption records sealed know their own mothers. How can
any of them understand what it is like to be among a select group of people who have been chosen by destiny, and by society, not to know?

Yet, just as the adopted are more romantic than anyone about mothers and mothering, they are also more disillusioned. Where is this mother for whom the child secretly grieves and fantasizes, and for whom the adult child still yearns? What kind of mother gives up her child and disappears without a word? What kind of mother surrenders her child out of love? What kind of mother is able to part from her child?

What is a mother, anyway?

A mother, according to the venerable Oxford English dictionary, is a woman who has given birth to a child; a woman who exercises control like that of a mother, or who is looked up to as a mother. Motherhood is the condition or fact of being a mother; the spirit of a mother; the feeling or love of a mother.

No dictionary can define a mother as well as a mother herself. An Abyssinian noblewoman speaks to us through the centuries:

> The woman conceives. As a mother she is another person than the woman without child. She carries the fruit of the night for nine months in her body. Something grows. Something grows into her life that never again departs from it. She is a mother. She is and remains a mother even though her child die, though all her children die. For at one time she carried the child under her heart. And it does not ever go out of her heart ever again. Not even when it is dead.[1]

The adopted child, who must grow up as if dead to his mother, has the need to believe that the woman who carried him in her body still carries him in her heart; just as he needs to believe that the woman who did not carry him in her body, but who cares for his daily needs, carries him in her heart. The task of adopted children is to reconcile these two mothers within them—the birth mother who made them motherless and the psychological mother who mothered them.

BOTH YOUR MOTHERS

I have learned over the years that there are many ways to have a mother, and many ways to lose one. While I was in Warsaw doing research on Korczak's life, Bieta Ficowski took me aside and confided the secret that her mother had kept from her until shortly before she died. On her deathbed she confessed that Bieta was not really her daughter.

Bieta's mother told her that during the war she had agreed to find hiding places for Jewish babies smuggled out of the ghetto. They were to be hidden for the duration of the war and then returned to surviving members of their families. However, she fell in love with Bieta and decided to keep her for herself. When the war ended, she could not bring herself to turn the child over to the Jewish authorities who were taking orphans to Palestine. She felt particularly guilty about hiding Bieta indoors on the day Jewish officials came into their courtyard inquiring about children. Only now, as she lay dying, could Bieta's mother reveal the truth.

Bieta was deeply shocked, but she forgave the only mother she knew. During her search for her Jewish family, Bieta learned that her mother and father, and all of her relatives except for an uncle now in America, had perished in the death camps. She had to absorb the fact that she was not who she thought she was. She had two mothers: one who abandoned her in order to save her and one who rescued her but withheld her identity from her. Bieta was still trying to work through her feelings of grief and anger for her loss and to reconcile her two mothers in some loving way within herself. Her husband helped her do this with a poem, "Both Your Mothers," that brought these two women together against a background of history:

> . . . But the mother
> who was saved in you
> could now step into crowded death
> happily incomplete
> could instead of memory give you
>
> for a parting gift
> her own likeness
> and a date and a name
>
> so much
>
> And at once it happened
> that someone hurriedly took care
> of your sleep
> and then stayed for a long always

and washed you of orphanhood
and wrapped you in love
and became the answer
to your first word

That was how
both your mothers taught you
not to be surprised at all
when you say
I am.[2]

To discover that one has two mothers may not be as dramatic for adoptees who are not Holocaust survivors, but it is just as shocking and difficult to come to terms with. Yet everyone has two mothers if we believe the psychological theory that we all split our mothers into the good one and the bad one. The psychological task, we are told, is eventually to realize that they are one and the same person, both good and bad. Some professionals believe that adoptees make one of their mothers the good mother and the other the bad one. But I think we could say that adoptees tend to split each mother into good and bad. This means that they have two good mothers and two bad mothers—four mothers in all who must be reconciled within themselves.

Think of it like this.

The adoptive mother is good in that she rescued the child, but she is bad in that she may have stolen the child. The birth mother is good in that she gave the child life, but she is bad in that she abandoned the child.

The adoptive mother is the authentic mother because she raised the child, but she is inauthentic because she is not the mother whom Mother Nature chose.

The birth mother is the authentic mother because she bore the child, but she is inauthentic because she did not mother it.

The child is attached to his adoptive mother by social history: she is the repository of his life experiences. He is still attached to the birth mother by his prenatal experiences: she is the repository of his original self.

What are adoptees to do with this conflicting imagery of good and bad mothers who rescue, steal, love, and abandon them? Who alternately stand in opposition and merge as one? To whom are they to be loyal? Which one of them is real?

Who Is the Real Mother?

From biblical times we have been asking who is the real mother, the one who bears the child or the one who raises it? King Solomon settled a dispute between two women claiming a child by ordering that he be cut in two by a sword so that each woman could have half. When the woman who had given birth to the child gave up her claim so that the child could live, she was declared the real mother. Blood was clearly thicker than water.

But in his play "The Caucasian Chalk Circle," Bertolt Brecht changed the verdict. The judge placed the child inside a chalk circle and instructed each woman to pull on an arm until the child was forced out to one side or the other. When the adoptive mother refused to take part in what would only tear the child apart, she was declared the real mother. In this case, adoption was thicker than blood.

So, who is the *real* mother? To be *real*—I turn to the dictionary again—means to have an existence in *fact* and not merely in appearance, thought, or language. Both mothers are *real* by that definition for both do *in fact* exist. The problem is that there is no definition in the dictionary for a *real mother*. We have to make up our own. For me, a real mother is one who recognizes and respects the whole identity of her child and does not ask him to deny any part of himself. This is difficult to do in a closed adoption system that requires the child be cut off from his heritage, and that pits the original mother against the replacement mother. If one mother is real, the other must be unreal. The stakes are high: the real mother has the power to cancel out the unreal mother, as if her motherhood never existed.

The adoptive mother believes that she is the *real* mother because she is the one who got up in the middle of the night and was there for the child in sickness and health. The birth mother believes that she is the *real* mother because she went through nine months of sculpting the child within her body and labored to bring it forth into the world.

They are both right.

The adoptive mother who loves and cares for the child is the real mother. And the birth mother who never forgets her child is the real mother. They are both real, and yet, because the child will remain burdened by the mystery of mothers, they are both unreal—as is the child.

Who Is the Real Child?

By denying that adoptees have two real mothers, society denies them their reality. And so it should not surprise us that adoptees do not feel real. They expend much psychic energy searching for the elusive *real child within*, only to find that child's identity hopelessly entangled in the reality and unreality of the two mothers. For deep inside every adoptee there is a chalk circle where he or she is pulled this way and that by two competing mothers. By the one who is there and by the one who is absent. (The fathers are still shadowy figures in this terrain.) The adopted child lives in fear of being torn apart by these two mothers, by divided loyalties, which is another way of saying that the child lives in fear of fragmentation.

Barry, a forty-three-year-old man adopted when five days old, described feeling he was in the middle of a "no-man's land," with his adoptive mother and birth mother on either side: "In different ways I was a part of both families, yet belonging to neither. My adoptive parents raised me, sacrificed for me, and loved me as much as they were able to. I was grateful—and hated them at the same time. I yearned to be with my birth mother with a passion unequaled in my life before or since. How could she give me birth and then give me away? I couldn't make sense of it. All I knew was that I needed that blood connection and didn't have it. I was stuck in that 'no-man's land.'"

It is still difficult for adoptive mothers and fathers to understand that the secrecy around the adoptee's blood connection can sentence their children to a no-man's land. Love is enough to forge the bonds between them, the adoptive mother thinks while the child is young and cuddly. But love based on a mother's own gratification at having a child to raise, rather than empathy for the child's inner struggle to cope with the mysteries of his existence, is not enough. It may not even be love, if we think of Janusz Korczak's and Alice Miller's concept of mother love as unselfish and putting the psychological needs of the child first. An adopted child can feel love and gratitude to his adoptive mother and father for their nurturing, and still feel resentment, as Barry did, for their keeping his heritage a secret.

Adoptees can find a way out of their no-man's land by escaping to a mythic realm beyond it. For here is the paradox: when one lives in no-man's land, one can invent and reinvent oneself at will. Not being entrapped by roots, the adopted can become anyone or anything they want, both real and unreal. Both mythic and divine.

It seems only natural that the adopted child, whose mother has mysteriously disappeared, would identify with a mythic hero who has also lost his mother at birth. Child heroes, such as Moses, Oedipus, Sargon, Romulus and Remus, were all abandoned to fate before being found and rescued by kindly people. They were forced to endure many trials, but had the superhuman resilience to survive. Carl Jung points out a striking paradox in child myths: while the *child* seems in continual danger of extinction, he possesses powers far exceeding those of ordinary humanity. Jung relates this to the psychological fact that though the child may be insignificant and unknown, a "mere child," he is also "divine."[3]

Adopted children feel akin to the children in fairy tales too: motherless babes who are suckled by animals; crafty changelings who replace human children; and magical children found in forests or on riverbanks. They identify with Starman, who is at home in the skies, and with Superman, who, after falling from another planet, lived a dual life much as they do—pretending to be a *real* person in everyday relationships and then disappearing on secret exploits that he shared with no one. Howard (whose story we will follow later) remembers not being able to read at grade level until he discovered that Superman was adopted. He began collecting and reading every issue of Superman's adventures, and he's been reading ever since.

But while the hero has a clear mission to fight for good over evil, to save maidens from dragons, or to found cities, adoptees can't help but wonder why they were put on earth. Searching for some meaning in their strange fate, they often feel they are connected to the divine mysteries of creation, and are destined to do great things in the world.

"Everyone is a child of God who gets lost," a Jungian analyst tells me. "Usually one attaches to the parents who become the main caretakers. But the adoptee makes the God connection, and develops a nonhuman relationship to the cosmos."[4] Because of the ambiguity of their origins, it is not unusual for adoptees to feel split in their identity between human beings and the gods—much like the legendary twins Castor and Pollux, one of whom was mortal and the other immortal.

Adoptees, then, live with a dual sense of reality: wanted and unwanted, superchild and monsterchild, immortal and mortal. One part of the self is tied to an earthly existence, while the other is in touch with a higher destiny.

One part is real, the other unreal. One part is chosen, the other abandoned.

The mother who relinquishes her baby for adoption, for whatever reason, does not perceive it as an act of abandonment, but rather as a way of giving the child a better life than she can offer. She is opting for what the Romans called "the cure for chance"[5]—the chance to make up for a hapless birth.

But the baby, vulnerable and helpless, is not ready to start gambling on chance. It wants its own mother, and can only perceive of her disappearance as an abandonment. As we will see, this sense of abandonment and mystery about origins will shape the child's life.

3

The Conspiracy of Silence

Secrets lie on the boundary between
self and others.
—AMY BUNIM LAWRENCE

DEEP IN THE CONSPIRACY OF SILENCE AROUND
adoption is the social history of the abandoned child. The very word
adoption has dark connotations that call forth images of exposure and
infanticide that society tries to repress. Freud turned to the myth of Oedipus, abandoned as a baby, for one of his basic theories on human behavior: the child's attraction to the parent of the opposite sex. But as an
adoptee who has always had an affinity for Oedipus, I recognize the
myth as an adoption story—a morality tale about the desperation of
birth families who dispose of their own kin, and the consequences of
secrecy in the adoptive family.

Oedipus is the quintessential adoptee, unaware of why fate has singled him out and driven by forces he does not understand. He was
abandoned because his father had been warned by the Oracle at Delphi
that he would be killed by his son. He grew up not knowing that he
had been left hanging by his pierced heels from a tree on a mountaintop. Exposed, abandoned, rejected, unwanted—whatever one wants to
call it—it was not an auspicious beginning. He survived only because a

kindly shepherd cut him down and gave him to another shepherd, who took him to King Polybus and Queen Merope of Corinth to raise as their own.

Like so many well-meaning adoptive parents since then, the king and queen did not have the heart to tell Oedipus the dismal truth: that he was not their natural son. A conspiracy of silence fell over the court. Oedipus didn't suspect that he was adopted (so Sophocles would have us believe) until he was taunted by a drunken man at a banquet. When he confronted his parents, they lied to protect their secret, assuring him that he was their own flesh and blood. And so Oedipus fled to another kingdom to escape the terrible fate the oracle had predicted for him: that he would murder his father and marry his mother. Of course, he wound up doing just that, since even the oracle didn't tell him he was adopted. He murdered an imperious stranger, his father, Laius, at a crossroads near Thebes (surely Oedipus was an angry young man), and married the widow, who was his mother, Jocasta.

At the end of the play, Oedipus blinds himself when he learns the truth of who he is. If only Oedipus' adoptive parents had not kept the story of how he came to them a secret, we sigh, the tragedy could have been avoided.[1]

FAMILY SECRETS

Now that the modern family is recognized as a psychological unit with its own rituals, myths, and value systems, we can see adoptive families—and all families—more clearly. A family that allows open and honest communication among its members is considered healthy. A family that cuts off communication with secrecy is considered dysfunctional. Oedipus' family, like all adoptive families that harbor secrets about the adopted child, is dysfunctional by these standards.

While some secrets can bring people together by giving them a sense of intimacy and sharing, secrets can be destructive if they cause shame and guilt, prevent change, render one powerless, and hamper one's sense of reality. When there are secrets in a family system, there is a conspiracy of silence. The conspiracy does not have to be agreed upon verbally, but can be unconsciously communicated to members of a clan. A conspiracy holds family members together like a negative energy force, but it also keeps them apart. Stronger than any one individual, it controls whatever interactions take place. It is the internal censor. It feeds on the emotions of its victims like the Minotaur in the labyrinth: it demands tributes of loyalty and submission. Invisible as radiation, it can be as lethal.

To understand the psychological fallout that adopted children experience in a family that keeps their background secret, it is essential to think about the nature of family secrets. I found it helpful to look at the three major kinds laid out by the psychologist Mark Karpel: the *individual* secret, which one person keeps from the others; the *internal* secret, which a few family members keep from another member; and the *shared* secret, when all the family members band together to keep outsiders from knowing what is happening inside.[2]

It is the internal secret that I am concerned with here, the secret that is kept from the adopted child. We also find this secret operating in stepparent families when children are not told the identity of a deceased or divorced parent (usually, but not always, the father) who disappeared from their lives when they were too young to remember. We find it in survivor families when children are not told that the mother or father raising them is not really their parent, that the real parent died in the Holocaust.

The secret in today's adoptive family is not that the child is adopted but *who* the child is. The adoptive parents often know things about the birth parents that they do not reveal. Once the child suspects that primal secrets are being kept from her, she may come to perceive her parents as adversaries who stand between her and her rightful parents. She may envy "normal" children, those raised by their real mothers and fathers, for knowing how to maneuver in the real world. Cut off from blood roots that could ground her in the universe, she feels like a foreigner who needs a guidebook to show her the way that others know naturally.

BEHIND THE CONSPIRACY

Adoption has always wavered between the legal fiction that a child is reborn into the adoptive family and the folk belief that blood is thicker than water. Before modern times, laws reflected the ambiguity in societal attitudes by leaving loopholes for the parties involved. The ancient Baby-

lonian Code of Hammurabi, the oldest set of laws to make adoption provisions, allowed all children, except those of courtiers, to return to their
original families if they so wished. And Roman law, concerned primarily
with property and inheritance rights, permitted birth parents to reclaim
their abandoned children if they paid the expenses incurred by the
adoptive parents. The 1804 Code of Napoleon, which was the beginning
of modern adoption legislation, stipulated that adoptees could maintain
their birthright.

It is hard to remember that until the last half-century, adoption was an
open transaction in this country, often an informal arrangement between
an unmarried pregnant woman and a childless couple who befriended
her. The birth mother may or may not have kept contact with the family,
but she had the security of knowing who was raising her baby, and the
adoptive parents had the security of knowing the background of their
child.[3] The situation changed when licensed adoption agencies were set up
in the 1920s to protect the interests of homeless and indigent children—
who, since the middle of the last century, had been used by wealthy families as indentured servants or sent out West on Orphan Trains to work on
farms. But by the late 1930s these agencies shifted their focus from the
needs of dependent children to those of infertile, middle-class couples
who desired healthy, white infants.

The original purpose of legal secrecy in the adoption field was to protect
the newborns from the stigma of being born out of wedlock, not to deny
them their birthright. Social workers urged the courts to seal away the
baby's birth certificate, which was stamped *Illegitimate*, and to issue an
"amended" one that substituted the names of the adoptive parents for those
of the birth parents. As the policy of sealing records spread rapidly from
state to state after World War II, however, it lost sight of its original purpose
and became a means of protecting the adoptive family from interference by
the birth family. Secrecy effectively pitted adoptive mothers against birth
mothers and kept adopted children separated from their birth families.

"There is no other situation in which the law of the land reaches into
the private lives of people so intimately to limit the right of association," a
professor of social work tells us.[4] A law professor, who is also a single
adoptive mother, points out: "The legal system ordinarily makes no
attempt to write out of existence, by sealing records, or other such mecha-
nisms, the various parental figures who walk out of their children's lives,
such as the divorced parent who relinquishes custody. It is only in regulat-

ing adoptive families—families formed in the absence of any blood link—that the government feels that it has to seal records so as to figuratively destroy the existence of the family that *is* linked by blood."[5]

Ambivalence and Shame

When we try to understand why state legislatures collude in this injustice to all the members of the adoption triangle, we begin to see that secrecy protects not only adoptive parents but everyone in society from their ambivalence and shame about adoption arrangements, and their own fears of abandonment. For adoption, as the child analyst Paul Brinich points out, includes elements that are drawn from the very roots of human psychology: fertility and infertility; love and hate; acceptance and rejection.[6]

Taking in a stranger's child requires a leap of faith and the repression of doubts on everyone's part. The public praises adoptive parents for rescuing "abandoned" children, while secretly pitying them for not having children "of their own." One can still hear comments like: "I wouldn't want to adopt—you don't know what you're getting." Or, "If it didn't come out of my body, then it isn't mine."

A woman writes me that even after adopting her daughter, she felt excluded from a special club of mothers. No one talked about birth experiences with her, and when she spoke about her daughter's arrival from Korea, everyone was enthusiastic and polite but she felt "special" and "excluded." Only after she gave birth to a second daughter did she feel admitted to the club: "I sensed that people no longer felt sorry for me that I was so desperate that I was 'forced' to adopt because I couldn't get pregnant."

Secrecy hides the ambivalence and shame that people feel about rejecting children who are handicapped or of another race. Yet their desperate emotional need for a child can eventually lift couples across racial and geographical boundaries until one baby is as good as another, and no price is too high. In a book of letters between two infertile women who were eventually able to adopt, one woman is courageous enough to admit her ambivalence and fears:

> But for now some secret thoughts that shame me: I wonder if she will be pretty (would our biological child have been?) or smart (an article in today's paper on identical twins raised apart gives credence to the increasingly popular notion that IQ skills are genetic . . . that envi-

ronment plays a lesser part than previously thought). In other words, can I and will I love her "as if" she is my own . . . can I make her my own? From what every other adoptive mother I know has told me, my fears are common.[7]

Secrecy also hides the ambivalence and shame of the birth mother, who may have wanted to keep her child but could find no way to do so in a society that encourages adoption not only over abortion but over preserving the relationship between mother and baby. A birth mother, urged by her parents and social workers to relinquish the son with whom she was reunited eighteen years later, recalls:

> I truly believed them when they said I would get over it. When I returned to the adoption agency begging for information and they called me neurotic, I believed them. I thought something was terribly wrong with me. I only saw my baby once as he was born. They took him away and advised me not to see him. I did not touch him, feed him or hold him. I feel very badly about that decision now. I felt very bonded to him in utero. I talked to him a lot and tried to explain why things were going to be the way they were. When he was gone, I was devastated.

Despite the trend toward openness in our society, we are told by many sources that shame and ambivalence still pervade the adoption world. The law professor Judith Resnik writes that "an anachronistic but potent stigma still clouds adoption: shame, felt by single mothers, infertile parents and illegitimate children alike."[8] Yet I notice that this stigma is often fanned by some adoptive parents themselves. As they blame societal forces—the psychological literature or the search movement—for its existence, they have the need to deny that the stigma they inveigh against comes more from within than without. Indeed, by constantly crying "stigma," and oversimplifying the issues involved, they close the subject off from any real understanding.[9] They are, as the psychoanalyst Helene Deutsch phrases it, "not free of prejudice against their artificial motherhood and their adopted children's origin. They want . . . to preserve the illusion that they are connected with the adopted child by a complete experience of motherhood, and to find a confirmation of this illusion in the child."[10] It seems that the more adoptive parents devalue biologic ties, the more they call attention to the pain of their infertility.

Infertility

Infertility, like adoption, goes back to ancient times. There have always been infertile people ready to adopt the infants abandoned by others. ("The kindness of strangers," the historian John Boswell calls it.)[11] Why else would Oedipus' parents, the king and queen of Corinth, have taken in a baby whose bloodlines were shrouded in mystery? And why would they keep it a secret, except for their embarrassment about their inability to conceive?

As couples wait longer to have children, there has been a rising rate of infertility.[12] It is a shock to learn that the child you dreamed of having—"a girl for you and a boy for me," as the lyrics of a popular song went—is never going to exist. Infertility can challenge one's sense of identity. It can cause one to doubt one's sexuality and parenting abilities, damage one's self-esteem, threaten one's marital relationship. It can make one feel angry, guilty, sad, and powerless. It can give one a sense of loss, which is considered a major explanation for depression—for women, loss of the experience of pregnancy, childbirth, and breast feeding;[13] for both men and women, loss of the "biological dream child."[14] Fertility specialists warn that adoptive parents need to come to grips with their losses before they can help their adopted children tolerate theirs; that preparation to adopt should include exploration of feelings of sadness and grief surrounding infertility, so that parents don't project their unconscious anger and fantasies onto the child. (The fact that many desperate couples spend their life savings on the latest high-tech reproductive methods to produce a child of their flesh and blood is not lost on adoptees who are asked to believe that they were "chosen" out of choice.) Once people accept that they will not conceive and make the decision to adopt, the trauma of their infertility may get suppressed, but not necessarily resolved. For, paradoxically, the child who rescues adoptive parents from childlessness is also a reminder of their infertility.

When we talk about adoption, then, we are talking about loss as well as attempts to rectify that loss. We are talking about being and not being. The child who could not be born to those who wanted it and the child who was born to those who did not want it. When we talk about adoption, we are talking about the conspiracy of silence that surrounds those mysterious unbegotten and misbegotten births. It is the silence and mystery that sink early into the adoptee's soul.

4

The Hidden Relationship

Cradled by our fall, we cried,
"Only what is born lives!"
O, stolen keys to forgotten doors;
the true mystery is how we got here.
—L. S. ASEKOFF, "KAFKA'S ANGEL'S"

BIRTH IS THE GREAT MYSTERY THAT ADOPTEES TRY to solve in order to feel alive. They say things like, "I didn't come from anyone, so how am I here?" They speak of how they "came to be" rather than how they were born. They paint pictures of babies falling through space, trailing umbilical cords still attached to shadowy female figures. "We were on a descent downwards," is the way one man explained it. "We may have been lucky to be saved by being adopted—but we still experienced falling." This sense of a terrifying free-fall through the universe is a consequence of adoptees' not feeling rooted in their own factual being and history. They feel a fundamental disconnection from themselves and those around them, which they describe as feeling as if they are in a fog, weightless, floating above the earth.

"When I meet adoptees, I feel I am meeting people who have no selves," observes Rachel, a graphic artist adopted at six days. "I feel they are spirits flitting around, that they don't own their souls. Instead of saying what is on their minds, they say what is expected of them—as if you could form a self by just pasting on images. They don't have a sense of being in their own body and feeling comfortable there. I know, because all of this is true for me."

This is *normal* talk for adoptees to make among themselves, although they often say they don't feel normal. It's not unusual for them to say they feel like members of a new species: "one that hasn't been discovered yet." They complain of not catching on to things that are obvious to others, of feeling off balance, of fading in and out, of losing energy—as if there were a slow leak in the self. They might say they feel that they don't exist or that they have an imaginary self. Sometimes they even say they feel they have no self—not "I feel I am not myself today," but rather "I am not my self any day."

What do they mean by that? When does the sense of self begin? Is a baby born with a self, or does it have a self only when it can talk and reflect upon its experiences? Did the adoptee have a self at birth? And, if so, what was it feeling?

THE EMERGING SELF

We still understand very little of the preconscious, preverbal experience of any infant, but the psychoanalyst Daniel Stern believes that infants begin to experience an emergent sense of self from birth, long before self-awareness and language. While acknowledging that we can never "crawl inside an infant's mind," he makes "working hypotheses" about the infant's subjective experience from recent infant research and his own observations. Stern posits that between two and six months, the infant has already consolidated the sense of a core self as a separate, cohesive, bounded, and physical unit. This will be followed by a subjective self, between seven to fifteen months, when it adds a capacity for psychological intimacy to that of physical intimacy. The infant's success in bringing together its developing selves will influence how it perceives itself, how it relates to the parent, and eventually how it will relate to others.[1]

Once when we were dining together during a conference, I asked Stern if he thought the adopted baby experienced those same psychological stages. He said he had never explored this. Most people haven't, but we can do some conjecturing on our own. Since most infants destined for adoption used to be put into foster care for one to three months before being placed with the adoptive family, we know that the baby experienced some stress: the trauma of separation from its mother, then adjust-

ment to a foster mother from whom it was separated, and then adjustment to the adoptive mother. We have to wonder how the baby's subjective self was reacting to these multiple dislocations and whether it was
able to consolidate a cohesive core self by six months, like other babies.

How convenient it would be if we could interview the baby who has
just been separated from its mother and put into another woman's arms.
How are you feeling about this? we could ask. Can you tell the difference between the woman who held you for a few days after birth and
the woman who is holding you now? Do you feel that you were abandoned and rejected by your mother, or is one mother the same as
another to you?

As a writer, I've managed to ask the baby within me these questions in
different ways over the years, even when I didn't know what terrain I
was mining. In an absurdist play I wrote long before I was in conscious
touch with my adoption issues, I had a newborn baby jump up from its
hospital crib and declare to its unwed mother: "Mama, I'll not stay with
you another minute. You are a disgrace to me. I'll go out and adopt
myself a respectable family, get myself a good name, and have no more to
do with you and your kind." And off she went packing, with a bottle
between her toothless gums.[2]

This baby was smart enough to leave before being left, something that
many adult adoptees are doing in their relationships to this day. But we
have to wonder: Does the baby destined for adoption know even before
it is born that it is going to be abandoned? Does the fetus get a physiological message of its dark fate from the turbulent wrenching of the
womb as its mother's body lies convulsed with grief? The baby can't tell
us with words, but we can look at some prenatal research materials for
clues.

THE PRENATAL SELF

Daniel Stern admits that he is seen by some traditional developmentalists
as making inferential leaps about what is going on in the infant's psyche.
Yet there is an even more speculative group of researchers working in
prenatal studies who are leaping even higher as they attempt to chart the
psychic development of the fetus. Just as Stern would like to crawl into
the infant's mind, these researchers would like to crawl into the womb
with the embryo and fetus and spy on what's going on. And with the

window that advanced technology has opened to the mysterious uterine world, it sometimes seems that they are doing just that.

In his book *The Secret Life of the Unborn Child*, the psychiatrist Thomas Verny, one of the pioneers in prenatal work, tells us that the unborn child is a feeling, remembering, aware being, and that what happens to it in the nine months between conception and birth molds and shapes its personality, drives, and ambitions in important ways. By the sixth or seventh month, it is capable of making fairly subtle discriminations in its mother's attitudes and feelings, and, more important, it starts acting on them. He describes the fetus's comfort as it listens to the reassuring rhythm of the mother's heartbeat, which is one of the major constellations of its universe. Its steady thump-thump comes to symbolize tranquillity, security, and love. In its presence, the unborn baby usually flourishes.[3]

Researchers can now chart the fetus's movements as it stretches and flexes, sucks its thumb, shakes with hiccups, twitches, and even opens its eyelids at seven months. They know the fetus is sensitive to stimuli from without as well as within. Audiologists have discovered that the unborn child prefers Vivaldi and Mozart to rock music, which prompts furious kicking, and that from the twenty-fifth week on, a fetus will literally jump to the beat of an orchestra drum. One experiment even demonstrated that the newborn can remember what it heard in utero, by measuring its reaction to its mother's voice reading the same story she read aloud to it before birth. Tests also show that a three-day-old baby can recognize its own mother's milk, as if it is programmed by nature to be with the woman who bore it.

Stern, as mystified as many other developmentalists by the prenatalists' findings, suggests that "for some events, recognition memory appears to operate across the birth gap." Prenatalists go even further. They now believe that the beginnings of awareness and early memory can be traced back to the womb.

What does the adopted baby remember from back there? I've wondered over the years as I observed the intense need of some adoptees to find and be reunited with the mother they were merged with in the womb. Does the baby know that the mother it was programmed to be with is missing, and that there is another mother in her place? Can you miss someone you didn't have a relationship with after that initial separation?

I was mulling over such questions when I came across some theoretical writing by Christopher Deeg, who is both a psychologist and an adoptee.

Deeg speaks of the baby's "hidden" relationship to the mother as the origin of the self. He speculates that the fetus in some manner "knows" the mother by virtue of intrauterine capacities. That it is capable of a "prepsychological dialogue" and of recording this physiological or biochemical transmission with its mother in its primitive psychic structure. He believes that the absence of the mother, despite the best adoptive conditions, poses a serious threat to the baby's equilibrium.[4]

If what prenatal research and Deeg's theoretical work suggests is true, we have to wonder how well a newborn who carries a recording of its prepsychological dialogue along with its genetic tape can flourish emotionally without its natural mother. As far back as the 1940s, the psychiatrist Florence Clothier, a pioneer in the psychology of the adopted child, was already concerned about this:

> The child who is placed with adoptive parents at or soon after birth misses the mutual and deeply satisfying mother-child relationship, the roots of which lie in that deep area of personality where the physiological and psychological are merged. For both child and mother, that period is part of a biological sequence. . . . It is doubtful whether the relationship of the child to its post-partum mother, in its subtler effects, can be replaced by even the best of substitute mothers.[5]

Clothier concluded that the adopted infant is "traumatized" by its separation from the mother at birth. It has to find a way to compensate for the "wound" left by the loss of the primitive relationship with her, "a relationship that gives stability and reassurance of safety."[6] Nancy Verrier, a therapist and adoptive mother, became aware of this wound when her adopted baby kept pushing her away and refused to be comforted. She calls it the "primal wound" because it happens at the beginning of life, while the child is still in a primal relationship to the mother: "The wound may make an infant feel that part of itself has disappeared, leaving it with a feeling of incompleteness or lack of wholeness."[7]

INFANT SPLITTING

Adoptive parents are understandably alarmed when they hear therapists speak about wounds and traumas—even though the professional, like

Verrier, may be an adoptive parent—because they interpret it to mean that the baby is hopelessly damaged before it even enters their home. Yet, clinicians are not writing off adopted children when they speak about trauma; rather, they are describing a vulnerability that responsible parents should be aware of. Adopted babies, like all infants, can be tremendously resilient if given the chance, but they have experienced a profound loss that other babies are spared. Adoptive parents who love their children must have empathy for, not fear of, the sorrow that their children carry in their souls. They must not turn from the pain, or turn on the professionals who describe it in the psychological literature.

The child psychiatrist John Bowlby, working in London, was one of the first researchers to document the anxiety infants experience when separated from their mothers.[8] Another English therapist, Harry Guntrip, believed that such infants actually withdraw from outer reality. "The basic nature of the infant, the 'natural self' that is the potential for the true self, retreats after being flooded with fear and anxiety," he wrote. "It is left undeveloped—in a state of being unborn. The infant can only retreat within. It cannot pack its bag and leave home." Guntrip went on to say that a vital part of the self can be lost and an inner deadness experienced when there is such a splitting of the infant ego.[9]

As for the adopted infant, Deeg sees it splitting off not only its anxiety but also its rage at the bad, abandoning mother in order to defend the self it shares with the idealized good mother, whom it internalizes.[10]

One doesn't have to be an adoptive parent to find this material difficult to absorb. Is it really possible that a baby filled with separation anxiety is capable of splitting off its original self and storing it in some secret chamber to which it cuts off access? Daniel Stern thinks not. He believes that splitting requires a level of symbolization beyond an infant's capacity. Yet I notice that adult adoptees often speak as if they have split off a part of the self back in those preverbal days: they speak of feeling unborn, having a dead space in the center like a hollow core, of carrying "a dead baby inside."

Who Is the Real Infant?

If we believe the British psychotherapist D. W. Winnicott that there is no such thing as an infant, only the mother-infant system—an infant in relationship with a mother or a caretaker[11]—we could say that there is no such thing as an adopted infant. There is only the birth mother–infant–adopted mother system: an infant in relationship with both the birth mother and the adoptive mother.

The birth mother and baby spent nine months together before parting in the hospital, while the adopted baby and adoptive mother are outside of nature's jurisdiction when they come together in the adoption system. But the adopted infant, just as helpless as any baby, and dependent for survival on someone to care for it, will accept nurturance from the person who provides it, and record new dialogue with its new mother over the "prepsychological" dialogue with its original mother.[12]

With so many internal communication channels running interference in those early months, we may well wonder whether the baby's seeming attachment to the adoptive mother is not an ambivalent one. And whether the adoptive mother, who usually has undergone her own trauma of infertility, is not also attaching ambivalently. Psychotherapists suggest that the adoptive mother has many reasons for feeling ambivalent: she may not feel entitled to be a parent or may feel she has stolen someone else's child; she may feel guilt toward the woman whose baby she has taken as her own and fear that she may change her mind before the adoption is legal; she may even be angry at the baby for taking the place of the child she could not have. Brinich suggests that insofar as the "alien" nature of an adopted child interferes with the adoptive mother's ability to tune in to the infant, there is potential for a lack of harmony, which may affect early patterns of feeding and sleeping, states of arousal, communication, and so on. He asks: "Can this infant and mother reach out to each other without holding back?"[13]

They seem to arrive at some accommodation, this mother and infant who have equal need for each other. There is very little research on adopted babies, but one recent study found that thirteen- to eighteen-month-old infants appeared to be just as attached to their adoptive mothers as nonadopted infants of the same age were to their natural mothers.[14] How are we to interpret this, given all the stress adopted babies have been through? I am tempted to quip that it proves the adopted child is already a skilled impostor, even at this tender age.

If only it were that simple. In truth, adopted infants *are* like other infants in responding to caretakers who provide their needs. Some adopted infants, especially those "elbow babies" who push their substitute mothers away, are known to hold out from the beginning, as if still loyal to that "hidden relationship" with the lost birth mother. But most babies are willing to be seduced by consistent nurturing that ensures their survival. The majority of adult adoptees whom I surveyed spoke of feeling very attached to their adoptive mothers as young children. It wasn't until they reached middle childhood or adolescence that they felt "disconnected" and "alienated." We have to ask what happened to take away their feeling of well-being. Psychologists are beginning to attribute this change in attitude to the adoptee's developing conceptual skills. They point out that from the age of seven, the child begins to understand the complexity of being adopted, and to get in touch with feelings of grief for the lost parents and anger at being different from children who live with their biological kin.[15]

Yet there is another dynamic going on here, one entangled in the web of secrecy in the closed adoption system. In the next chapter we will attempt to unravel it as we see how the young adopted child struggles to make sense of her separation from the birth mother and membership in the adoptive clan. And how the adoptive parents, themselves shaped by the restrictions of the closed adoption system, neglect to give their children what they need most to develop a whole sense of self: their full narrative.

5

The Broken Narrative

Heaven was in labor. Earth was in labor,
And the purple sea was in labor.
The blood-red sea had birth pangs.
The hollow step of the seaweed emitted flame,
And out of the flame sprang a little boy:
Fire for hair, and fire for beard,
And his eyes were suns.
—OLD ARMENIAN SONG

THE RIDDLE

The riddle of where babies come from is perhaps the first problem to engage a child's mental powers, Freud tells us.[1] A child asks her mother a riddle: "Did I grow in your tummy, Mommy?" The mother answers, "Yes," and the child doesn't have to brood about it anymore. But when the adopted child asks the same question, and the answer is "No," the child is burdened with her own private riddle: "Whose tummy did I grow in?"

The adopted child will keep asking, "Did I grow in your tummy, Mommy?" hoping to trip the mother up and get a yes. The child is really asking for the beginning of her personal life narrative, a birthright that everyone takes for granted. The narrative starts anytime after conception, and even before if it tells how Mommy and Daddy met. It grows as we grow, changes as we change. It usually includes how we kicked in the womb, the ease or difficulty of our birth, and what kind of baby we were.

A friend of mine recalls that when his seven-year-old (biological) daughter was a little younger, she would approach him four or five times a year with "tell me the story." And then he would tell her once again about how he met her mother through a friend, and how they started dating, and how they got married, and how they loved each other, and how she began growing in her Mommy's tummy. It made his daughter very happy and secure to hear the story that began not with her but with her parents who created her. Sometimes her grandparents and other relatives showed up in the details of the story of before she was born. The child knew without having to be told that her narrative was connected to the narrative of her parents, grandparents, and great-grandparents down through the generations, and so she was connected. Her narrative revealed her identity. It told her who she was. If there had been essential people missing from the narrative—her Mommy, Daddy, grandparents, and other members of her clan—it would have been difficult for her to feel connected as she did.

For most children, like my friend's daughter, their narrative is as much a part of them as their shadow; it develops with them over the years and cannot be torn away. Unless, of course, they are adopted.

Narratives can be broken by historical or personal events, such as war, divorce, death, or desertion. Or by infertility and adoption. We are talking about broken narratives when we talk about adoption because everyone's narratives are broken. The adoptive parents' narrative is broken when they are unable to have a biological child to continue their family line. The birth parents' narrative is broken when they are unable to keep the child who would have continued their family line. And the adopted child's narrative is broken when she is lifted out of her own genetic and historic family line to fix the break in the adoptive parents' narrative. Because of the secrecy in the closed adoption system, the continuity of the adoptive parents' narrative is made possible by the discontinuity of the child's.

"The particular human chain we're part of is central to our individual identity," according to Elizabeth Stone, who writes on how family stories shape us.[2] Not to know our full story is to live with some of the disorientation and anxiety of the amnesiac. She refers to the persistent need of many adopted children to know more about where they "really" come from. Something intangible and crucial is missing. To know themselves, they seem to need more of the collective family experience that predates their birth.

"The story about who we are is a sacred story," says Lee, an adopted woman. "When people take it or keep it from us, they rob us of ourselves. They destroy the most sacred thing of all. They kill our Source." Lee got this insight after talking with a friend who had just returned from working on a reservation with Native Americans. He told her that in native society, if you rear someone else's child and that child is of the Bear Clan and you're of the Turtle Clan, you've got to tell him what it means to be of the Bear Clan. He's got to be given a name that fits with Bear Clan customs. He's got to know that he's got his whole identity and that identity goes right back to the myth, right back to the beginning of time. *That* is strength. *That* is power. *That* makes it possible to feel good about who you are. And if you don't know who you are, you don't know where anything else fits.

TELLING AS NOT TELLING

In the closed adoption system, if you rear someone else's child, you tell him about how he entered your clan and very little about the clan from which he came. His identity is supposed to start from the moment he became part of your family, and he is expected to live as a child without a past.

The problem, as the psychoanalyst Don Shapiro sees it, is that adoptive parents must deal with their own origins in order to understand their children's need for theirs.[3] In this country of immigrants, many people are cut off from earlier generations, but not from the parents who gave birth to them, or the narrative, however full or truncated, that the parents pass along. But adoptive parents in the closed system seem to think nothing of cutting their children off from the birth family's narrative, which means cutting them off from their biological and historical origins.

In her wonderfully irreverent novel *In a Country of Mothers,* A. M. Homes has the adopted protagonist tell her therapist how she was told she was adopted right after birth: "I came home from the hospital and they said, 'Hi, how are you? This is the house, this is the kitchen, this is the front hall, we'll take you to your room. Oh, and by the way, you're adopted, but don't think twice about it.'"[4]

In *Lost and Found* I spoke of how adoptive parents once dispatched the natural parents in unnatural ways, such as automobile or plane crashes—stories that seemed to be composed in a psychological vacuum but had a metaphorical truth in that birth parents and child were meant to be as if dead to each other. I also cited some of the books that parents gave their children, such as *The Chosen Baby* story, which begins with the baby waiting for its adoptive parents at the adoption agency, as if it had been miraculously conceived in a filing cabinet or delivered there by a stork.[5] The absence of the baby's birth parents in such books may account for why generations of adoptees have felt that they were not born as other people were, or not born at all. An adopted man who went in search of the missing parts of his narrative said: "The 'chosen baby' story simplified a complex, powerful, and emotional drama which involved many families and would alter their lives forever."

With all the changes in the adoption field in the past few decades—especially the scarcity of healthy white babies—there is no longer one standard plot to cover how an adopted child comes into the family. I realized this when I was writing my picture book, *Tell Me a Real Adoption Story.*[6] The adopting parents in my story networked in their community with doctors, lawyers, friends, and strangers until they learned of a pregnant woman who could not keep her baby. But many parents meet their Asian children at the airport, or travel to South America or Eastern Europe to make arrangements. Finding a child to adopt can be as arduous as trying to have one is for infertile couples.

No matter how adoptive parents today manage to find their babies, many are still giving them the same old mixed message: you are ours, but you are really not ours. They still tend to be deliberately vague about the reason the mother gave her baby up: she was too poor, she was too young, she loved you too much to keep you. They tell the child that she is adopted, but they do *not* tell her what she needs to know about the tummy and the families from which she came and to which she is still biologically connected. *Telling*, then, is really *not telling*.

Claire, the adoptive mother of five-year-old Nicole, came to me in great pain. When Nicole was four, she asked if she grew in her Mommy's tummy.

"No," Claire answered.

"How come?" Nicole wanted to know.

"Mommy's tummy was sick."

"Whose tummy was I in then?"

"Someone else's," Claire said. And then Claire went on to explain that the woman who gave birth to Nicole couldn't keep her because she was all alone and had very little money. That seemed to satisfy Nicole for a while.

When Nicole was five, Claire tried to teach her the facts of life by reading her a book called *Where Did I Come From?* Nicole began to cry when they came to the part where the umbilical cord was cut. Asked to explain why she was upset, she said, "I couldn't be fed through the umbilical cord." As for why not, she responded, "I was from the poorhouse. There was not enough money to buy food." Nicole had taken Claire's story about her birth mother's poverty literally and was filling in the vacuum in the narrative by herself.

That same year a woman smiled at Nicole in the supermarket. The woman was blonde with blue eyes, like Nicole, and looked more like her than her adoptive mother did, who had dark hair and brown eyes. Nicole slipped away from her mother and wrapped her arms around the woman's legs. "She must think I'm someone else," the woman said when Claire came to retrieve her. In the car going home, Claire asked Nicole who she thought the woman was. "My mother," Nicole replied. "What do you mean?" asked Claire in alarm. "You know what I mean," Nicole said. "My *real* mother." Claire couldn't think of anything to say except to warn her not to go up to strangers because they could go off with her. Nicole probably did not want to go off with that woman who looked so much like her that she could have been her mother; she just wanted to find that mother on her own, since her adoptive mother did not seem able to.

Nicole cried a lot that year, and began to hit her playmates. Once when her mother tried to comfort her, Nicole asked, "Where did I come from?" And when Claire explained once again that she was from another lady's tummy, Nicole pounced with: "Where is she? I want to find her. Can't she live with us?" As long as her mother remained an outsider, some part of Nicole would have to be an outsider too. She was trying to bring everyone together so that she could have a whole family and be whole.

Claire tried to jockey for time by telling Nicole, "When you are older I'll help you find her. Now is not the time." Nicole hasn't brought the subject up again, and she has stopped hitting other children at school. But Claire still finds herself in a state of panic: "I worry that Nicole will like her better than me and want to go live with her." Claire is expressing a fear that many adoptive parents have. But the young child who knows only one Mommy, the one who gets him up in the morning and puts him to bed at night, to say nothing of all the love and attention in between, is not about to go off with a Mommy he doesn't know just because he came out of her tummy. He wants to learn about that Mommy or see her, but he does not want to leave his cozy room, his toys, his pets, or his friends for her. The adoptive parents are his parents if for no other reason than that they caught him and claimed him when he was falling alone through space. If adoptive parents could understand this, they would not be afraid to let their children know about, and even connect with, their origins.

In this vignette we can see how the adopted child tries desperately to find the missing parts of the riddle of the self. Adoptive parents say they are keeping the communication lines open with their child by talking about adoption as the subject comes up, but even when the child gives desperate signals that she needs to know more—grabbing strange women in supermarkets, expressing anger and frustration by hitting her schoolmates—they do not open up the narrative with enough real facts to make the child feel real. Many admit remaining purposely in the dark about their child's heritage so that they would be telling the truth when they later said they did not know. And so over the years the parents keep communication lines open about the *mystery* rather than the *actuality* of the birth parents, and deny their child the building blocks of the self that she needs to become whole.

In situations where the adoptive parents have met the birth mother before the child was born, which is happening with some frequency in open adoption, they may embellish the child's narrative with a description of her. But while open adoption means a continuing relationship with the birth mother to some parents, it often means sending photographs through an intermediary for the first year and then cutting off communication. By the time the child is old enough to hear how his parents met his mother, she may no longer be on the scene. The child wonders why this "other" mother doesn't come to visit if she liked the adopted parents enough to *choose* them to raise her baby. Why she doesn't call or write. Why she doesn't have a name. As have previous generations of adoptees, this child eventually figures out that her adoptive parents have no intention of including her birth mother in their lives.

Many adoptive parents compare their method of telling/not telling to explaining sex gradually over the years. The irony is that the very young child will learn more about sex than about his own origins, for while parents teach words like *uterus* and *vagina* and *penis*, they never connect real people to those body parts. "We'd tell you, but we just don't know," becomes the refrain when the child asks about his parents. Or, "When you're old enough you can find out." But the child hears the parents' lack of conviction behind their words. "I got the message they didn't want to think about me being born," said one adoptee who was very confused on being told she grew in her Mommy's heart. She tried to imagine herself all curled up in there, or squeezed somewhere between her Mommy's heart and tummy.

In their book *Talking with Young Children About Adoption,* two therapists, who are also adoptive mothers, place the blame for their not knowing about their children's families of origin on "adoption practice." It should provide pictures of the birth parents, they write, as well as information about their personalities, physical traits, and interests, family trees and medical history, and a letter from each birth parent explaining why the child was given up for adoption. "The letter could be opened in late latency or adolescence, when the question of 'why' recurs at a deeper level. Without such a practice, the adoptive parents are asked by their children to put into words what they do not fully know."[7]

The authors seem not to grasp the deep level of the "why" that already exists in the heart rending questions of the children they quote. One child asks her mother why the lady whose tummy she grew in can't come to her birthday party. A boy asks his adoptive father if his other mother could live in a tent in the backyard. He was shrewd enough to know that she wouldn't be allowed in the house.

Despite being professionals, these two mothers seem as infantilized as their children by the closed adoption system. Why do they have to be beholden to an antiquated adoption practice when they could very well insist on the information they need to answer their children's questions? Failing that, they could locate the birth mother on their own, even if it means traveling back to the child's country of birth, and keep an *updated* file on her life, even if only through correspondence, so that she does not become frozen in time like a figure on a Grecian urn. Giving real information to their children while they are still young—as some parents do in open adoption—will enable them to integrate their two heritages into a whole identity. It is not impossible that the adoptive parents might even like their child's birth mother enough to invite her to one of those birthday parties, if not to live in a tent in the backyard. The greatest birthday present adoptive parents could give their child is the gift of his own heritage.

The authors do include the story of one adoptive mother who decided to be prepared with the answers to the questions her year-and-a-half-old twins might one day ask. She requested the agency to put her in touch with the birth mother, the only one who could give the real explanations. Opening a closed adoption, as this mother did, is becoming more common in this country as adoptive parents come to understand that filling their children's needs is what real parenting is all about. Removing the secrecy around her children's birth mother was rewarding for everyone, as we can see from her report:

> Visits with Mommy Michele and her extended family have become normal, happy events. We share a Christmas holiday meeting, try for an annual birthday celebration, and usually manage about two other get-togethers a year. Comfortably juggling schedules, we arrange visits with no formalities, no rules, no set dates. In between, we chat on the phone and catch up with news. . . . [The twins] are just now, at age four years nine months, beginning to assimilate the term *birth-mother*. They announce to all that they have a birthmom and that they were in her womb and that I am their adoptive mom. . . . Having Mommy Michele, Mommy, and Daddy answer small questions at the time they arise we hope will reduce big traumas later on for all of us. Because we continue on the course of open adoption with comfort, conviction, and love, there is a great sense of security.[8]

When this adoptive mom asked one of the twins how it feels to be adopted, he answered, with a smile that seemed to have started at his toes, "Great!"

The child in a closed adoption will not be so lucky. When she asks "Did I grow in your tummy, Mommy?" she is trying to be born. Nothing but factual knowledge of her birth mother, which other children take for granted, will convince her that she was born. She wishes she had been in her adoptive mother's uterus because then she would be real, like other children who know their mothers. There is a terrifying abyss between the tummy of the unknown mother who carried her and then let her go and the adoptive mother's tummy in which she wishes she had grown. She may seem content not to get real answers, but in her nightmares it is that abyss she will fall through.

Mother's Dough

Native Americans understand intuitively that all children deserve a symbolically crafted life story that includes origins; that "if you don't know who you are, you don't know where anything else fits." Mental Health Professionals also understand the psychobiological need to stay connected with one's roots. "Without origins, the adopted child cannot rest in the crib of history," the psychologist Jerome Bruner told me on learning about the secrecy in the adoption field. He recalled that his mother used to save some old dough to bake bread: "It's called Mother's Dough. You need a piece of the past to make the present."[9]

An incoherent adoption story that lacks Mother's Dough—a bit of old dough to blend with the new—will mix things up in a child's psyche, causing confusion about beginnings and endings, connections and disconnections. A surreal prose poem by Charles Simic could well describe the absurdity of the incomplete adoption narrative as perceived by the child:

> I was stolen by the gypsies. My parents stole me right back. Then the gypsies stole me again. This went on for some time. One minute I was in the caravan suckling the dark teat of my new mother, the next I sat at the long dining room table eating my breakfast with a silver spoon.[10]

An incomplete story, no matter how lovingly presented, runs the danger of being perceived as surreal. Befuddled adopted children often wonder whether they have been stolen by one set of parents and might be stolen right back by the other. Poor mothers and rich mothers become interchangeable. At times the children take their nourishment from the "dark teat" in the gypsy caravan (read birth parents) and at other times from a silver spoon in the conventional world (read adoptive parents).

Gail and her brother tried to make sense of their mother's upbeat story about how they were selected (but from where?) and how wonderful they were (why?). Her brother felt that their mother went overboard on the "you're so superior" bit. Gail's response was to think, "I'll never be good enough, so what's the point in trying?" Her brother's was to be the "best juvenile delinquent" in their small community.

When a nonadopted child loses even one parent, everyone is aware of the child's need to grieve. But no one considers that the adopted child also needs to mourn. How can you mourn someone you never knew? people ask, disregarding the child's prenatal bond, as well as the human need for biological and historical connection. By denying the complexity of their child's background, adoptive parents deny him the reality of his loss, and hence his own reality.

THE REPLACEMENT SELF

At whatever age it occurs, the moment of telling (which, as we have seen, is not really telling) will be forever etched on the adopted child's soul. She may look the same after that, but she will never be the same again. She may say she is glad to have been chosen, but she would rather have been born. Some part of her will have turned into a changeling, a baby left by the fairies as a replacement for the human baby they abduct. In legend, the changeling replaces the child who is the legitimate heir in the family.

The adoptive mother tries to take care of the baby, but the changeling may resist. One mother spoke of being disappointed that her baby was not huggable. Even the food he liked as a child was different from her family's taste: "I watched him grow like a plant whose name I had forgotten. I felt like I was putting nothing into him. I didn't know what he contained."

The infant substitute does not look like a changeling to the adoptive parents, but folklorists say that to anyone who has the fairy vision the fraud appears in true form. Adopted children see that fraud when they look into the mirror and the changeling looks back at them.

The changeling comes into the adoptive family to replace an infant or child who has died or never existed. In her novel *In a Country of Mothers*, A. M. Homes has her adopted protagonist try to explain to her therapist what it feels like to be a replacement child:

> How would you describe your relationship to your brother?
> My relationship? He died before I was born.
> Do you think of him as your friend? Your enemy?
> "My ghost," Jody said. "I am him, he is me."

In my own case, my birth mother had an older, married half-sister who was her mother's favorite. That sister died with her baby in childbirth shortly before my unmarried, seventeen-year-old mother delivered me. The legitimate baby was dead, and I, the illegitimate one, was alive. But my grandmother did not intend for me to replace the grandchild who should have been. She forced my mother to surrender me to adoption. I then became the legitimate replacement child for the biological child my adoptive parents should have had. And they became my replacement parents.

In his book *Tragic Drama and the Family,* the psychoanalyst Bennett Simon tells us that the replacement child bears the burden of parental guilt, shame, and ambivalence that attended the death of the previous child.[11] In some instances, the dead child is idealized and the replacement child becomes the bad one who does not deserve to live or be happy. Often the replacement child becomes the object of both parental anger and guilty oversolicitousness.

The adoptee who replaces either a dead child or an unborn child, who is as if dead because it never lived, must bear the burden of the parents' unresolved infertility and grief over not having their fantasy child, while trying to be what that fantasy child would have been.

Susan said that she felt like a shadow of the Susan who was never born: "I was playing the role of the daughter who didn't exist. To me that child was perfect. I never measured up. I felt that nothing I did was good enough."

Ruth was named after her adoptive mother's stillborn baby girl. Her adopted brother, who had been named Paul after a stillborn boy, was given back to the agency when he proved to be emotionally unstable. He was replaced by a healthy infant boy, who inherited the name of Paul.

In what Simon calls "the calculus of life and death," adoptees wonder why they lived and the legitimate child who should have been did not. They wonder whether they have a right to be alive.

THE UNBORN SELF

Without concrete information about the circumstances of your birth, especially about the woman who gave you life, the adoptee often has the sense of not having been born at all. The "amended" birth certificate is a fake, listing, as it does, the names of the adoptive parents rather than the birth parents. And the fact that the real birth certificate is sealed enforces the sense of nonexistence. The adoptee feels alone in the world. Connected to his adoptive home by the fragmentary adoption narrative and disconnected from his real biological narrative, he has lost his place on the intergenerational chain of being. I call this *cosmic loneliness*.

"Adoption is a major cutoff," the psychologist Harriet Lerner once told me while we were discussing the harm secrets can do to a child. "When you cut off a child's birth parents, you cut off that child's birth."

You also cut off what Daniel Stern calls the "narrative point of origin."[12] This "key experience" will lie buried in the child's psyche until the adoptee, at whatever age, is strong enough to claim it.

6

Artificial Self, Forbidden Self

When I was to be a child,
Someone else was a child,
not real I
(this can still be excused).
—TADEUSZ KANTOR, "I SHALL NEVER RETURN"

Every man is involved personally
in whether or to what extent
he is being "true to his own nature."
—R. D. LAING, *THE DIVIDED SELF*

THERE IS AN EDWARD GOREY DRAWING (THAT ELICITS both wonder and dread) in which a boy stands on top of a ravine looking out into the distance, while his teddy bear, having slipped from his grasp, falls into the abyss below. The adopted child, having perceived the terrible truth that children can be lost from their parents, is both the boy and the teddy bear.

PSYCHIC TRAUMA

One definition of psychological trauma is an experience that is sudden, unexpected, abnormal. It exceeds the individual's ability to meet its demands. It disrupts one's sense of self and identity; it threatens one's psychological core.[1] This is what happens when a child learns that he is adopted. Hearing that one was not born to one's mother is a profound and unrecognized trauma. It is as if the child has received a "deadly traumatic telegram," as the psychoanalyst Harold Blum puts it.[2] The child finds it incomprehensible.

This is not to say that the child is irreparably damaged, as some adoptive parents fear is meant when professionals speak of wounds or traumas. Children are known to be resilient, to suffer all kinds of early abandonments and other traumas and to recover. But when the adopted child learns that he both *is* and *is not* the child of his parents, the shock connects to that earlier preverbal trauma the baby had at separation from the mother and has retained as an inner experience.

Even this would not have to be so devastating for the child were it not compounded by yet a third trauma: the secrecy that disconnects him from his parentage and history. He is forbidden to know to whom he was born. Blum suggests that the revelation of adoption can be softened in the context of a "lovingly secure parent-child relationship." This is true but, unfortunately, not even the most loving adoptive parents (and this is their tragedy as well as the child's) can soften the psychic toll that secrecy exacts from the child in that it interferes with the child's struggle to form an early sense of self.

The Survival Bind

Having to live in two worlds at once, inner and outer, drives a child to seek compromise positions in an attempt to hold on to both worlds, according to Guntrip.[3] Adopted children try to straddle the two worlds for a while. They ask questions over and over in an attempt to make some sense of what has happened to them. They may even think that a mistake has been made and that the "first" mother will come back for them. Many adoptees have told me of waiting for their mothers to return. We can see this as the first stage of grief: denial that the birth mother would leave them behind.

Rachel never felt she belonged in her family, which was often in turmoil because of her father's compulsive gambling: "I felt that someone had invited me to dinner—a long dinner—and I couldn't get out of it. I had the feeling that my real mother was my guardian angel watching over me, and that she would come back for me. I used to sit and wait for her on the curb in front of my house."

Thoughts of being kidnapped and rescued often go in tandem in the adopted child's psyche as part of the denial that the birth mother has disappeared for good.

Rachel recalls: "I was in the uncertain position of feeling grateful for being saved from a disaster from which I had no consciousness of even having emerged. It's as if you suddenly discover your life came with a certain set of strange conditions—gratefulness to your rescuers being first among them."

"I think my parents got a lot of admiration for rescuing me and my younger brother," Alan says. "Their roles as rescuers and my role as the rescued create a relationship that does not allow the adoptee much opportunity to feel or express any negative feelings toward the rescuer. For the rescuing parents there can be a need to promote their child's neediness in the service of maintaining relatedness."

Sometimes the adopted child has nightmares that she has been or will be kidnapped and may or may not be rescued. Birth parents and adoptive parents alternate as the kidnappers and rescuers. The wish to be kidnapped by the birth parents may surface as a fear of it actually happening.

Sally, an unmarried woman in her forties, always felt "lucky" and "rescued," but for years she had a recurring dream of King Kong climbing into her bedroom window and kidnapping her: "He stole me away from my very own bed in my nightie. The dream no doubt reflected my feelings about the circumstances of my adoption: that my parents took me from my birth mother."

THE DIVIDED SELF

Implicit in the parents' loving message to the child is: "We will love you as our own unconditionally—under the condition that you pretend that you are really our own." The child is being asked to collude in the fiction that these are his only parents and to accept that his birth heritage is disposable.

There is a double message here of "being and not being," according to a team of Argentine psychiatrists. The parents are saying: "You are not to be what you were born to be, but what we want you to be."[4] The prohibition of finding out about their origins is transmitted in all of this. Only if adopted children commit themselves fully to the identity of the adoptive clan can they have the adoptive parents' love. Already abandoned by the birth mother, the adopted child feels no choice but to abandon her and, by so doing, to abandon his real self. This early, potential self that is still attached to the birth mother is unacceptable to the adoptive parents and, therefore, must become unacceptable to the child.

There is no more consequential step than abandoning the real self, Karen Horney stressed throughout her work.[5] The child forced to give up the real self cannot develop feelings of belonging. There is instead a feeling of basic anxiety, of being isolated and helpless. Adopted children often try to shut out the subject of adoption. This means that they must separate one part of the self from the rest of the self—a pattern known as dissociation, disavowal, numbing, or splitting. Clinicians are agreed that children cannot form a healthy sense of self if they must disavow reality, yet this is what adopted children are asked to do. They are too young to articulate what is going on inside them, but adult adoptees, looking back in sorrow as much as in anger, understand what they did to survive.

Rachel recalls: "When I was five, I realized that my mother wasn't going to appear. I gave up and became a quiet, docile child. I realized the necessity of forgetting about her. With that forgetfulness, some indefinable and yet crucial part of me went into hiding."

Mark, a musician in his thirties, remembers the exact moment he tuned out. At the age of four, he asked if he could meet the mother he had been told about when he was two and a half: "It was the first time I wanted and needed something they wouldn't consider. They said I had to wait until I was eighteen, which is like ninety to a young child. I didn't ask any more questions after that. The fact of my adoption burst like a bubble in my mind, then sealed over. It became important for my sense of coherence as a self to imagine myself as not adopted."

D. W. Winnicott and R. D. Laing both used the terms True Self and False Self to describe the split in the human psyche that many children make.[6] I believe it is more accurate to call the split in the adopted child the Forbidden Self and the Artificial Self, neither of which is completely true or completely false.

The Artificial Self

The Artificial Self has many of the characteristics of the Good Adoptee, whom I described in *Lost and Found* as being almost selfless in a desire to please. Like the adoptive family in which it has been placed, the Artificial Self is artificially created. It is a social construct, an *as if* self living *as if* in a natural family. Wanting to fit in at any cost, it will deny its own needs for the sake of others. It is canny in that it senses what is acceptable and what is not, and will do anything to avoid confrontation. In that sense, it takes on the attributes of a false self, which Laing says is in compliance with the intentions or expectations of others, and acts according to other people's definitions of what one is instead of according to one's own definitions of what one wishes to be.

"I was forever to be the grateful, unquestioning adoptee and guard against any behaviors that would possibly betray my biology," Alan says. "I never wondered about my birth mother beyond her selfless and necessary act of giving me up. I never wondered about her life or family before or after the moment of her surrender. I had no notion that a birth father played any part in this at all. I never thought of myself as being born, only adopted. Certainly a part of my compliance in not wanting to know more about my birth mother was that she must be defective, immoral, or incapable as an adult."

Rachel recalls: "For years I played the game of 'This is my only family, I have no other.' I continue to play that game. At times it is confusing to sort out what about me is genuine and true, and what about me was developed as a survival strategy to be able to stay in my adoptive family. I developed a sixth sense for knowing what kind of daughter they wanted me to be. I became something behind a blank mask where others could draw the face they wanted to see and behind which I furiously nurtured that of myself which I'd been able to salvage."

The Artificial Self is compliant, afraid to express its real feelings, such as sadness or anger, for fear of losing the only family it has. It cuts the natural parents off from consciousness until they are no longer available, except when they surface in daydreams or fantasy. It denies its need for origins.

Alice, a divorced woman in her mid-forties, says: "I became the good, very compliant adoptee, suppressing my guts, never showing anger. The expected role I played became 'me,' except there was no 'me.' My self got lost underground, and I never thought of birth parents as a reality. 'Me' didn't belong. 'Me' didn't exist."

The Artificial Self may behave like the perfect child but feels empty within. It may look real to others but does not feel real. Having cut off a vital part of itself, it sometimes feels dead. As one woman said: "I never felt entitled to be alive. I had a subtle feeling of unreality, as if I was living a borrowed life."

Rachel remembers that whenever she passed a construction site where some huge gaping hole had been carved out of the earth, she would feel both fatally drawn to it and terrified. "It was as if any physical void would see its own nature reflected in me and, recognizing me as an ally, sweep me into its vortex. Or perhaps it was I who secretly felt the desire to enfold myself there, feeling that was where I truly belonged. To openly acknowledge the void—the manifestation of absence—as my true progenitor would have been the most honest statement I could make about myself."

The Artificial Self tries to structure its psychic reality to match the reality of the family in which it finds itself. Some adoptees are so successful at splitting off a part of themselves that they stop asking questions about the birth mother early and do not fantasize or dream about her.

Robin, adopted at four months, was the perfect adoptee until she was forty-four years old. "I knew I was cute and I always believed that if I could just be good enough, care enough, do well enough in school, I would be kept and could somehow change my parents' lives and possibly protect my older adopted brother, who was always in trouble. My adoptive mother was a cold, controlling woman with a sharp tongue which she used to ridicule my father and make demands. I felt she was a princess and I was there to make her life perfect. That meant sacrificing my *self* to fit her needs. In school I was overeager to please teachers and friends. I never wanted or had an enemy. I was a good athlete, a good student, and never was angry or mean. I was really kind of disgustingly perfect. My weak points were a poor self-image. I felt stupid, unattractive, and really sad and alone inside. I felt not a part of the real world—different.

When Robin married and had two children, she desperately wanted everything and everyone to be happy. But her perfect world fell apart when her teenage daughter went around filled with anger. She sought help to understand what she had done wrong that her daughter was so angry. The therapist helped her realize that what she had done wrong was not allowing her and everyone else in the family to live a natural, necessary emotion called anger. "After a few years of therapy, I was able to get in touch with my own anger—and my *self*," Robin says. "I realized that I had not asked questions about adoption, fantasized or dreamed about my birth mother because I felt indebted to the people who had taken me in and to whom I owed my existence."

Robin learned that when you numb one part of yourself, you numb vital emotions as well, and this can have an intergenerational effect. Many adoptees, however, are not as successful as she was in blocking everything out.

Marilyn, who was adopted at two months and is now a twenty-five-year-old graduate student, tried to get by on her Artificial Self, but was in touch with her ambivalence. "I always felt I had two selves," she says, "the culturally accepted one with my adoptive family and the private one that was not real to others, but that I knew was real." Marilyn was very close to her parents, especially her father, an educator, whom she tried to please by being the top student in her high school class and by winning a scholarship that he steered her toward. "This remains one of my proudest accomplishments," she says, "although it is bittersweet because I almost feel I was forced into winning it, and I wonder what would have happened if I hadn't." Would her father still have loved her if she hadn't lived up to his high standards? Because of the lack of security of the blood knot, adoptees are more susceptible than others to such doubts.

Marilyn remembers herself as an intense child, bright and articulate, though the happiness of her childhood was "mitigated over the years by emotional complexity." Unlike Robin's parents, hers spoke openly about adoption, but credited God for bringing them together. When she was nine, she realized that her parents' promise to help locate her birth parents someday did not have "the requisite emotional backup." It was then that she blocked out any thoughts of adoption so completely that when an eleven-year-old classmate, also adopted, asked her if she would ever want to search, she replied, "No. Why would I ever want to do that?" (Many years later, however, she did begin a search.)

During high school Marilyn looked for role models in her teachers, and became so close to some of them that she was voted "pride of the faculty" in the popularity poll. "I believe that I looked for my mother in every woman I have ever known—teachers, friends, counselors," she says. "I felt painfully disconnected from my true self and my peers. When I acted in school plays, I got to be someone else, but this type of charade became difficult for me when I realized it wasn't only on stage that I was acting."

Like Robin, she felt she had to be extra good because her brother was drinking and taking drugs during that time and causing her parents a lot of problems: "I resented the inordinate amount of attention he got, but I didn't dare express my anger for fear everyone would leave me."

The Artificial Self builds rigid walls around it, and over the years it fortifies them with ever more denial. But every once in a while some life crisis manages to shake the fortifications, foreshadowing the time when massive anxiety will suddenly come crashing through, much as an expected wave sweeps with ease over the seemingly sturdy walls of a sand castle.

When Marilyn was fifteen, her mother gave birth to a son, causing her to get in touch with her feelings about adoption again: "It was extremely painful to watch my mom go through her pregnancy—to know that someone had been pregnant with me and had given me away, and not to know if she had cared for me. It was anguishing not to feel completely a part of anyone, anywhere, and not to be able to talk about it for fear of alienating and distancing the only family that I knew. During this time I cried myself to sleep every night thinking about myself and my birth mom and how unfair it was to have to live without ever knowing her or having that part of myself. I never seriously contemplated taking my own life, mostly due to my belief in God and that there is a time and a place for everything, and that it is not up to us to decide. However, living my life became increasingly difficult, and I became acutely aware of my inside self and my outside self during this time."

Many adoptees struggle with feelings of disconnection when their parents give birth, not believing their parents' insistence that there is "no difference" between getting a child and having one. It is what the sociologist and adoptive father David Kirk calls "rejection of difference" as opposed to the more healthy "acknowledgment of difference."[7] "There is a difference," says Marilyn, "and my adoptive parents' denial of it kept them from seeing *my* needs. They saw no correlation between their having another child—a birth child—and my having another mother—a birth mother."

When adoptive parents deny the reality of a difference between the biological child and the adopted child, they think they are assuring the adoptee of their love, but they are, in effect, denying the adoptee's reality.

The adoptee continues in her artificial role rather than risk losing her place in the family, but goes underground with her forbidden thoughts, which make her feel more isolated and alone.

The Forbidden Self

The Forbidden Self, which often acts like the "Bad Adoptee" I discussed in *Lost and Found,* is the self that might have been had it not been separated from its mother and forced to split off from the rest of the self. While most adoptees, like Robin and Marilyn, try to please their parents when they are young, at some point the frustration, sadness, and anger of being cut off from the reality of the past becomes too much for them and they can't pretend anymore. "I couldn't numb myself," one woman said. "I couldn't fit into the lie." And another: "No matter how good I tried to be, I always felt that I was a bad person."

The Forbidden Self goes underground for vitality and authenticity, harboring a jumble of fantasies about the birth parents and the life that might have been. Like Laing's "inner self," it is "occupied in maintaining its identity and freedom by being transcendent, unembodied, and thus never to be grasped, pinpointed, trapped, possessed."[8]

As we have seen, Marilyn considered her Forbidden Self to be her inner, private self. "It's the self I grew, raised, and took care of," she says. "It had happy and sad feelings. It was the part of me that wasn't real, but I knew it was real. It was my only link to the biological past I might have had. I couldn't share it with anyone for fear of its being destroyed." When Marilyn's parents "dragged" her into family therapy because they couldn't cope with the behavior of her older adopted brother, she refused to reveal her "secret inside place" to the counselor. "I remember telling her quite flatly that I didn't want to talk about adoption."

The Forbidden Self keeps itself hidden in order not to be flushed out and destroyed. It refuses to disavow the reality that it has other parents somewhere or to abandon what it feels to be its true, or potentially true, self.

"I see adoption as all about dominance and dependency," Marilyn says now. "Adoptive parents mistake possession for love. That's the tragedy. That's the origin of the sense of loss I have. I was expected to lose my identity on their terms. Out of a sense of loyalty to them I kept my feelings of needing to find my origins a secret for so long. I disavowed myself.

I finally realized that not allowing myself to be a whole person and play-ing the game on their terms was not being true to myself."

The Ghost Kingdom

Carl Jung said that among all possible ghosts that haunt us, the spirits of the parents possess the greatest significance.[9] Having been banished from the adopted child's everyday world by the closed adoption system, the birth parents become little more than the ghosts I described in chapter 1. ("Hereditary ghosts," the Finnish psychiatrist Max Frisk labeled them.[10]) I call the spectral place in which these ghosts reside as the Ghost Kingdom. It is an awesome sphere, located only in the adoptee's psychic reality.

The Forbidden Self, and occasionally even the Artificial Self, slips into the Ghost Kingdom to rendezvous with the lost mother and the lost baby, who never had a chance to grow into the child it should have been. One man described it as "a forbidden world, like a hole—wonderful, terrify-ing, ghostly—that you could fall into completely." Once there, it is not necessarily a peaceable kingdom, for the adoptee is free to express not only love but anger at being, as one woman put it, "cast out into the world with strangers."

Like children of Holocaust survivors who lead double lives, one in the present-day experience and one in the "time tunnel" of an imposed iden-tity with the dead children they replace, adoptees live their everyday experience in their "pretend" family and another in the "time tunnel" of the Ghost Kingdom they share with the idealized and denigrated birth parents.[11] If we can grasp the unreality of the realm wherein adoptees perceive their most real selves to reside, we will understand the adopted person's own sense of unreality and how, at any age, conscious thoughts of reunion with the birth mother back in the womb, which the Ghost Kingdom represents, can bring with them terrifying images of disintegra-tion into nothingness.

Adoptees, then, are caught between the loyalty they feel to the adoptive parents who rescued them and the invisible loyalty to the mother who gave birth to them. Troubled as they are by feeling ungrateful, they remain ambivalent about accepting their adoptive parents as the "real" ones. Yet because they have not had real experiences in the real world with the birth mother, they cannot accept her as real either. Their split loyalties prevent them from resolving their issues with either set of parents.

Adoptees may go in and out of the Ghost Kingdom as they go back and forth between the Artificial Self and the Forbidden Self at different periods of their lives. For example, they may be compliant as children and then, in an adolescent struggle for authenticity, rebel against the adoptive parents, whom they see as inauthentic and a barrier between them and their authentic self.

David, adopted by a Jewish family at nine days, was the model adoptee until he turned thirteen. He kept his room and his possessions in perfect order, was polite, and seemed unconcerned when a brother was born two years after he came into the home and a sister twelve years later. Naomi, his mother, remembers that he asked a few questions about his adoption while he was growing up, but she told him nothing except that his birth mother, who was not Jewish, loved him and wanted him to have a good home.

In accordance with Jewish law, David's parents had him converted to Judaism when he was five. Just before he was to study for his bar mitzvah at the age of thirteen, he learned that boys who were converted could choose whether to take part in this ceremony initiating them into Jewish manhood. David's parents were startled when he announced that he did not want to be bar mitzvahed because his birth mother wasn't Jewish. They informed him that because he was their son and had grown up in the Jewish tradition, he had no choice in the matter. He went through with the ceremony and seemed to enjoy all the attention and presents he received.

But David changed after that from the compliant, lovable boy who always tried to please his parents into an angry, unkempt teenager who cut himself off from all family activities. Unable to articulate his feelings, he acted them out. He fell in with a bad crowd, began drinking, and did badly in school. He seems to have equated getting bar mitzvahed with betraying his non-Jewish birth mother, to whom he also felt loyal. Had his parents been able to understand this and discuss it with him, had they taken that opportunity to give him the information they had about his birth mother, had they given him a choice, they would have become his allies rather than his opponents. Once it had become his choice, I believe David would have chosen loyalty to his adoptive parents (where an adoptee's main loyalty lies) and agreed to be bar mitzvahed. From the moment he lost that battle of wills, however, he made his adoptive family the loser in the only way he knew how—by becoming a loser himself.

David's parents tried everything they could to help him and themselves. When he wouldn't stay with therapy, they joined Tough Love, a parents' group that devises radical strategies to counter a child's rebellious behavior. But the source of the pain of adoptees is different from that of other acting-out adolescents, and nothing will work for them until their parents gain insight into the adoption issues at play. Only when David became violent did his parents manage to get him hospitalized, for seven weeks (which is all their insurance would cover). After that, unable to keep a job, he spent his days sleeping and his nights at his computer bulletin board.

David's mother refused to give up on him. When she saw a local notice of a meeting of Adoptive Parents for Open Records, she overcame her fear and decided to attend. It was a seminal experience. She saw a birth mother for the first time—in fact, she was sitting next to her. "My whole feelings changed," she says. "I realized this was a *real* woman, with a husband and kids. I heard adoptees talk about their need to know their birth mothers. I thought maybe this was what was bothering David. I felt I couldn't be his mother if I didn't help him."

That night Naomi pulled out David's adoption folder, which contained his birth mother's name and address, and handed it to him. Her disheveled son, who in fits of rage had broken furniture, knocked holes in walls and ceilings, and thrown heavy objects at mirrors, began to cry. They cried together. "I never felt closer to him than at that moment," Naomi says. She was surprised that David didn't leap at the opportunity to write to his birth mother, but he gave her permission to do so instead. She waited nervously for the response, which came two weeks later with expressions of gratitude along with pictures of the birth mother, her husband, and her two children, all of whom knew about David. She was only sixteen at the time of his birth and had been pressured by her stepmother to give him up. She wrote that she had never stopped thinking about him.

After three months, David is still reluctant to answer his birth mother's letters. He wants his adoptive mother to be the bridge to that formerly forbidden world to which he does not yet have the psychic strength to connect. He is holding on tightly to his adoptive identity—the only one he has—and being loyal to the parents he has been opposing. Naomi says she can look back through the years and see all the times when her son was reaching out with his questions, but she couldn't respond because she was threatened by his birth identity. She is waiting until David will be able to communicate directly with his birth mother and to repair the split in himself.

The Luck of the Draw

Many factors influence how much splitting adopted children do and how well they cope. If they have the luck of the draw, they will find themselves placed with parents of similar temperament, talents, and physical characteristics—parents who are empathic to their needs and not only keep the communications lines open but go out and get the answers to their child's questions. By the age of seven, most adopted children are still open and trusting with their parents as they begin to probe for more concrete information about their birth mother and the circumstances of their birth. What is her name? Where is she now? Can I see her picture? Can I meet her?

Without the luck of the draw, adopted children will find themselves with parents who use them to serve their own emotional needs. They may be placed in homes where there is alcohol addiction, emotional, physical, or sexual abuse, divorce, or mental instability. Adoptive parents are not immune to the vices and pitfalls that claim other parents. When their parents fail them, children will close down, withdraw into the Ghost Kingdom.

How well adoptees overcome the traumas inherent in adoption and the additional ones they encounter in their specific families will be determined by their genetic susceptibility to stress—some children have more than others—and their ability to find an empathic teacher, friend, or mentor to give them emotional support.

THE FAMILY ROMANCE

All children keep some kind of secret place tucked away to which they can escape and fantasize about having better parents, especially in midchildhood when, as Freud told us, children begin to look at their parents more critically. They imagine that such insensitive people could not possibly be their *real* parents; that they were probably just dropped off by parents of noble birth, who will soon return to claim them. Freud called this the family romance.

The adopted child's family romance has much in common with other children's, with the difference that the adoptee lives in actuality the family romance that other children live in fantasy. The adoptee really does have another set of parents out there somewhere. The adoptee's fantasies begin when the child learns of his adoption, not in mid-childhood, when most children struggle with their ambivalence about their parents. Their fantasies differ from those of the nonadopted in that they are negative as well as positive, and usually about the mother. The lost mother may be a famous movie star or a favorite teacher, but she can also be a prostitute or a drug dealer.

Adoptee fantasies, which reflect one's deepest hopes or fears, can fluctuate with one's moods. "When I was angry with my adoptive mom, my birth mother was a beautiful, wealthy woman," a female adoptee recalls. "And when I was feeling angry at my birth mother, I fantasized that she was old, poor, and an alcoholic. I must have thought I was an immaculate conception because I never fantasized about or truly understood that there was a man involved in all this."

Fantasy as Structure for the Adopted Self

Adopted children spend an exorbitant amount of psychic time in fantasy. They may seem to be sitting quietly in their rooms, or just looking out the window, when really they are deep in the Ghost Kingdom imagining scenarios that might have been or still might be. "Fantasies are an underground way of relating," says Mark. "I used to be riveted by Jules Verne's *Journey to the Center of the Earth* because it showed a whole other reality under the surface of this reality. That's how I imagined my life."

Jung said that fantasies are the natural expression of the life of the unconscious. I see adoptee fantasies, both positive and negative, as an essential part of the building blocks of the developing self, as the fragile center beam around which the edifice of the adopted self is built. These fantasies are not just the passing fancies with which most people empower themselves at various periods of their lives but actual reality for the adoptee's inner, secret self. They are the mother replacement: the comfort zone that the mother did not provide. They serve the function of the surrogate rag doll that experimental monkeys are given after the real mother has been taken away. They are also a form of grieving, of conjuring up the lost mother, in the same way that children grieving for lost parents are known to conjure up their ghosts.[12]

Adoptee fantasies serve a different purpose from those of the nonadopted: they are an attempt to repair one's broken narrative, to dream it along. They enable the child to stay magically connected with the lost birth mother. Guntrip distinguishes healthy fantasies from pathological ones. The healthy ones prepare us for action in the outer world; the pathological ones are accompanied by withdrawal from the real world to avoid working things out. The adoptee's fantasies, based as they are in the Ghost Kingdom, cannot connect with the outer world. They run the danger of becoming pathological when they interfere with the child's functioning in everyday life.

Positive Fantasies

Sometimes a young child reveals a cherished fantasy when she does a school assignment. Asked to describe a wish that she would like to come true, an eight-year-old adopted child wrote: "I wish I could see my real mom and dad because it would be fun I think. I would take flowers to my mom and take a tie to my dad. I would be so happy to see them. . . . That's been my wish since I was five."

Often adoptees fantasize that they might encounter their birth mother by chance in some public place.

Lisa remembers daydreaming on the bus coming home from school that her mother would get on: "We would look at each other and know we were mother and daughter. She would go to my house and tell my parents she was taking me away with her. They wouldn't care and would let me go. And life would be great. Sometimes I dreamed that she was rich and would love me, and other times that she was poor and we struggled. But I felt I was loved. The only negative thoughts I had were that she rejected me, and that she might be a prostitute."

Adoptees hold on to positive fantasies of their birth parents as an escape from the mysterious reality in which they find themselves, and as a way of holding on to some self-esteem.

Helen imagined her birth parents as beautiful, rich, intelligent people who had been killed in a plane crash only weeks after she was born: "For a long time, it never occurred to me that they might be alive. Later, as I got into the double-digit age bracket, I thought of my mother as possibly unwed, but still glamorous; perhaps a teenage girl who fell into a mad, passionate affair with a dissolute artist who later died of consumption. My heroine was Marilyn Monroe. I identified with her, the orphan seeking a sense of self through the adoration of crowds.

Perhaps Marilyn was my mother. Perhaps my father was Jack Kennedy, or Bobby, or Yves Montand, or Howard Hughes. I, too, wanted to be famous, wanted in some obscure way to 'show them'—my parents, or the world—that I was somebody worthwhile."

Some adoptees have serial fantasies—running scenarios that they add to and change over the years.

At thirteen, Emily, who was adopted at three days, made up elaborate stories about her birth mother. Sometimes she was rich and married, with eleven children and sundry pets, all of whom Emily named. At other times her mother was poor, and beat and starved her children and animals. In junior high, as a latchkey kid, Emily began to fantasize that her birth mother would be waiting in the hall for her when she came home from school. Each time she turned the key in the door she expected to find her. Her mother would have a car waiting outside that would take them to the airport. They would fly back to the state where she was born, and where her mother now resided with her husband and all her children. Each time the front hall was empty, Emily's heart sank. But she continued to hope. Her imaginary scenarios with her birth mother took on a life of their own and became more real than her life at home and school, which she began failing. What had begun as healthy fantasies now interfered with her functioning in her every day life.

Negative Fantasies

As we have seen, negative fantasies have a way of intruding into positive ones, because they are the ones that adoptees fear are true. The very anonymity of the birth parents—people with no names or faces—devalues their status, and suggests that it is lower than that of the adoptive parents. The shame embedded in the secrecy surrounding an adoptee's identity can taint her self-worth, which is tied to that of those missing parents.

When Helen was sixteen, she wrote a story about a promiscuous single mother named Rita, who blackmails the wealthy father of her son into providing money for the boy's support: "Rita was my nightmare mother, a tough-talking, hard-drinking bottle blonde who had always been what is discreetly called 'popular.' She was the figure that would haunt me as I grew into what should have been adulthood without ever feeling myself an adult, feeling less, not more, sure of myself the older I got."

An adoptee's negative fantasies often reflect her feeling of being an unwanted child who is not entitled to live.

Born on the day *Roe v. Wade* made abortion legal, Ann believed that her mother probably resented having had to go through with the pregnancy. In the seventh grade she had a nightmare that her mother kidnapped her, while screaming that she wished Ann had never been born: "I have in my head that since women can now legally kill their unborn children, my birth mother should be allowed to kill me. Over the years I've imagined that she tortures me, sets fire to me, smashes my hands with a hammer, and tries to cut off my arms and legs. Then the fire department saves me. She gets charged in court, but I testify that she is my mother and can do whatever she wants. I ask that the charges be dropped. Sometimes she ends up liking me and sometimes hating me."

When adoptees' fantasies are negative, Harold Blum sees them as denigrating both the adoptive parents and the unknown biological parents, as well as the adoptees themselves: "In addition, the adoptee may also show self-denigration and self-blame as a 'rejected' child of the natural parents and as an artificial child of the 'pretend' parents," he writes.[13] "The boundaries between who is the real parent and who is the real child, between reality and fantasy, may be blurred where reality has been validated or anchored in fantasies and where familial secrecy surrounds adoption."[14]

The Mystery of Reality

The blurred boundaries that adoptees struggle with contribute to what Robert Jay Lifton calls the mystery of reality. "The adoptees' condition highlights questions about what is reality for all of us," he points out. "Their struggle to grasp cognitively what is real is an extreme version of what everyone is struggling to grasp."[15]

He believes that we are separated from animals by our ability to reconstruct reality through images. These images are influenced by the culture around us. Natural children, who have parents, siblings, and other blood-related relatives, are grounded in a reality from which they can spin their images. But adoptees do not feel grounded or connected by any such reality. Much of their imagery is not centered on the adoptive family in which they live as if they belong, but rather in fantasy and imagination. They have a sense that their very perceptions are deceiving them. They have lost the ability to distinguish between what is real and what is supposed to be real.

We will see how this mystery of reality affects the adoptee's emerging sense of self.

7

Stuck in the Life Cycle

Those who do not have power over the story that dominates
their lives, power to retell it, deconstruct it, joke about it,
and change it as times change, truly are powerless, because
they cannot think new thoughts.
—SALMAN RUSHDIE

THE MYSTERY OF WHO THEY ARE BECOMES ESPECIALLY
poignant when adoptees reach adolescence. It is then that they feel the
prison walls of even the most loving home close in on them. If your personal narrative doesn't grow and develop with you, with concrete facts
and information, you run the danger of becoming emotionally frozen.
You cannot make the necessary connections between the past and the
future that everyone needs to grow into a cohesive self. You become
stuck in the life cycle, beached like a whale on the shores of your own
deficient narrative.

IDENTITY ISSUES

Erik Erikson, whose theories of identity have influenced modern thought,
speaks of the psychological tasks that the young person must solve in the
early stages of the life cycle: basic trust and trustworthiness, self-esteem, a

sense of right and wrong, independence, and initiative. Failure to achieve a strong sense of self by accomplishing these tasks leads to what he calls identity confusion: doubt about who you are, what you want to be, and what you want to do.[1] Erikson's sensitivity to identity issues may well have been influenced by his being adopted as a young child by his mother's German-Jewish husband and his lack of knowledge of who his real father was.

"Adoption was the great theme of Erikson's life," a childhood friend of Erikson tells me. "He talked about it all the time, speculated on the possibilities. What if he had been raised by his mother and his real father? What if his mother had stayed in Denmark instead of going to Germany to give birth to him?"[2]

The secrecy, born of shame, that permeates adoptive relationships makes both half and full adoptees into speculators. As Winnicott wrote, it is "dreadful" not knowing whether something is a "fact or mystery or fantasy."[3] No matter how much they probe, adoptees can get no new information from their parents. Questions only make their parents tearful or angry, as if the very mention of adoption could hurl them back into their former childless state, and throw into doubt the authenticity of their family. One man recalls that each time he asked his mother anything about his adoption, he saw her disengage: "Her eyes got a faraway look in them. She was no longer looking *at* me, but *beyond* me."

Their parents' discomfort can't help but make adoptees wonder if there are still things being withheld from them. They can only speculate about what it is that is so secret. Sometimes their persistence will yield another piece in the puzzle that the closed adoption system never meant to be completed.

Powerless to master their past, it is no wonder many adoptees have a hard time getting through adolescence. Some try to stay securely within the confines of the Artificial Self, feeling safe within its constrictions, but not a few pay the price with eating disorders, phobias, and an underlying depression, which rises out of unresolved grief and loss. Other adoptees, courting the true self in the dark corners of the Ghost Kingdom, take an oppositional stance to anyone who tries to control them, be they parents, school teachers, or legal authorities.

Who Am I?

"Life history intersects with history," Erikson wrote,[4] but it is an intersection that adoptees who are denied access to their past cannot find.

They perch ambivalently on their adoptive family tree, whose roots reach back to lands other than those from which their forefathers came. Their ancestors, whose suspect genes and blood fevers even now run amok within them, sent forth shoots from another tree—but where, and when?

"You don't know who or what you lost. Your family is wiped out. You lose everyone, everything," said Howard, a lawyer, who was adopted by a Jewish family from a Jewish agency, but wasn't sure he was Jewish.

The unnaturalness of not knowing your origins makes you feel unnatural, as we can see in this poem by an adopted woman.

I am Frankenstein:
created, not born.

I am Edward Scissorhands:
functioning but not quite finished.

I am the Incredible Shrinking Man:
with a disease no one can name.

I am the android from the Twilight Zone:
my behavior programmed into my circuits.

I am adopted—the freak whose motives will always
be misunderstood

> *—the creature unable to hold your hand*
> *—the earthling with an alien disease*
> *—the monster created by acts of mankind, not acts of God*
> *—the unhuman mandated by law to fill the place of a real*
> *human who could not be here.*

Who Do I Look and Act Like?

Most people take their blood relatedness as much for granted as the air they breathe. Sometimes I browse through books of family memoirs to ferret out references to roots, shared talents, and physical resemblances—things that all but the adopted accept as their birthright. Under the closeness and conflicts of family life, I sense the primal connectedness that people share through genetics and family history.

One night at a dinner party I listened as my host mused about his children: his son looks like his grandfather, but does not have his disposition; his first daughter has his reserved and deep nature; his second daughter looks like his wife's brother and shares his interest in science. Without being conscious of it, he was telling me how his children are connected to the family.

Adopted children never hear their parents make such conversation. They don't know who they resemble or who resembles them, whose interests and talents they share. They suffer from what is called "genealogical bewilderment"—a lack of knowledge of one's real parents and ancestors.[5]

"I've always been a people watcher, always searching for the lost faces I never knew," an adopted man admits. He is describing "visual hunger," the sensory need to see someone who resembles you.[6] He is also revealing what the psychiatrist C. Murray Parkes calls the "separation anxiety" of someone yearning for a person lost to him. Such searching behavior, often accompanied by hyperactivity and restlessness, can be seen as a grief reaction to unresolved loss and, as Parkes points out (and as we shall see in chapter 10), may result in a literal search by an adopted person for the lost birth mother.[7]

Adolescents stare for hours into the mirror hoping to see—what? Perhaps an image of the self in their reflection, as Otto Rank said people have always hoped for as they look into mirrors or, like Narcissus, shimmering water. Adoptees search in the mirror for a glimpse of their mother's eyes, their father's nose, a grandparent's lips, some clue to who they are and what they might become.

Howard remembers his distress as an adolescent when he checked on himself in the mirror. He was the tallest boy in his class, already towering over his adoptive parents. His voice and body were changing so rapidly that he almost suspected his skin would turn green and he would develop horns. "And why not?" he asks. "If half the world believes God impregnated a woman, why couldn't a Martian have impregnated my mother?"

Rachel says that families are a hall of mirrors. "Everyone but adoptees can look in and see themselves reflected. I didn't know what it was like to be me. I felt like someone who looks into a mirror and sees no reflection. I felt lonely, not connected to anything, floating, like a ghost."

Patricia Storace, an adopted woman, creates her reflection in her poetry:

Mother and Father,
lavish and careless
you left kisses everywhere
on the sheets on the glasses
on the walls on the night—
before you knew kisses were permanent.
One settled on my face,
and trembles there—
my mouth its imprint.[8]

What Religion and Nationality Am I?

If, as the sociologists tell us, each family has its own particular culture, the adopted child has lost his culture as well as his name. He moves to the internal rhythms of his unknown progenitors, even as he struggles to fit into the family in which he finds himself. The adoptee cannot say, like Kurt Vonnegut, "In any case, what the heck? I didn't get to choose my ancestors, and I look upon my brain and the rest of my body as a house I inhabit which was built long before I was born."[9] Nor can he say, like Wallace Stegner: "I got the genes and the luck."[10] The adoptee doesn't know who built the house he inhabits, whose genes he got, or whether he got any luck.

Howard, tall and blond unlike his Jewish adoptive parents, worried as an adolescent that he might not be Jewish. If he wasn't Jewish, and wasn't baptized, who would claim him in heaven after he died? He would be alone eternally. As his adoptive father lay dying, Howard pleaded with him: "Please claim me when I come up there."

Janet was told that she had the same Irish and German heritage as her adoptive parents, even though they knew that her birth mother was French-Canadian and her father Italian. Her adoptive father wanted her to think she was German because he didn't like Italians. Janet felt doubly betrayed: her parents had lied about her lineage, which was her birthright, and tried to wipe out her nationality, an authentic part of her.

Separation Anxiety

As we have seen, separation anxiety is a grief reaction to unresolved loss. When they are little, adopted children often have trouble staying overnight at a friend's house, and going to school or to camp. (Howard said: "I had such anxiety I couldn't make it through nursery school.") Later they have trouble leaving home for boarding school or college. While other teenagers are separating from their parents and turning to people outside the family circle, many adoptees fear to venture far from the only place that stands between them and the void. Separation is associated with the visceral feeling of loss from the time of that first separation from the birth mother. Each developmental stage carries with it the threat of new loss—not only of one's adoptive parents but of one's self.

Stan says: "The natural maturational push to move away is conflicted with the terror of loss. No one named this process for me and my family. We only knew that it was strong. Separating, differentiating, and sexual development—although predictable and natural—rearouse issues of loss, infertility, and sexuality, all of which resonate within adoptive families in very special ways."

Adolescents sense this same fear of loss in their adoptive parents, which makes them even more fearful. As one woman put it: "We were tied together in a dysfunctional way by our elephant in the living room, the adoption secret. My parents were not whole without me, and I was not whole without them." Another woman, who still has separation problems, says: "It is difficult for me to say goodbye to my friends. In fact, the word *Bye* has always bothered me. I prefer *See you* because it feels less final."

Adoptees in families with natural children may have even more problems with separation. One woman, who was a teenager when her mother gave birth to a girl, said: "I made a conscious choice. I could either be disposable (as they no longer required a stand-in) or I could become indispensable. I chose the latter." She was so successful that her father would not let her go away to college; she was too badly needed at home to help her mother with her sister and adopted brother.

Helen, who "fell apart" when she entered high school, remembers that she suddenly fell apart again in college. "I was in a strange city, where no one knew who I was and no one cared, and suddenly the identity I'd constructed for myself was air, and it blew away. I was nothing, I came from nothing, and I often thought of returning to nothing. I hid in the closet of my room, my only refuge from four roommates who had come to college to party, not to have an identity crisis." She returned home after the first semester, entered a local college, made new friends, and had a measure of success, but when she began graduate school "it started all over again." This time she went into therapy to talk about her "ambiguous feelings" about her birth parents. "The therapist told me my feelings were based in fantasy—as if they could be anything else! He advised me to stop feeling sorry for myself and get out in the *real* world. That was my last visit to a therapist."

Identity Hunger

According to Erikson, young people who are confused about themselves have "identity hunger."[11] I like this term because it suggests the starved part of the adoptee's psyche—the part that hungers for the nourishment that the mystery about their heritage has denied them. "The secrecy in adoption cuts off your legs just as you're trying to jump over all the hurdles," a male adoptee told me. "There is the presumption that something is wrong because it can't be told. And when a child is raised with secrets, he feels his whole life to be wrong."

Erikson pointed out that the lack of a sense of identity may cause one to reject the desirable role models offered in the family and to choose a negative identity as a way of regaining some mastery. Adoptees who receive the unconscious (and sometimes conscious) message from their adoptive parents that their birth parents don't quite measure up to their standards may find it easier, and more authentic, to take on the negative identity of those devalued birth parents than to meet the high expectations of the adoptive parents. They may do badly in school, hang out with an irresponsible crowd, and have difficulty holding jobs, thereby living out some of the worst fears of their adoptive family.

In answering my questionnaire, some women described their adopted brothers as lacking a sense of direction that would give purpose to their lives; as fluctuating between being extremely passive or self-destructive. Perhaps it is difficult for a male adoptee to be assertive in our competitive society when he doesn't have control of his own personal history. By taking on a negative identity, he may feel he is choosing the truest part of himself. He may reject his adoptive family's social status and go to live among marginal people whom he imagines are like the people he comes from. He may even confabulate stories about his life, giving himself a different name, a different family, and a different history, depending on his immediate needs.

Adoptees often have a hard time in adolescence, when physical development stirs up buried questions about their sexual origins.

"I wasn't confused about my sexuality," one man said. "My parents were." A female adoptee's father told her: "If you get pregnant, I'll throw you out on your ass." Her mother suggested she might want to go on the pill since "some girls' hormones are so strong they can't wait for sex till they get married." Sensing that their adoptive parents worry that they will become like their "wayward" birth mothers, adopted girls often have an unconscious compulsion to act out a self-fulfilling prophecy. Some become pregnant as teenagers and give up their babies for adoption, as if the one way they can identify with their birth mother is to act out the one thing they know about her: her pregnancy and relinquishment of her baby.

Both male and female adoptees may give themselves freely to others out of a sense of worthlessness or as a way of trying to get close to another person. Physical intimacy gives them the illusion of love. The psychologist Stanley Schneider believes that some adolescent adopted girls turn to men in a desperate yearning for "lost maternal love."[12]

Lisa, who is twenty-one, says it makes her feel loved when a man holds her. "I smoked my first joint when I hit thirteen, and found out that if I party, people will like me, think I'm cool. I always had pot or beer I was sharing with the guys, and after a while I was sharing myself with them also. To get money, I would baby-sit or steal. I started doing coke, then crack, then tripped on acid. I always thought the guy I was with would love me to death. It would be perfect. It never turned out that way. Once I attempted suicide when a guy dumped me."

Last year Lisa became pregnant with a baby she had conceived during a three-month binge on cocaine. She said she wanted to give the baby all the love and closeness she never had. "Why should I care that I don't know the father's background?" she asked in response to my question. "I don't even know my own." Like other adoptees with identity hunger, Lisa hoped she could feed off the identity of her lovers. Then she hoped her baby would fill that empty void. She miscarried in her second month, then entered a drug rehabilitation center.

ANIMALS AS SURROGATE SELVES

From the time they are children, adoptees are usually shadowed by a pet of some kind, more than likely of unknown origins. They tend to identify with animals, perhaps because they share some state of grace that is outside the human condition. Girls are particularly drawn to cats, especially if they come from a shelter.

One woman, whom I shall call the Cat Girl, was told that soon after she was brought home from the hospital at two weeks of age, a stray cat attached itself to her family. Her mother took in all the strays after that. "In my mind, I became a stray cat like them," she says:

> My father's nickname for me was "Kitten." My parents thought I could do everything perfectly, but I knew that was a lie. When I wasn't in school, I was locked in my bedroom with my cats trying to become one of them. I learned to sit and sleep in odd positions. My parents gave up trying to communicate with me early on, and when they were away I ate with my cats on the kitchen floor, lapping milk and eating their foul canned food. I practiced jumping from increasingly dangerous heights until I could consistently land on my feet, and walked on thin ledges to improve my sense of balance. Personal hygiene became an obsession.
>
> From the outside my life appeared quite lovely. I was one of the best students in school, elected to offices, chosen for beauty pageants. And yet I lived a double life. In my mind, I was a rejected, abandoned stray who had no rights, and I looked down on anyone who could not see that. I was simultaneously arrogant and diffident. There could be no intimacy with my parents because adoption stood in the way. Instead of binding us together, it became a locked door between us that we didn't know how to open. Any questions I raised about adoption were met with the usual "You're hurting your mother" or "Why would you care about *that woman* who didn't want you?" I have spent thirty-five years with no intimate relationships, living out the fantasy that I was a stray cat whom curiosity would kill. I know that I am not a cat—but I have only acquired that knowledge recently. I wonder how many more stray cats are out there.

The Cat Girl's extraordinary behavior is hardly typical of most adoptees, who raise generations of cats without becoming one. Still, the bizarre quality of it captures the feeling that many adoptees have of being a stray who has been taken in, and is not suited for ordinary human attachment. They may feel more comfortable with animals than with people.

I've had my fair share of pets over the years: dogs, cats, birds, snakes, and iguanas. When I went to Hawaii with my husband for three months to hole up and work on this book, my animals had to remain at home. (Alas, one cannot bring pets—especially iguanas, which are Public Enemy No. 1—into that island state.) Soon after we arrived, I happened to notice that there was a little shop at the corner of our street that was selling puppets and stuffed animals. Without thinking, I started bringing them home, the way the Cat Girl collected her stray cats. Soon the room was a miniature zoo.

What is it with animals and adoptees? I thought. Why am I doing this?

I began to see animals as early attachment figures that the adopted child latches on to. Unlike the transitional object that a young child may keep as a buffer against the world until he is brave enough to go it alone, there is nothing transitional about an adoptee's stuffed or live animal. It is needed for life. The sense of loneliness and disconnectedness is so deep in most adoptees that they feel they can never get close enough to others. The live or stuffed animal grazes loyally in the interstices between them and the rest of the world.

We could say that adoptees project much of their need for the idealized mother onto their animals. These furred and feathered friends give the unconditional love that would have been given by her. Think of it this way: just as the Egyptians had inanimate objects placed in their graves to accompany them through eternity, so adoptees, of all ages, have live and inanimate animals to accompany them through life.

Animal-assisted Therapy

Therapists who are seeing adopted children and adolescents should consider letting their own pets become an integral part of the treatment process. Freud wrote of the "extraordinary intensity" with which he loved his dogs, of their "affection without ambivalence," of the "simplicity of a life free from the almost-unbearable conflicts of civilization," and the "intimate affinity of an undisputed solidarity."[13] Although he never revealed why, Freud kept his chow dogs in the office while treating patients. This master of the unconscious must have consciously known what professionals are just discovering today: animals calm and reduce stress in patients, and in the therapist, too.

I have found animals wonderfully effective with uncommunicative adopted teenagers brought to me by parents who have despaired of finding anyone their kids would open up to. My black Standard poodle Ariadne, self-trained in clinical procedures, had her technique—megalicks—down to a science. During my first counseling session with invariably silent and sullen adopted adolescents, she would put her head gently, but firmly, on the client's knee—which had a biofeedback effect. The adoptee's hand would automatically search out the most effective rubbing spot, usually the top of Ariadne's head, which, in turn, triggered him or her to ask questions about the vicissitudes of Ariadne's life, which then triggered an outpouring of the adoptee's own vicissitudes. At the close of the session, Ariadne would plant a warm, wet megalick on what she considered her client's most needy spot (therapists, take note): the ear.

If Ariadne's subtle canine approach did not work, her partner, Annabelle, a calico farm cat, took over. Her dramatic technique (not to be confused with psychodrama) was to cringe pathetically in a nearby chair. The adolescent would unfailingly walk over to comfort her, which triggered questions about Annabelle's traumatic past: a harrowing saga that made the adoptee's troubles seem insignificant. (In brief, Annabelle and her two-week-old littermates were about to be shot by a farmer in California when they were miraculously rescued by a woman to whom he had confided his plan. Then, during the brief period that my daughter took her in, she was abused by a neighboring tomcat. A few months later, Annabelle's carrying case, with her in it, went astray in an East Coast airport, and she spent four perilous weeks in a shelter before I was able to locate her.) Annabelle's story never failed to open up the most recalcitrant adolescent adoptee, who became eager to return for future sessions in order to see her.

Billy

My conviction about the effectiveness of animal-assisted therapy for adoptees was confirmed when I met Billy during a visit to Green Chimneys, a residential treatment center and farm in New York.[14] The 108 children there are, for the most part, from minority families that have been decimated by poverty, drugs, and violence. There are always some adoptees and foster children. The animal population consists of sheep, cows, goats, pigs, and horses, as well as wild birds and animals who need rehabilitation. The latest arrival was a one-winged bald eagle, incapacitated by the 1989 *Exxon Valdez* oil spill.

Billy, an adopted teenager, differed from the other children at the residential home not only in his South American origins but in that he knew nothing about his birth parents or the country and culture from which he came. He was like an alien dropped from another planet, mingling with the others, pretending to belong. He did not know why he hadn't had the energy to rise in the morning at his adoptive home and go through the motions of living, such as getting to school. It is not uncommon for adopted children, and adults, to suffer from this lack of psychic energy, caused in part by having split off much of their vital self. Because the secrecy in the adoption system extends to children adopted from abroad, Billy had no real facts about himself and was not able to communicate with his adoptive parents about his needs. He was becoming one of those traumatized adopted children who lose any sense of being able actively to influence their destiny, and move into a state of learned helplessness.

Billy didn't talk much until we wandered out to the barn and patted the sheep and goats who nuzzled us. One lamb had lost its mother at Easter and had to be bottle-fed by the children. We talked about how sad it was for the lamb to be without its mother. This was an opening for Billy to admit he knew nothing about his mother or why he was given up. I assured him that it was natural for him to wonder about her. We looked up his native land together on a map in an encyclopedia in his classroom, and read about its geography and culture. I knew he would tuck all this away somewhere in his psyche, and integrate it slowly. Being able to touch the subject of one's mother, to make her real, is a first step toward becoming grounded, developing self-esteem, and having hope.

RACIAL ISSUES

Before you go to war for any purpose, you should stop to think of the innocent children who will be injured, killed, or orphaned.
—JANUSZ KORCZAK

Children of International Adoption

Adopted children of another ethnic heritage, such as Billy, are known as transracial adoptees. To understand the identity problems they face in adolescence, we must go back to the history of how they came to this country, first on the winds of war and then on the wings of poverty and political upheaval.

The earliest influx of transracial adoptees to the United States were mixed-blood children, known as Amerasians, spawned by our soldiers during the American occupation of Japan, and then during the Korean and Vietnam wars. As a foreign correspondent in Korea at the end of the war, and in Vietnam, I saw what war does to innocent children. I saw the young victims in the orphanages; I saw them in the hospitals; I saw them in the streets. Vietnamese children separated from their families were known as the Dust of Life.

Since those war-torn years, Asian children have been scattered like dust by the social chaos in their decimated countries. The shortage of healthy white newborns in this country inspired many infertile couples to overlook racial and religious differences and take in the babies of poor Asian women—unwed factory workers who could not return to their villages with an illegitimate child, and poor mothers who already had too many mouths to feed. Until the last few years, more than half of our transracial adoptees came from Korea. Throughout most of the 1960s and 1970s, as many as three thousand were delivered annually by plane to various U.S. airports by reliable caretakers, who, in exchange, were given travel expenses.

I remember sometime in the 1970s boarding a 747 in Tokyo that had originated in Korea and was bound for New York, via Seattle. On my way through the plane I chanced upon a scene that seemed out of a Fellini movie. On every seat in the central section lay a full-blooded Korean baby swaddled in blankets. There must have been about sixty in all. An eerie silence filled the air, as the infants slept or stared solemnly up at their attendants. Their grave beauty startled me. When I returned to the area during the flight, I found a few restless babies being carried up and down the aisle on comforting shoulders. I soon was carrying one on mine, and the precariousness of the infant's unknown fate made me feel that I was carrying my earlier self on this fragile shuttle hurtling eleven thousand miles through the skies. I wanted to hold her for as long as this journey took, then flee home with her and give her everything I could to make up for the loss of what she was leaving behind in her ancestral land. But, as an adoptee, I knew I could not make up for the pain of the loss of her mother, who, out of poverty, desperation, the dream that her baby could make it better alone, the fantasy of some wealthy foreign couple raising her like a princess, had left her near some police box, knowing that she would be quickly found and taken to an international adoption agency.

"What is her name?" I asked one of the women escorting the babies. She didn't know. "Do the babies have any family identification or any history attached to them?" She looked at the little cloth bracelet with its destination number on the infant's wrist and then looked over its clothing. "I don't see anything," she said. "I guess it's because these babies were abandoned." That is how I first learned that the American families waiting at the airports for their children were given no background information except that dread word *abandoned*.

The sense of being abandoned, of being unwanted, was the heritage around which these children were expected to build a healthy sense of self. The children wouldn't know, because their adoptive parents weren't told, that their mothers were instructed to leave them at the police box so that it would look *as if* they were abandoned. It was a matter of everyone saving face, especially government officials, who made abandonment a legal requisite for the baby to leave the country. The Abandon-the-Baby Game became so successful that international agencies sent representatives around the country looking for pregnant women, wed and unwed alike, who might find it financially as well as socially expedient to take part in the game rather than abort. The policemen in the police boxes, the social workers in the foreign and Korean agencies, and the government officials, who took their cut, were all in on the profitable game. It wasn't until the international press happened to uncover it while covering the 1988 Olympic Games in Seoul that the government, out of shame, drastically reduced the number of babies it exported abroad and began making provisions to provide for them at home.

Over the years I have seen in my consulting room many of these docile babies who turned from cuddly toddlers into depressed adolescents. Their pain and confusion about their identity is much like that of American-born adoptees, except that they have an extra handicap in trying to form a cohesive sense of self. They have lost not only their mother but their motherland and their mother tongue. They have acquired an American name and an American family, but their facial features and the color of their skin reveal another identity, a Korean one, that they can neither wash off nor claim. Many remember being called "chink" or "flatface" at school and taunted with shouts of "Ching Chong Chinaman." No one sees them for who they are, but then they don't know who they are. They often feel alienated from the white community and rejected by the Korean community. Like all adoptees, they may idealize the lost birth mother when they are in adolescent rebellion against the adoptive mother, while at the same time feel unforgiving toward that woman who abandoned them. So, too, they may, at moments of disillusionment with America, idealize the country they have lost, while harboring resentment that it abandoned them.

American parents feel helpless and angry that no one warned them of the pain their adolescents would feel at being abandoned. No one told these parents when the plane landed with its precious unidentified bundles that their love would not be enough, that they should go to Korea before too many years passed and find the people who knew their child's story, or even a fragment of it. I tell adoptive parents to stop letting the agencies, lawyers, or independent facilitators infantilize or intimidate them and to research their children's heritage on their own before the trail becomes cold. This often means returning to the country of origin while the child is still young. The agencies in the home country have information that is not necessarily passed on to their American offices and, even if it is, might not be given to the adopting parents.

The veteran investigative journalist Ruth Gruber became aware of this in the mid-1970s when she went to Korea and Vietnam to ferret out the true stories of NBC reporter Marjorie Margolies's two adopted children, Lee Heh and Holly.[15] In Korea, she learned that Lee Heh had two older brothers in an orphanage in the port city of Inchon, and she heard the family history from them. When their mother was dying from tuberculosis, she asked her sister to leave six-year-old Lee Heh at a police box, as if abandoned, so that she could be put in an orphanage and sent to America for adoption. The aunt warned Lee Heh not to tell anyone she had relatives, so that she could pass as an orphan. Lee Heh kept her secret, as children do, at her own personal cost.

In Vietnam, Gruber discovered that Holly had not been left in a garbage can, as her records showed. Her mother had given her up because she could no longer cope with hunger and hopelessness.

In a more recent situation, young friends of mine took my advice to return to Korea when their son was only two. They learned that he had been sent to the agency in Seoul from a small town in the south. Taking an interpreter with them to their child's birthplace, they unearthed his records in the mayor's office. The documents revealed that the baby had been left by his unmarried father at the gate of a wealthy family, which was the traditional custom in Korea when a poor family could not keep an infant. The father had attached a note saying he would return after trying to reconcile things with the mother. When he didn't appear after a few months, the family turned the baby over to the authorities, who made arrangements with an international American agency in Seoul. My friends are now in correspondence with the wealthy Korean family. Even if they are not able to trace the birth father, their son will have an authentic beginning to his narrative and gratitude for his parents' loving attempts to reclaim his heritage.

Some American families wait to go back to Korea until their children have finished high school, or send them there on a "motherland tour" sponsored by the adoption agency, but it is usually too late by then to locate the children's birth families. One caring adoptive mother who accompanied her college-bound son, Josh, to Korea, accepted the Korean orphanage director's advice not to visit the police box where he had been left as a baby. "I was Josh's first legal guardian, and I say his life began right here," the director told them. The adoptive mother watched as Josh looked thoughtful, and then agreed, "Yes. My life began right here."

"It was a special moment," the mother would write in a magazine article. "In a sense, our son had let go of whatever and whomever might have come before."[16] But had he? She goes on to admit that Josh was moody and difficult all that summer back in the States. Why shouldn't he be? Had the orphanage director conceded that it was too late to go to the police box to find people who would remember him, Josh might have felt better. It would have been an acknowledgment that he had been born of a woman, not of an orphanage. But even more important, Josh had a right to see the police box, the closest he might ever get to his mother or whoever placed him there for her. If the orphanage director was still at his post eighteen years later, the policeman could well have been at his, too. Stranger things have happened when adoptees go in search. It is not impossible that an orphanage director might not want foreigners talking to policemen who are key players in the Abandon-the-Baby Game that is still going on, if not at the same accelerated pace.

Now, when the source for adoptable babies has shifted to countries in

South America and Eastern Europe, some adoptive parents complain of having to spend time in residence while waiting for legal arrangements to be finalized. In the long run, however, it is better that they have a chance to see their child's country of origin, to learn something of its culture and people, and, if possible to meet the birth mother. Elizabeth Bartholet, a Harvard lawyer with one biological son from a former marriage, has written extensively of the difficulties she had with the bureaucracy during her two trips to Peru to adopt her two sons. Pages are devoted to her uncomfortable quarters and the inconveniences of maneuvering in that poor country, but no scholarly or compassionate discourse on why so many native women are desperate enough to give up their newborns; nor is there a personal attempt on her part to learn something about either of her sons' birth mothers. Having come as a late convert to adoption after a decade of failed experiments with reproductive technology, Bartholet decided that biological ties are unimportant to her—and so should be to everyone else, including her adopted children. Her declaration that her adopted Peruvian sons, "with no blood ties linking us together," are clearly the children "meant for me" dismisses the mothers with whom her sons share a blood tie, the importance of that bond, and the grief the boys must feel at its loss, regardless of their love for her.[17]

In contrast to Bartholet's story, I remember the adoptive mother who called me after she returned from Peru with her baby several years ago. She had read *Lost and Found* and was determined to meet the birth mother of her child. She persisted even when officials tried to convince her that it would be impossible to locate this Indian woman in her marketplace stall at the foot of the mountains. The adoptive mother found a guide and for three days roamed through the marketplace until they found the birth mother. She had a dark braid over her shoulder and a young child strapped to her back, which told the adoptive mother that the newborn had been one too many. The two women looked at each other sympathetically, their tears the only common language between them. The adoptive mother felt she had been sanctioned by this woman to raise her son. And she had the greatest gifts an adoptive mother can give her child: the beginning of his narrative and her memory of the warm feelings she shared with his other mother.

One of the luminous things about adoption is that its mystery holds the possibility for miracles. I have found that much of the despair that transracial adoptees experience comes from feeling that they are cut off from their origins by vast distances that seem psychologically as well as physi-cally insurmountable. The parent or therapist who accepts the impossi-bility of any adoptee, and especially one from overseas, ever connecting with the past also abandons the child to that fate. I was to learn from Celia, who came from the Philippines when she was seven, that no child has to be permanently cut off from her roots.

After she had been found wandering the streets of Manila when she was three, Celia was taken by the police to an orphanage, where she was labeled "abandoned." For the next four years she lived in a series of fos-ter homes until she was selected to be sent for adoption in America. Her adoptive mother brought Celia to my office when she was fifteen. She had run away to live in New York's Chinatown the summer before, as if trying to connect with people who looked like her. She did not remember her original name, but she had vague recollections of living with old grandparents and having a father who visited her occasionally. Celia had become lost when she tried to follow her father after one of his visits. Although Celia could draw a picture of the one-room house she had lived in and the lane she walked down that last time, it was all very hazy in her mind.

By chance, at an international child welfare conference in Washington, D.C., I met the director of the Philippine adoption services. She volun-teered to put a story about Celia in the newspapers. At least three fami-lies claimed her, and one proved to be hers. Celia learned that when her parents divorced, her father had given her to his parents to raise and let her mother keep her two older brothers. Her vague memory of grandpar-ent figures proved to be true, and she turned out to be two years older than the age recorded when she was found. Her Philippine family was overwhelmed with joy to know she was alive and to reunite with her dur-ing the brief trip she was able to make there. Neither Celia nor I had imagined that such an extraordinary event could ever happen. She still has the difficult task of integrating her two worlds, but she has the mate-rials with which to build a coherent self.

"Foreign adoption is not the solution, but a tiny, insignificant Band-Aid on a huge, gaping wound and an enormous amount of denial," a Korean adopted woman tells me. "We exploit and export living, breathing prod-ucts known as children."

She is justifiably angry. International adoption has gone from the res-cue of war orphans to the legal, and in many cases illegal, trafficking of children. We are seeing the exploitation of poor women in undeveloped countries as they are encouraged to give up their children to fill the increasing needs of infertile couples in developed countries—which, in turn, fills the pockets of those who facilitate these arrangements. Yet we are in a tragic catch-22 situation. Until we help Third World govern-ments take responsibility for their own social and economic problems so that destitute mothers can keep their offspring, children will be the inno-cent victims of malnutrition, disease, and homelessness. But even as we "rescue" these children from life-threatening situations in their countries, we should heed the words of the Commission on Human Rights that we find ways "to enable biological parents to have the means to retain their children instead of offering them for adoption due to a lack of other options."[18]

There is no question that adoptive parents feel a profound love for their transracial children. Yet all too often that love denies the child's need for connection to his roots. Taking *in* a child from overseas should not mean taking *away* her heritage, but rather should mean helping the child to integrate one with the other.[19]

"Identity issues loom with special intensity for transracial children in the early years and the late years of adolescence," says the clinical social worker Warren Watson. He calls those periods the Front Door and the Back Door of adolescence.

Watson, whose practice in Minneapolis is made up primarily of Korean and South American adoptees, says that the Front Door begins at puberty, when all adoptees look in the mirror and ask, Who am I? and wonder how tall they'll get and what genetic diseases they might have. The Korean adoptees, who have less access to their records, have the added mystery of who left them at the police box where they were found, while South American adoptees have no idea which Indian tribe they come from.

The Back Door begins at eighteen, when transracial adoptees leave home, but don't know how to be separate and still stay connected. Not knowing where they are going, and with nothing to grab on to, they are thrown back to their early abandonment issues.

"No matter how good their family, or how connected they feel, they are aware that they look different, feel different, and are different," Wat-son says. While the younger adolescents display mostly sadness as they wonder why they were given up, the older ones act out more, breaking family and social rules. They may steal cars, drink, indulge in sex, and fight with their parents, who often place a high premium on middle-class values. Watson finds that the most rebellious adolescents come from families that are rigid, deny the differences in their children, and have unmatched expectations. For their part, the children believe that the different culture they came from doesn't match up with the strict religious mores of their parents, especially when the Christian message of sin makes them feel a sense of shame about their conception and abandonment.

Watson tries to help these adolescents break through their defenses in order to get in touch with their feelings and express their grief. Those who can speak openly with their adoptive parents about their feelings and fantasies about their birth parents and country of origin will feel better about themselves. He still recalls the fourteen-year-old Colombian boy, adopted at fourteen months, who told him: "I just want to go back for a visit. Even if I can't find my birth parents, I can see what I saw, smell what I smelled, and feel what I touched."[20]

Biracial Adoptees

> I don't think there's anything inherently wrong with adopting children of another race, but you need more than pity to be a good mother. After adopting, you still have to raise it.
> —ADOLESCENT BIRACIAL ADOPTEE

I was matched to my parents by religion and race, as was the custom in traditional adoption until the shortage of available white newborns like me forced infertile couples to consider other options—which meant becoming color-blind. Biracial children, as American mixed-blood children are called, are the same as other children in the eyes of their adoptive parents, but, unfortunately, the eyes of a racist society will see and respond to every mark of difference. For this reason, the National Association of Black Social Workers came out in 1972 against the adoption of black or biracial children by nonblack families, calling it "racial genocide." This policy has held until recently, when white couples are once again actively seeking to adopt children of color who are in the foster care system.

Biracial children are considered black in this country, even though one of their parents is white. The uniqueness of their identity in belonging to both races, which makes them *both* black and white, has not been recognized by society. Whichever race they are adopted by, these children carry an extra burden because the secrecy in the adoption system keeps them from knowing their full ethnic heritage.

Amanda was adopted by white, upper-middle-class parents who felt the moral obligation to give a home to a needy child after having one biological son. "They were doing the latest fad," Amanda explains. "It was the in thing to adopt black kids in the sixties.' She was told that one of her parents was a person of color, but which parent and which color were not clear. Her mother said it was her birth mother who was either East Indian or African-American, while her father said it was the birth father. People thought she was East Indian or Italian. She didn't "have a clue" what she was. The black kids in the little Florida town where she lived for the first few years of her life treated her like a curiosity at first, and then beat up on her because they thought she was "uppity" to hang out with white kids. In middle school a black student broke her jaw when she couldn't tell him what she was.

Amanda feels that adopted biracial children are at more of a disadvantage than nonadopted ones: "My friend Gloria, whose mother is white and whose father is black, is always harassed by Hispanic kids because she doesn't look Spanish enough. She doesn't get upset, because she knows what she is. But an adopted person like me doesn't know." Amanda's friend Carl, who had a white birth mother but was adopted by a black family and has a "black identity," made her feel it was a disadvantage to be adopted into a white home: "He says it's obvious I had a white adoptive mother because she didn't teach me how to manage my hair, and that I would have a stronger sense of how to combat racism if I grew up in a black family."

A sadness settled on Amanda in adolescence and developed into a deep depression. Her adoptive mother lost interest in her after she divorced her husband, and Amanda didn't get on with her new stepmother. She became addicted to drugs and alcohol, and ended up in a residential treatment center for the last two years of high school. When a prestigious college accepted her, she felt it was because they needed another black student. Only the maternal support of a professor got her through alcoholic binges and suicidal gestures. "If my natural mother had stuck by me, I wouldn't be suffering like this," she thought. "I would be connected."

When, in her early twenties, Amanda found her birth mother, she met a white woman who was also adopted, and deeply ambivalent about having a biracial daughter. "You don't know what I went through because of you," her mother said. "I was married to a white man. You were black. My adoptive father was threatening to disinherit me." She made it clear that she wouldn't have agreed to meet Amanda if she hadn't been raised by a white family.

Now, at twenty-five, Amanda thinks of herself as mixed race. "We are our own race," she tells her biracial friends. She doesn't think it matters whether a biracial child is adopted by a black or white family, as long as there is love. "My European heritage is as important to me as my African-American side," she says. But she feels she will not understand her black heritage until she finds her father. And her birth mother refuses to give her his name.

Max, also biracial, in his twenties, and adopted by a white family, believes that people "oversimplify" the race issue. He wants to find his birth father more than his mother because he feels that not only race is involved but gender, too. He was told his birth mother was white, but his father might be half Native American and half black. He hopes this is true about his father because he thinks he would be more accepted on a reservation, where tribal identification, unlike racial identification, has a specific history and culture. But he looks black. And he has a lot of anger for the way he was treated by the other kids in his white community. When he finally met some black students in high school, they called him an "Oreo"—black on the outside, white on the inside. "They thought I was pretending to be something I wasn't," Max explains. "I couldn't speak black English."

Max feels that the best environment for a biracial child is a mixed one. But he suspects that the child would do better in a black family or a family of color: "Racism is something you have to deal with," he says. "White parents can't prepare you. I have not been able to escape the fact that I am a person of color and, therefore, regarded as a second-class citizen in the eyes of many people. As a mixed-race person who has been rejected by people of all races, I feel pretty insecure about my heritage."

On the other hand Peter, after years of struggling with his mixed-race identity in a white family—years that included prison terms for drug use and breaking and entering—says: "I don't look at things in black and white anymore. Who is to say what's black and white? I belong to the human race. I'm a human being."

We can see that separation from and lack of knowledge of one's racial or ethnic identity can be a stumbling block for children born in this country as well as for those born overseas. The issue of whether black and mixed-race children can thrive in a white home is being raised again by would-be adopters, who point to the thousands of children of color languishing in foster care.

Joyce Pavao, a family therapist in Boston specializing in adoption, and an adoptee herself, says that her first choice would be to place a child with his extended family or, if that were not possible, within the larger community of his race and religion. She would rather have children adopted by white families than spend years in foster care, but only if those families were willing to stretch themselves. They would have to see their family identity as biracial, which would mean changing their life-style and moving into an integrated neighborhood for the sake of the child. They would have to understand what the adoption specialist Annette Baran has been saying for decades: "You stop being white when you adopt a black child." Both Pavao and Baran believe that biracial adoption should have some degree of openness, that the child has the right to stay connected in some way with his origins.[21]

The rights of the adopted child, along with the rights of all children, have been addressed in the 1989 United Nations Convention on the Rights of the Child, which states that the child has a right from birth to a name, to acquire a nationality, and, as far as possible, to know and be cared for by his or her parents. A separated child has the right to maintain contact with both parents.

When these goals are met, the adopted child will not have to go underground with his feelings of sadness, powerlessness, and anger. In the next chapter, we will learn what happens when these feelings get out of the adoptee's control.

8

The Antisocial Tendency

He is a fake child.

No doubt he was born of a woman, but this origin has not been noted by the social memory.

As far as everyone and, consequently, he himself are concerned, he appeared one fine day without having been carried in any known womb: he is a synthetic product.

Since his earliest childhood, the unknown mother has been one of the chief figures of his mythology.

He both worships and hates her, smothers her with kisses and seeks to debase her.

Whenever the child tries to reach beyond the bureaucracy of which he seems an emanation to his true origins, he finds that his birth coincides with a gesture of rejection. He was driven out the very moment he was brought into the world. The child senses that a woman tore him from herself, alive, covered with blood, and sent him rolling outside the world, and he feels himself an outcast.

—JEAN-PAUL SARTRE, *SAINT GENET*

THE ADOPTED BOY WHO WAS DETERMINED TO BE "the best juvenile delinquent in the community" once bragged: "The secret is to look like a Mormon and act like a Sicilian." He achieved his goal and ended up, like so many angry and depressed adopted adolescents, bouncing around between hospital psychiatric wards and residential treatment centers.

I thought of this boy and others like him when I read Winnicott's article "The Antisocial Tendency."[1] Winnicott saw hope in a child's acting out, which he identified as a reaction to perceived losses in the early mother-child relationship. He felt that the child was seeking something of which he had been deprived as a way of a "self-cure."

What are adoptees seeking? I see those who act out as crying for attention and help, while fighting to preserve their integrity. Just as Winnicott spoke of the "true self in cold storage,"[2] we could say that these adoptees are trying to thaw out the true self, to bring a dead self to life. Their antisocial behavior is the unconscious strategy they seize upon to feel authentic, vital, and alive—their form of self-cure. In order for therapists to help with the cure, they must, in Winnicott's view, manage "to meet and match the moment of hope."[3] Therapists should not be asking why adopted children are angry, but why shouldn't they be?

THE ANGRY SELF

Anger, the other side of depression, is always waiting to be tapped in the adoptee, especially in adolescence. "Adolescence is about separation, identity, and sexuality," says a male adoptee who is also a therapist, "but the biological unknowns for adoptees complicate and handicap this process. It was a tough time for me. Although I remained a model student at school, I became an unhappy and angry teenager at home."

Children who are not given permission to express their negative emotions while they are growing up do not get practice in venting them appropriately. Adopted children, who get the message that not only were they chosen, but they were chosen to be the light of their parents' lives, often do not feel entitled to express any negative feelings, such as grief or anger at being cut off from their origins. Some become so successful at splitting off their feelings and keeping up a cheerful facade that they do not even know when they are angry.

Michael, who had been a compliant child, remembers telling a friend that he never got angry, and being amazed when the friend responded: "Michael, you're furious right now." It made him start wondering why he didn't feel his anger. He decided that he felt depressed and worthless instead: "There was toxicity throughout my system, but I was so split off, I wasn't aware of it."

Paul, a Roman Catholic priest who prided himself on his even disposition, was surprised at being called angry in seminary evaluations. But he was even more surprised at his rage when a nun refused to give him information from his adoption files. "If I had a gun in my hand, she would be dead," he said. "I was ready to kill."

Anger that adoptees have built up over the years can erupt as uncontrollable rage. There is the unexpressed anger that they are adopted; anger that they are different; anger that they are powerless to know their origins; anger that they cannot express their real feelings in a family climate of denial. When this anger is allowed to build in a child over the years, it will eventually surface as aggression—stealing, setting fires, destroying property—and, if left unresolved, as violence. When treatment is sought, the adoptee is usually identified as the patient, but therapists are beginning to pay attention as well to the unconscious hostile interaction between parent and child.

The psychologist Stanley Schneider, an American who directs a residential treatment center for adolescents in Jerusalem (many of whom come from Canada and the United States), believes that there is a greater tendency in adoptive families for a child to act out the unconscious hostile and sexual impulses of a parent. Schneider sees the adopted child's internal world as a seething caldron containing four elements of anger:

the anger of the parent(s) who gave the child up for adoption
the anger of the child's adoptive parents
the child's anger at the natural parents
the child's anger at the adoptive parents.[4]

If the adoptive mother and father are having difficulties in their marriage, they may project onto the child their underlying feelings of hostility toward each other. One parent may be angry at the other for being infertile. They both may be angry at the child for not being the child they might have had. They may even harbor unconscious anger at the birth mother for conceiving, when they could not, and producing a child who does not live up to their ideal.

The birth mother and birth father are both angry at fate for getting them into this situation. The mother is angry at the father for deserting her, at her parents for not helping her to keep her baby, and at the system, which did not provide the support that would have enabled her to raise the child.

The child is angry at the birth parents, especially the mother, for giving him away. He is also angry at the adoptive parents for taking his birth parents' place and not providing information about them. He is angry at the system for sealing his records. And at fate for making him different.

Upon reaching adolescence, the adopted child, according to Schneider, has to contend with all these elements of anger. They may explode into tremendous rage, which manifests itself in destructive acting-out behavior.

CUMULATIVE ADOPTION TRAUMA

It is no longer a secret that there is a disproportionate number of adoptees in hospital adolescent psychiatric wards and residential treatment centers across the country—but professionals disagree about the cause. The rationale one hears that middle-class adoptive families are more inclined to seek psychotherapy does not explain why their adopted children are disturbed enough to need it. Other reasons given are genealogical bewilderment (lack of knowledge of origins);[5] interaction between parents and child, such as the parents' overreaction to the child's sexuality; good medical insurance for in-care treatment; a proneness of insecure adoptive parents to hospitalize children unnecessarily; genetic impairment in the child; and the consequences of the birth mother's anxiety and poor prenatal care. I suspect another cause might be the difficulty that many young adoptees have repressing their grief and anger and sense of powerlessness in the closed adoption system, which has been called a seedbed for a personality disorder.[6]

Reports in the psychological literature that adopted children often show identity problems because they do not know their antecedents have proved threatening to some adoptive parents, who attack these findings as "cultural prejudice and myth" and interpret them to mean that adoptive families are "defective," that adoptive children are "doomed to psychological pathology," and that adoption is "somehow inferior to biological parenting."[7] The need to idealize the institution of adoption in order to ward off their own fears unfortunately prevents these parents from being in touch with their children's pain. It is as if they want to believe that if the professionals don't write about the problems they observe, then those problems don't exist.

Perhaps the most alarming professional paper on adopted children was delivered in the mid-1970s by the Mexican psychiatrist Luis Feder, who first used the terminology "adopted child pathology" and "adoption syndrome." After studying two hundred adoption case histories, Feder concluded that the "traumatic vicissitudes" of adoption—from the abandonment by the rejecting, feticidal birth mother to the unknown motivations of the adoptive parents—can cause pathology in the child. This pathology could "flower" into narcissistic character disorder, delinquency, homosexuality, fantasies of or attempted suicide, incest, psychotic episodes, homicide, fratricide, and parricide.[8] His pronouncements sound as distressing today as they did then, but later in this chapter we will see how prophetic some of them were.

More recently, David Kirschner, a Long Island psychologist with twenty-five years of experience in treating young adoptees, gave the name "Adopted Child Syndrome" to the pattern of disturbed behaviors and characteristics he observed in his young patients. The children's symptoms include pathological lying, stealing, truancy, learning problems, running away, setting fires, sexual promiscuity, an absence of normal guilt and anxiety, and extreme antisocial behavior that often gets them in trouble with the law. He found their personalities were characterized by impulsivity, low frustration tolerance, manipulativeness, and deceptive charm that covered over a shallowness of attachment.[9]

The idea that there could be an adopted child *syndrome* is understandably very frightening to adoptive parents and is perhaps the most controversial issue in the field today. Some professionals who agree with most of Kirschner's findings are uncomfortable with the term *syndrome* because it implies pathology in medical usage, although Kirschner means it as behaviors grouped together.[10] One writer, an adoptive mother, called it a "pseudosyndrome" and accused those who use it of "scare tactics" that will frighten away those who want to adopt.[11] This need to wage a semantics battle to deny the complexities of adoption is unfortunate, for the professionals who write about the pain and trauma of the adopted child are publishing their observations in an effort to help adopted children and their families. As the child analyst Steven Nickman, himself an adoptive father, writes: "The family with its support systems, and ultimately society at large, bear a responsibility for recognizing the dilemmas of adopted children and youth." By living up to this responsibility, they can help "avoid contributing to the development of full-blown character disorders in later life."[12]

I have seen enough evidence in the constellation of disturbed behaviors exhibited by adopted children and adults I have worked with to accept that there is an adoption syndrome. I prefer, however, to call it *cumulative adoption trauma* because, as I mentioned in chapter 1, there are a series of traumas. They begin to accumulate from the time the child is separated from the mother at birth, learns that he is not the biological child of his family, and then dissociates in order to live as if he does not need to know whose child he is. In order that the term cumulative adoption trauma not sound the clarion call for alarm, I suggest that it (like the syndrome) be seen on a broad continuum: from mild to serious to pathological disturbance. My own work with nonclinical adoptees who have grown up in the closed adoption system reveals that virtually all of them can be located somewhere on the continuum, even if mostly on the lower end, as they struggle with issues around self-esteem, lack of trust, and fear of abandonment, to name just a few.

Acting-out adoptees—those with antisocial and self-destructive tendencies—make up the broad middle range. A small, extremely disturbed subgroup who exhibit criminal and murderous behaviors, and make headlines, are on the pathological far end of the continuum.

Acting Out

Among the acting-out behaviors that we find in the middle range of the continuum, the most common are lying and stealing, running away, and addictions to drug, alcohol, or food.

Lying and Stealing

Winnicott places stealing at the center of the antisocial tendency, along with lying.[13] Since adopted children often feel that they are living a lie that is endorsed by society, how can they know what truth is?

A young woman says: "Being adopted is a life of lies. Who I am born, I am not. Now I am given to someone else. Now I am this person. I was Italian. Now I am Irish. I see I am different, my hair, my skin. Flesh tells me. I lie constantly for no reason. Stories. Always telling stories. No one understands why. When they notice." A man says: "Living a lie that is endorsed and fueled by society makes it easy to evolve into a person who is incapable of knowing what truth is. This is costly to oneself and eventually to society."

According to Winnicott, "the child who steals an object is not looking for the object stolen but seeks the mother over whom he or she has rights."[14] Many adoptees recall stealing from their parents' wallets when they were young because they felt they had been stolen from their mothers and ripped off by the adoption system. Stealing can also be seen as a form of revenge, taking the "reparations" adoptees often say they feel they deserve. Or it can be an expression of rage. One woman, who described her stealing as a "vicious act," saw it as a substitute for hitting people.

Laing saw stealing as a way of taking control. "If you steal what you want from the other person, you are in control," he wrote. "You are not at the mercy of what is given."[15]

Walter, an artist in his thirties, is always quoting from George Orwell's *Nineteen Eighty-four*, especially the passages "who controls the past controls the future" and "the past had not been altered, it had been destroyed." He says: "You trade your identity, sever the past, rewrite history when you're adopted. In high school I felt I lived in a totalitarian state of mind. I had an altered birth certificate and a destroyed history. It's a tragedy—all that energy going into the lie. To steal someone's mind is the perfect crime."

Walter has been stealing from the time he was a child: candy bars from stores, money from his parents' wallets. But it was usually for the "sport" of it; he'd return things more often than not. "I can understand how someone becomes a criminal," he says. "Stealing is like drink, just a different form of self-destruction. I am in battle between the sacred and the profane." He was recently caught for the first time, in his hometown while visiting his seriously ill father. It was an inexpensive item, and he sensed that he would be discovered.

The worst part was having to face his parents: "I was sorry I had besmirched their name, that it might be in the paper. I felt defeated, hopeless, worthless, ashamed, even suicidal as I drove home to tell them. I wanted to run my car off the road. And yet I felt a psychological pressure to confess to my father. I imagined he would say: 'How can I help you?' And I would reply: 'Help me get information on my birth mother.'

"But that's not the way it happened. My father asked if I had done this before. I confessed I had, and asked him why he thought I did. 'You have a hole in your conscience and you'd better plug it up' was all he said."

Running Away

Running away has been called the "roaming phenomenon" and a "symbolic search" for the parents.[16] We could say that the adopted adolescent is not running *from* but *to* something. One man remembers that he would head toward Denver, where he was born, with the thought that his birth mother might be there. It didn't matter that he didn't know her name and had no way of looking her up.

Some adoptees go to live in a friend's house, as if wanting to try another family out for size. This substitute family can satisfy their fantasy of what it would have been like to grow up with their real family. Others run for the sake of running, as if they can somehow escape themselves or their fate. "Running away from yourself is the hardest thing to do," according to one woman, who ended up a ward of the state at thirteen.

Drug, Alcohol, and Food Addictions

Adoptees who become addicted to food or alcohol often feel that they are hiding out from grief and pain. "I need something to fill me up," one woman said. "I can't stop stuffing myself." And another said: "Even before adolescence, food meant nurturance. I became a compulsive eater, snitching and hoarding food until a binge."

Bea, adopted at six days by a professional family, describes her teen years as very destructive: "In eighth grade I was one of 'three most popular girls,' a cheerleader, and an A student. Starting with my freshman year of high school, I was like a different person. I drank, smoked pot, did acid, popped pills, stole clothes, and slept around. My grades were C's and D's. I hung around with the drug crowd from backgrounds unsimilar to mine, generally uneducated, lower middle class. I was angry, hostile and—honestly—I thought I was having the greatest time of my life."

Ralph, adopted at three months, spent much of his adolescence in trouble, including four years in juvenile detention for taking drugs. Yet he doesn't feel he was a bad boy. He didn't know what to make of his pain. In his desperation to belong to a family of his own choosing, to feel alive, he tagged along after the tough boys, where the action was.

The Suicidal Self

"There are no statistics on the number of adoptees who attempt suicide, or those who succeed," I told a group of professionals and adoptive parents at a community meeting on adoption a few years ago. I added that if there were, we might be surprised at the large number. An electric charge went through the audience, seeming to unite everyone there against me, the bearer of bad news. The next day I received a call from the child analyst who had organized the meeting, asking permission to erase my comment on suicide from the tape. She explained that it was too disturbing for adoptive parents, and as long as I had no statistics, she felt justified in making this request.

I told her she could delete it, but I am not proud of having done so. The adopted child in me had surfaced, wanting to please the authorities. Since then, I have wondered why the impulse of professionals and parents is to avoid rather than to probe this subject. A rash of adolescent suicides in the nonadopted community brings out specialists who ponder the cause and seek a solution. Why shouldn't this be done in cases where adopted children are involved? Does the idea of adoptee suicide suggest parental, professional, and societal failure? Is there a resistance to connecting adoption and suicide?

In a study on the relationship between parental loss and suicide, the British psychiatrist Steven Greer, influenced by the pioneering work of John Bowlby, concluded that parental loss in childhood, particularly when this occurs in the first four years of life and involves the loss of both parents, "may predispose patients with neurotic disorders to suicidal behavior."[17] He found that the relationship between parental loss and attempted suicide appears to be independent of the absent parent's sex, the cause of parental loss, and the subsequent childhood environment.

Adopted children lose both parents early in life, even though this loss is not acknowledged by their adoptive parents and their community. While reading through the two hundred questionnaires filled out by adoptees for my research, I was struck by the large number who had contemplated or tried suicide during adolescence, or had adopted siblings who succeeded. One woman wrote of her brother who hung himself at the age of twenty in the basement of their home. "He always felt like a loser," she said. "He gave up on everything, including his life." The family found a copy of an anonymous poem called "The Man in the Glass" among his things. Its message is that you can fool others, but not the person who looks back at you in the mirror:

When you get what you want in your struggle for self
And the world makes you king for a day.
Just go to a mirror and look at yourself,
And see what THAT man has to say.

For it isn't your father or mother or wife
Who judgment upon you must pass;
The fellow whose verdict counts most in your life
Is the one staring back from the glass. . .

You may fool the whole world down the pathway of years
And get pats on the back as you pass,
But your final reward will be heartaches and tears
If you've cheated the man in the glass.

Here is a typical sampling from the questionnaires on the subject of suicide from adult adoptees who on the surface are leading satisfactory lives:

A man adopted at ten weeks: I was always suicidal. As far back as five or six. I remember saying I wish I were dead.

A woman adopted at six weeks: I had no sense of self as an adolescent. I felt unreal, split. I was depressed most of the time. I thought I was crazy. I attempted suicide a few times.

A man adopted at three weeks: I got depressed occasionally (usually when I wasn't stoned) and even contemplated suicide.

A woman adopted at four weeks: I often felt suicidal and attempted it twice—had my stomach pumped once and a shotgun taken from under my chin the other time. I could never cut myself.

A man adopted at three months: I felt I wanted to commit suicide, but I was already dead so I didn't have to.

Over the years, I have kept a special folder filled with clippings on adoptee suicide that friends and acquaintances have sent me. One of the most poignant notices to cross my desk was a death announcement submitted by a bereaved father to the Alumni News of an elite women's college. He wrote that during the last two years of his adopted daughter's life, "she suffered from a complete nervous and physical breakdown, in part from the rejection she felt as an adopted child. This resulted in a profound depression from which she could see no relief other than by taking her own life." He added proudly that she had recently completed a master's thesis on "Lewis Thomas and the Role of Man in a Biology Watcher's World," and closed with: "She leaves her adoptive parents."

Not too long ago, Mi Ok Bruining, an adopted Korean woman, sent me the poem she wrote for Peter Young Sip Kim, a Korean adoptee who committed suicide a month before his thirty-first birthday:

We talked of suicide often,
of your two previous attempts—
when you were alive and still of this earth.
It was never a morbid topic for us—
but a secret desire and seductive fear
we shared as kindred spirits.

When I tell my friends of your death,
Peter, of our profound loss—
they ask: Why? Did you and I know?
Because, I reason: it was about being adopted
and feelings—of being different,
never belonging, never feeling whole
nor complete, feeling rejected and discarded
and yes, you and I know.
    .   .   .   .
I tell my friends of your suicide, Peter,
because your sadness and regrets
and anger and rage must not be forgotten.[18]

I have only recently discovered any statistics on adoptee suicides in a research study on adolescents that showed higher levels of depression and anxiety in adopted compared to nonadopted boys. Among the findings were that adopted boys were more at risk for suicide and have attempted suicide at a higher rate than their nonadopted peers.[19]

The group that did this research has a large federal grant to study the mental health of adopted teenagers. The project came about through the initiative of the adoptive parents of an eighteen-year-old college student named Andrew, who put a bullet through his head in the family's home during a weekend visit.

Andrew was a fun-loving, tender child who was always for the underdog, his adoptive mother told me. As the youngest of three adopted children, he would tag along after his sister, Mary, who was six years old when he arrived as a nine-day-old infant. When she talked of finding her "other" mother, he talked of finding his. The middle child, who was four years older than Andrew, would walk out of the room when these discussions came up. Ironically, he would be the one to search first. After the name of his birth mother was inadvertently given to him by the adoption agency when he was seeking information for a passport application, he looked in the phone book and found it. His birth mother welcomed him, and he became especially close to his grandparents, who lived only seven miles away.

Mary was not to have the same luck. When, after graduating from college, she asked the adoption agency to act as an intermediary, she was told that her mother refused to have contact. Mary's life went into a tailspin: it took several years to recover from the negative impact of drugs and abusive relationships. Andrew seemed to change after that, too. He felt as if he had lost his sister. He began to write poetry about death and to do so badly in high school that he almost didn't graduate. "I feel sometimes I don't belong in this world," he'd say, and brood over not knowing anyone he resembled physically. He did not speak anymore of finding his mother. When his adoptive father asked him the summer before his death whether he might search for her, he exploded with anger, saying, "She's probably a whore." That same summer, in the depth of depression, he told a friend that he needed to know his birth mother but had decided not to look for her because he was afraid of what he might find. "I've closed that door," he said.

There were, of course, other problems in Andrew's life. He had never been able to hold a job, to finish things, or to control his explosive temper. His mother remembers that once during a minor argument with his parents, Andrew picked up a kitchen chair in a blinding rage. She was afraid, for in that moment he was not the Andrew she knew. Later, during a discussion about his anger in family counseling, he said, "I don't remember what happens when I get angry. I black out."

That final summer, while his parents were on vacation, Andrew showed further signs of instability. He lost his driver's license, was fired from the job his father had arranged, and changed his mind at the last minute about going into the marines.

In the fall, Andrew went to a college in the same state. He made friends quickly in the first five weeks, even found a girlfriend, but had trouble with one course. In early November, the day before his suicide, he phoned his mother and said he wanted to come home for the weekend. He mentioned a fight with his girlfriend, but gave no hint of his plan. Nor did he tell his mother that he had just received his midterm report card with an F in the course that had bothered him. His mother noticed he seemed disorganized when he arrived. He gave a number of reasons for not bringing his dirty clothes home to be washed: no time to collect them, no room in the car. Later, she would understand that he knew he was never going to need those clothes.

On the last day of his life, Andrew made a point of having a long talk with his mother. He asked about her studies and encouraged her to pursue her vocational goals no matter what obstacles she might encounter. It was his way of saying goodbye. When his father called from the office to say he would be late coming home for dinner, Andrew said, "Goodbye, Dad," in a choked voice that left his father feeling uneasy.

Andrew went out with his friends to eat, have a few beers, and go bowling. His parents were in bed when he returned about 1:00 A.M. A friend he called said that Andrew sounded depressed and had trouble hanging up. Andrew tried to phone his girlfriend, but her mother said it was too late and told him to call back in the morning. According to the coroner, it must have been about 3:00 A.M. when he shot himself in the basement family room with the gun he used for hunting. He left a sprawling poem, one line of which was "So much to lose!"

The suicidologist Edwin Shneidman points out that there is rage, guilt, anxiety, and dependency in the psychodynamics of suicide. The predisposing conditions are feelings of abandonment, helplessness, and hopelessness. "Every suicide comes from unfulfilled needs," he writes. "It is an attempt to stop the unbearable anguish or intolerable emotion."[20]

As we have seen, adoptees often have feelings of abandonment, helplessness, and hopelessness. Andrew seems to have identified with his sister when her mother refused to see her. He must have sensed that he, too, would be rejected and that he did not have the psychic strength for it. Everything he did after that seemed to send him on a downward spiral. He often apologized to his adoptive parents for failing them. "I am going to the ancestors of other worlds," he wrote in a poem shortly before his death. Perhaps he felt it took less courage to find his birth family in the next world than to risk finding them in this one.

Parents of children who commit suicide always feel guilty and sense that the community somehow blames them for the death. Andrew's mother remembers pounding the kitchen table in anger that morning when she and her husband discovered their son's body. "Adoption! These kids never feel like they really belong in this world. Who will understand?"

This anguished question eventually sent her "into a whole new world of discovery." She would have to be the one to understand. She attended meetings of adoption support groups, where she listened to adoptees who were searching for their roots and to birth mothers who were searching for children they could not forget. At adoptive parent groups, she heard mothers and fathers who were searching for answers to their children's erratic behavior, just as she was searching for answers to Andrew's suicide.

"Andrew was angry at adoption," she would write eight years later in a book on grief. "Even though he was close to us who were his adoptive family, he needed to know and claim his birth family. When I imagine the pain he felt, I feel ill. The child I cradled and fed. The scratched knees, the fevers, the bruises we mended. And then a pain THIS DEEP! I still want to fix it! I am so helpless. Forever helpless."[21]

The book she has written, her lectures to parent groups across the country, as well as the knowledge that she has instigated a research study on adolescent adoptees, have helped her feel less helpless. After learning about the psychology of suicide, she feels free from guilt. "I am not responsible for my son's death," she writes. But she has taken on the responsibility of educating other adoptive parents about the psychology and needs of their adopted children. By possibly saving the lives of other children in the future, she is giving meaning to Andrew's life and death.

Adoptees Who Kill

How do we go from suicidal adoptees whose rage is turned inward to those who kill?

"Behind every suicide is a homicide," David Kirschner tells me. He believes that many of the adoptees who murder were more suicidal than homicidal. "Their histories show that they often made repeated suicidal attempts first. They smashed up cars, took pills, courted danger. You don't hear about the suicide attempts in the media. They're not sensational enough."[22]

The painful truth is that at the extreme end of the antisocial continuum we find a very small subgroup of adoptees who commit violent crimes, such as serial murder. It is as difficult for me to report this as I am sure it is for the reader to absorb, but we must pay attention to this group, for, as the criminologist Jack Levin points out, adoptee serial killers have become household names.[23]

I remember when David Berkowitz ("Son of Sam") terrorized New York City in 1976–77 by shooting and killing six young women, and wounding others in parked cars, and my fear that he might be lurking somewhere when I walked my dog in the evening. I can also remember my shock when I heard that he was adopted. I received many calls from adopted friends with reactions such as "My God, he's one of us!" Then, sixteen years later, as I was completing this book, Joel Rifkin ("The Rip-per") also adopted as an infant, and labeled the worst serial killer in New York history, confessed to strangling seventeen women and dumping their mutilated bodies in rivers and woods over a wide area. In different parts of the country, other male serial killers—many adopted shortly after birth—have also targeted young women as their victims and made the headlines.[24]

While one cannot say that the fact of being adopted in itself explains the murderous behavior, one cannot discount it as a contributing factor. In his book *The Confessions of Son of Sam*, the psychiatrist David Abra-hamsen discusses the deleterious effect that the "mystery of his origins" had on the young David Berkowitz, and decides that crucial to turning him into a murderer was that he was adopted.[25]

One could hypothesize that adoptee serial killers vent their rage on prostitutes or seemingly loose women, as if to get revenge on the woman who bore them illicitly and abandoned them. This is borne out by Erik-son's observation that since a person retains an image of his mother as a young woman, Berkowitz could have been shooting the mother who abandoned him.[26] Abrahamsen reports that six months before his killings began, Berkowitz had searched for and found the mother he had been told died in childbirth, and was troubled to learn that she gave him up for adoption while keeping his legitimate half-sister. It made him feel like "an accident, a mistake, never meant to be born—unwanted." He fumed that his mother was sitting in parked cars with his father. Abrahamsen concludes that Berkowitz chose his victims as "substitutes of his mother and/or sister, and of himself," as the only way "to prevent them from having illegitimate children who would have to go through all the misery, unhappiness and pain he himself had experienced," and "to relieve and release his unbearable emotional tension."

In trying to make sense of what he had done, Berkowitz wrote Abra-hamsen from prison: "I believe it is vitally important for workers in the mental health field and the public at large to understand what was on my mind and what really motivated me to commit my crimes. No doubt another 'Son of Sam' (multiple murderer) will follow in my path—the path that has previously been cleared before me."[27]

It is essential not only to probe the motivations of those who have fol-lowed Son of Sam but also to study why the majority of the small sub-group of adoptees who kill take the path not of serial murder but of par-ricide.

When Leslie Walker, a political reporter for the *Baltimore Sun*, wrote *Sudden Fury: A True Story of Adoption and Murder*, on the 1984 trial of Larry Swartz, a seventeen-year-old adoptee who killed both of his adoptive parents, she didn't know that the story she told was not exceptional.[28] Evidence shows that a large number of murders of one or both parents are committed by teenage or young adult adoptees (those adopted soon after birth as well as later). The criminal lawyer Paul Mones puts this statistic at 15 or 20 to 1, adoptees over nonadoptees. In the last two years alone, he has represented twelve cases of adoptees who killed one or both parents.[29] As with serial killers, there is almost no psychological literature on this subject and no archive of national statistics, which is needed if we are to understand the true extent of such crimes.

Unfortunately, a report of bad news of any kind about an adoptee makes people think it stigmatizes *all* adoptive parents and children. When, in 1986, I did an op-ed piece for the *New York Times* on the trial of fourteen-year-old Patrick DeGelleke, whose parents were killed when he burned their house down, I was attacked in the press by adoptive parents and adoption lobbyists for my sympathetic report on the precedent-setting use of the Adopted Child Syndrome by defense witnesses David Kirschner and the psychiatrist Arthur Sorosky.[30] In the article I pointed out that while most adoptees have no choice but to adjust to the condition of being cut off from their heritage, there are some who cannot control the inchoate rage caused by their feelings of rejection by the birth parents and the sense of powerlessness over their fate. I warned that it is time society became alerted to cases such as DeGelleke's and began looking into the stresses caused by the closed adoption system, but some adoptive parents among my readers seemed more alarmed by the mention of a syndrome than by the crime itself. "Suddenly a defense testimony for one child had turned into an indictment of an entire group of children," one woman wrote. Others denied that adoption has any relationship to psychopathology.[31] Sadly, twelve such parricide cases have been reported in East Coast newspapers since then,[32] and, undoubtedly, national statistics would reveal many more.

The psychiatrist Emanuel Tanay sees the killing of parents in any family as a last resort to hold the self together and resolve a "catastrophic conflict."[33] In the case of adoptee murderers, the catastrophic conflict arises out of the child's dissociated response to the trauma of separation from the mother and the secrecy about his origins. I find it significant that an adoptee who commits parricide usually kills *both* parents, not just one, as if the adoptive mother and father have become a fused unit that represents everything that has cut him off from his authentic self and rendered him unable to function in the world. Yet, unlike the natural child who kills an abusive parent, which is the case in the usual parricide, the adoptee may love and be dependent on his adoptive parents but, in his dissociated state, be unable to control the rage that he projects onto them.

Patrick/Steven

At six feet, six inches, nineteen-year-old Patrick Campbell towered over me when I interviewed him in a county jail in Connecticut in 1989. His baby face and slow manner of speaking reminded me more of Li'l Abner than a killer who had murdered both his parents. After that meeting, I corresponded with him, but did not see him again until I testified at his sentencing hearing a half-year later, in July 1990.

Patrick was adopted at sixteen months in Michigan by a professional couple who had requested a child with a high IQ to be a brother to their natural daughter. The social workers must have known that Patrick's unmarried birth parents were poor, rural people, but they gave him to this upwardly mobile couple. The Michigan agency furnished no information about where the baby had been since his mother had relinquished him at birth, nor would it release this material to the Connecticut court for the murder trial.

Patrick grew into an awkward, hyperactive child, who infuriated his exacting father by playing with younger children and performing badly in school. He said his father whipped him a lot with a belt as punishment. He spent a lot of time alone in his room talking to someone named Steven—an imaginary friend, the perfect boy he might have been had his birth mother kept him.

At the age of ten, Patrick was reported to the police for exposing himself in front of a young girl. He was treated by a private psychiatrist until a repetition of this act was the impetus for his parents sending him to a residential hospital for most of his high school years. His records there show that adoption was not an issue that was taken up by the staff, and, contrary to his wishes, he was sent home to his family for his last year of high school.

When Patrick kept late hours after graduation, his father gave him an ultimatum: go into the military, get a job, or move out. It was similar to the order that a psychiatrist advised John Hinckley to give his son: shape up or ship out. Neither father understood that his son would only unravel psychologically without family support.

Patrick got out. Again he was abandoned, alone in the world with no cohesive self to help him survive. For two years he lived on the streets in a neighboring town, sleeping under bridges with the homeless and druggies. Steven, the kind, good self who had been with him from childhood, was still at his side and was responsible for attracting his girlfriend, Mary.

A few weeks before the murders, Patrick felt disoriented and tried to check himself into a hospital. He was turned away when his parents, who were contacted, refused to take responsibility for the bill. On the morning of the killing, Patrick said he woke up in a black mood and knew there was something really wrong with his head. He was upset because his best friend had gone out with Mary, and she had moved back into her home. He felt rejected by both of them, abandoned again, frustrated, and filled with rage.

Still, Patrick told me, he did not intend to kill his parents when he began the two-hour walk along the railroad tracks to their house. He didn't know why he was headed there, but he sent Steven, his better self, back to Michigan to be with the birth mother he had fantasized about all his life.

Once before, Patrick had broken into his home while his parents were at work, raided the refrigerator, fallen asleep on the couch, and was kicked out when they returned. This time, after removing his sister's air conditioner, he climbed in through the window, and avoided the kitchen. Instead he drank some blackberry wine from the bar. Then something snapped. It was as if someone possessed him—he believes it was the devil. He went down to the basement, picked up a hatchet and a sledge-hammer, and waited by the door for his parents to come in through the garage. He said he never felt such power. He bludgeoned each of his parents to death when they returned home, and burned their bodies in the backyard before taking off in his mother's car to see his girlfriend.

It was a gruesome crime, committed by a mind that had a psychotic break. In my testimony at Patrick's sentencing hearing, I spoke of cumulative adoption trauma as a mitigating factor that should be considered by the court in order that Patrick might be sent to a mental hospital rather than to a prison for hardened criminals.[34] I described the genealogical bewilderment and emotional stress that adopted children experience because of not knowing about their parentage; how the cumulative trauma leads to depression; and how the anger and rage are split off in such a way that some adoptees, unable to deal with their catastrophic conflict or to hold themselves together, can only act out violently. In such adoptees there may be other contributing factors, such as genetic vulnerability, neurophysiological impairment, or extreme physical or verbal abuse. But I suggested that the closed adoption system that forces a child to dissociate, in order to live an as-if life in the adoptive family, inflicts an unrecognized abuse that Patrick and his parents were victims of, as are all the families in which these tragedies occur. The Connecticut courts, however, have yet to accept cumulative adoption trauma or the Adopted Child Syndrome as a psychological factor in such cases. Patrick was sentenced to prison for forty-five years.

Before he was led away, he was allowed to have a brief first meeting with his weeping birth mother, whom the public defender had located in Michigan and brought to the court for the hearing. An emotionally responsive woman, she explained to Patrick that she had been between marriages, with hardly enough money to feed her five other children, when she made the difficult decision to give him up. Family photographs revealed that he resembled his inordinately tall half-siblings on his father's side.

In one of his early letters to me about his birth mother, Patrick wrote that if he could have seen her and talked to her, things would have been different for him. In the letter he sent her after she had been located by the court, he asked her not to be mad at him, and asked only one question: "If you did keep me, what would you have called me?"

The Breaking Point

"Patrick Campbell was acting out in metaphor all of our rage," an adopted woman tells me. "It came from the same dark, murky depths—the shadow side of the adoptee. It is frightening to think that I could have been a murdering, angry child." An adopted man admits that he doesn't know how he managed to control his rage, which at times in adolescence reached murderous dimensions.

According to Laing, the schizoid person's experience is split in two main ways: there is a "rent in his relation with his world" and a "disruption of his relation with himself." Laing believes there is a comprehensible transition from the sane schizoid way of being-in-the-world to a psychotic way of being-in-the-world.[35]

If we try to understand this in terms of the adopted child, we can see how he splits in order to survive and takes on a functioning self, the Artificial Self, as a way of being-in-the-world. If that split self feels too depleted to go on, a part of the Forbidden Self, where rage and anger have accumulated, could take over with disastrous results. It could become intent on destroying everything that stands between it and what might have been, as if, by so doing, it could erase fate.

Kirschner has testified in court that the adopted person is at particular risk for extreme dissociation under stress, and specifically under the stress of real or perceived rejection by family or friends. This threat of loss or rejection can trigger a brief reactive psychosis, as it did in Patrick Campbell. Kirschner leans toward the belief, as do I, that Patrick may have multiple personality disorder. Steven, his good alter, had been sent away, and "an alternate personality functioning as Patrick's superego had relinquished control over his behavior."[36] In his last letter to me after the sentencing hearing, Patrick revealed that Steven had been sitting right next to him in the courtroom. Steven added a few lines of greeting, and then Patrick signed both of their names.

It is interesting to note that in Patrick Campbell's case the split-off self is the idealized good self that would not commit such a crime, while in other cases it is usually the bad alter who commits the crime. Martin Tankleff, an eighteen-year-old high school senior who bludgeoned both his parents to death in 1991, asked during his confession to the police: "Is it possible there is another Martin Tankleff?"[37]

In 1993, a New Jersey Superior Court judge allowed the defense to use the concept of the Adopted Child Syndrome in the trial of twenty-two-year-old Matthew Heikkila, who two years previously had murdered both of his adoptive parents with a sawed-off shotgun. It was a precedent-setting decision in that state, and Kirschner's testimony was considered a deciding factor in persuading the jury to vote against the death penalty.[38]

Matthew, a troubled high school dropout, was known to be jealous of his younger brother, Joshua, born to his parents nine months after Matthew's adoption. It didn't help that Joshua, an outstanding and popular student, was everything that Matthew was not. Matthew's only success was with women, but shortly before the murders he had been rejected by two girlfriends, one to whom he had been engaged and the other whom he had just impregnated. He also felt rejected by his birth mother, who, he had recently learned, used a false name so that she could not be found. Adding to all this, he expected rejection by his adoptive parents. At a therapist's suggestion, they had him sign a contract that he would have to leave home if he broke any more rules, skipped church, or continued using drugs. It was an ill-advised contract that he quickly broke. What may be a simple threat to other acting-out adolescents—"If you don't behave, you're out of here"—may feel like the threat of annihilation to the adopted person, who is always fearful of fragmentation. It may seem like the equivalent of a death sentence. "They were going to kick me out," Heikkila told Kirschner. "So I had to do it. It was self-defense." An adopted person sees himself as fighting for his life in that psychotic moment when he kills his adoptive parents.

The tragedy in this case, as in the other ones, is that the therapists who tried to treat Matthew over the years were not knowledgeable about the psychology and possible pathology of the adopted, and so could not recognize the dangerous potential of his fragmented and aggressive behavior. Nor could they help his parents, who, in their denial that his being adopted made any difference, had closed off the subject of adoption as a trouble spot and left it to fester in him. When Matthew threatened his father with a gun, and later tried to commit suicide, the warning signals were there, but neither the professionals involved nor the family understood the severity of the situation.

The Heikkila defense attorney said that knowledge of this case should help prevent such things from happening in the future, and I agree. Prevention lies in educating society. Even though I am primarily concerned with the subjective experience of ordinary adoptees, I feel responsible for reporting on the deviant behavior of the few adoptees who resort to murder. As I pointed out earlier, we are not stigmatizing adoption when we look honestly at what is happening. There is much that we can learn from these cases about adoption pathology in general and about how to prevent acting-out and violent behavior. We can no longer afford to ignore the special vulnerability of adoptees in our present closed adoption system to patterns of severe dissociation that can result in tragedy.

9

The Adult Child

Anxious the bird lost from the flock—
The sun sets and still it flies alone,
Back and forth with no place to rest,
As night wears on, its cry grows sadder—
—T'AO CH'IEN, A.D. 416

No one has yet put into words the
psychological complexity of being adopted.
—ADULT ADOPTEE, A.D. 1990

TERESA, AN ADOPTED WOMAN IN HER MID-FORTIES, writes me that she finally has a satisfying marriage and career, but the adoption questions still "haunt" her. While her adoptive mother was dying, a friend of the family remarked that as *adopted* daughters, she and her sister could not be trusted to make good decisions about the care of their mother. "Does this never go away? Will no stage of my life be free of the questions and doubts and subtle accusations by others that I am not a worthy, full adult?" she asks. "Will I ever feel like a whole person? Will I ever be able to know that the good things that come my way reflect who I really am?"

Such questions haunt many adult adoptees who, on the surface, lead successful lives. Adoption is an invisible trauma, and so few can guess an adoptee's basic insecurity about coping with life or sustaining a relationship with others. We have all heard people mention the well-adjusted adopted children or adults they know—or, rather, think they know.

Adult adoptees, unlike adolescent adoptees, are not overrepresented in mental health facilities. To accept this as a marker of health, however, is to overlook the fact that those adoptees seeking private therapy or support groups for alcohol or drug addiction, eating disorders, depression, or marital failure do not become part of the clinical statistics.[1] Noting the relative absence of adoptees in clinical psychoanalytic literature, Brinich speculates that the psychological importance of adoption can recede in adulthood when the child has grown into independence; or that a blind spot develops in both patients and their analysts.[2] Nickman suggests that the reason for the sparseness of psychological literature might be that the topic can mobilize primitive anxieties in analysts no less than in other people: sadistic and voyeuristic feelings, rescue fantasies, early fears of abandonment, and core anxieties about one's place in the world.[3]

The disheartening truth is that the psychological importance of being adopted does not recede in adulthood, as Teresa found out, but lies waiting to take center stage at various transitions in the life cycle. My own research on adoptees who have grown up in the closed adoption system underscores Guntrip's observation that there is no quick and easy way to make a mature and stable adult personality out of the legacy of an undermined childhood.[4] One who is not grounded in his factual history will feel insubstantial, without a firm sense of self. Adoptees speak of feeling bewildered, embarrassed, innocent, and powerless, as well as guilty for their resentment at having been chosen for this strange fate. As one woman said: "It hurts that I can't have what natural people have."

Adult adoptees often describe themselves as shy loners or floaters, lacking self-confidence. They may change jobs often and have problems with control and power, intimacy and commitment. They are self-negating. They may look secure, but they suffer from feelings of shame, inner badness, and defectiveness. They fear homelessness, betrayal, disintegration, and going mad. But, most of all, they fear abandonment.

The message adoptees give to friends and spouses is: "Do anything you want to me, but don't abandon me."

THE ABANDONMENT COMPLEX

Inside every adoptee is an abandoned baby. It lies coiled in the core of the adopted self like a deep sorrow that can find no comfort. "The condition of abandonment is not unique," the Jungian analyst Nathan Schwartz-Salant tells me. "But the extremity of abandonment in the adoptee is unique."

Sally confides: "My fear of being abandoned borders on terror and paranoia. I have a recurring dream in which I'm abandoned by earth. I envision myself as a fetus in the amniotic sac floating away from the planet, and all that's in sight are the earth and my severed umbilical cord." Mel admits: "I feared abandonment as a child, and I still fear it at age forty-four." Deborah says: "I can't abandon people even after saying hello."

Jung said that abandonment is necessary if the child is to evolve toward independence, and that the child cannot do this without detaching himself from his origins.[5] But the Jungian analyst Gilda Frantz, who was abandoned by her father as an infant, believes that if children are abandoned before they are old enough and strong enough to cope with the experience, they may be unable to integrate its purpose or meaning.[6] This is certainly true for adoptees, who go through life unable to make sense of the purpose or meaning of their being cast out into the world alone. They have an "abandonment complex," if we accept the definition of yet another Jungian analyst, Harriet Gordon Machtiger, who writes: "Individuals with loss and abandonment complexes are torn between an overwhelming yearning to return to a symbiotic state of existence and an equally strong urge to assert their separateness as individuals."[7]

To flee or to merge—that is the dilemma that faces adoptees. They often have the need to merge with others as a way of overcoming their loneliness and dependency, while at the same time they have the need to escape coming yet again under someone else's control. Pulled between a fear of being deserted and a fear of being entrapped, they give mixed signals. "It's like I want to connect, but I'm afraid of you so I can't" is the way one woman described it. Another woman spoke of avoiding rejection with men by testing and pushing away, rejecting first so that she is not rejected. A man getting a second divorce said: "I constantly want my freedom of action, but still find it very difficult to let go of the relationship."

And so adoptees usually find themselves hovering between two extreme states of being: the Free Spirit Self, which believes it could take off at any moment, but doesn't because the fear of aloneness is stronger than its wings; and the Dependent Self, which seeks vitality by merging with whomever seems safe (but usually isn't) or seems to offer unconditional love (as if anyone could). These antithetical impulses can lead to disastrous relationships and a number of failed marriages before an adoptee understands the psychodynamics at play.

Seeking Mother in the Lover

Adoptees often try to make older or more mature people into idealized parents. I have noticed that young female adoptees frequently seek out mother figures in women who may be teachers or counselors, and later seek maternal, nurturing men in marriage. One woman, who has been married three times, spoke of looking for mothers, not mates: "I went for the families as much as the men: I wanted a Jewish mother and I got one in my first marriage; in my second, I got a mother-in-law who was the ideal of what I wanted to be. Finally, in my third, I found a really nurturing man, and I didn't need his mother."

Male adoptees may seek out the lost mother in their lovers or wives, often choosing older, maternal women or safe, dependent women who won't leave them. The most essential quality in a loved one for both men and women is that he or she be abandonment-proof. But the problem with sacrificing romance for safety is that one may get stuck in a boring relationship in which the spouse becomes another parent figure to be rebelled against. As one woman in the process of divorce said: "I'm now ready to have a husband rather than a father."

At forty-seven, Hank describes himself as an adult who is still an emotionally immature child. Not too long ago he had a thriving professional practice that supported a wife, three kids, and a large home with a two-car garage. He also had a drinking problem ("to feel good about myself") and a woman on the side ("to prove I wasn't tied down and didn't have to play by conventional rules"). He didn't feel guilty because he believed that his wife (whom he'd taken to calling "Mama Mae") was self-sufficient and didn't need him to nurture her. Now that she's left him for someone else, he realizes how dependent he was on her nurturing. He feels abandoned. He lost his professional license due to his drinking problem, and his life has shrunk to a few rooms over a garage.

Eileen avoided intimacy until her mid-twenties because she was afraid of getting pregnant before being ready to commit herself. "I knew that my morals and personal experience would not allow me to have an abortion, for I could have been aborted myself," she says. When she was engaged at twenty-four, she still withheld her secret Forbidden Self—the part that was tied to her natural mother: "I couldn't risk not being understood, having my inner self shattered." Eileen revised the beginning of the marriage ceremony so that she would not be "given away" in the traditional sense. She explained to her parents that she had been given away once and did not want to be given away again.

It was only when she began searching, a year later, that Eileen was able to reveal her secret feelings about her lost mother to her husband: "I realized my pain was too big for anyone to handle alone and that, by keeping the secret, I was denying my whole identity and preventing myself from being a whole person." Being able to share her Forbidden Self with her husband has given her the intimacy she never had before. "My marriage is the one place I belong," she says.

Love in the Ghost Kingdom

Adoptees who cannot find a satisfying relationship with the opposite sex often retreat to the Ghost Kingdom, where their fantasies may prove more safe and rewarding than their experiences in the so-called real world.

Arthur, a writer who married and divorced twice before settling on a farm with three dogs, speaks of fantasy relationships as perhaps the most defining experience in his personal world. "I fall in love with birth mother substitutes, who, of course, never live up to my ideal," he says. "In my mind there seems to exist some fairy-tale realm that defines my private world. I search there, I love there, I grieve there. Without it, my experience is routine, drab, obligatory. And, looking back, my life has always been this way. I lived with my adoptive family, but I loved with my birth family. Just last week I fantasized about a relationship with a blonde young woman I saw at my athletic club. I admit a 'real' relationship would be more substantial than a fantasy one, but, hey, fantasy is reality too. When I am dying, I will still be expecting to be saved by that special woman who will take me away and make everything right."

We can see such fantasy women as the elusive siren some adopted men pursue: the mother goddess. The pattern often is to idealize and then denigrate a woman, to cast her off as they were once cast off, and move on to the next one. "Loving them and leaving them" may be the ultimate revenge for having been left so early. Some adopted men speak of being angry and aggressive toward women at the end of a relationship, without understanding the source of their rage.

Michael, a forty-one-year-old professional, played the Free Spirit, going from woman to woman, unable to commit to anyone. "I had no self-worth, no insides," he says. "I didn't know there was more to me than a penis, or how much I hated women. I seduced hundreds of them just so I could reject them. I couldn't be intimate or real. It was too scary."

When Michael stood at the altar for the first time at the age of twenty-one, he felt he was at his funeral, not his wedding: "I was there for primitive reasons, her taking care of me. I was mentally abusive—critical. Don Juan gives an illusion of connection, but when it becomes real, he's out of there."

A few years ago, at a psychoanalytic workshop, I listened to a case presentation on a successful lawyer who had been adopted when a few weeks old by Italian Catholic parents. The analyst spoke of Phil's extreme repression of childhood memories and his total lack of emotion, as if something had been rendered lifeless within him. He had all the symptoms of trauma, without a trauma that he was aware of or that the analyst could recognize.

Phil had left three wives and four children, for whom he felt nothing. "All women are whores," he said. "They're always ready to spread their legs for any man." He was a tyrant with his wives and girlfriends, forbidding them to dress seductively and beating them if they showed interest in other men or seemed negligent toward the children whom he would eventually abandon, along with them.

It was fourteen years into the analysis (with a break of eighteen months after the twelfth year) that the therapist had the insight that Phil's problem had roots in an early, intense childhood trauma that he had totally shut out of his consciousness, and that was connected with his biological mother. Making an active intervention for the first time, he confronted Phil with the idea that he must have fantasized his mother as a slut who would spread her legs for any man and who had conceived a bastard she had to get rid of. Phil was irate, but the analyst didn't retreat. "She abandoned you, threw you away," he went on, in an attempt to put Phil in touch with his "overwhelming rage, denigration, and mistrust of all women—especially those who were mothers."

At first Phil denied ever thinking or dreaming about his birth mother, but soon he was working with the therapist on fantasies of who this mother might have been—a woman who tricked a man into making her pregnant, or a prostitute on the streets. Before long he could recover shreds of memory from the past, especially his feelings of anger and humiliation when, at the age of five, he learned from his cousin that he was adopted. The cousin said Phil didn't really belong in the family since he was not his father's real son. After that, Phil was able to uncover other painful memories and deep, disturbing feelings, which he had acted out with punitive behavior toward women.

We can see that cumulative adoption trauma, like other traumas, plays havoc with memory. Many adoptees report that large chunks of their childhood got repressed along with everything else. And many, like Phil, act out those disavowed feelings with an aggression that alienates the very people with whom they want a relationship.

The Impostor: Fear of Intimacy

A person has to have a good sense of self to be secure enough to get close to another without the threat of being unmasked as a fraud. Adoptees who have spent their lives covering over their real feelings often avoid intimacy for fear of being discovered for the impostors they know they are. Let down your guard, they think, and everyone will see that under the confident self you present to the world, there is really a weak and frightened child. Better to keep your distance to avoid being abandoned again. As one man said: I'm afraid that when I get into a relationship, she'll see that I'm just a phony, not real. You've got these fake spots—you're a half-person."

Adoptees take on the role of the impostor early in life: from the moment they try in earnest to live as if they are a natural member of the family in which they find themselves. Some part of them is acutely aware that they are playacting—pretending to be someone they know they are not, while not knowing who they are. "I spent my whole life trying to act like real people do," said one woman. And another: "I've always felt I was given the wrong part in the wrong play. It was a script written for someone else."

Ben remembers feeling like an impostor while standing at a grave with his mother's relatives: "I was watching them and thinking: 'Who are these people? I don't look like them. I don't belong with them.' I was living a lie. And I was playing my part so well, I felt like a heel. I don't think anyone suspected, but deep down I felt I didn't deserve to be loved, respected, or given anything. Because I was really an *orphan*."

Rachel says that her happiness as a small child disappeared during her struggles for authenticity in adolescence and young adulthood: "My parents thought they knew me, but they didn't accept me for who I really was. If they'd known, they would have abandoned me. I saw myself as two people: one in front who was adopted, and the shadow, who was the real me, lagging behind."

Feeling the impostor can affect an adoptee's professional accomplishments, as well as his ability to achieve intimacy. No matter how high he
climbs in his field, he still has the feeling that he's put something over on
others. Hank remembers feeling like an impostor when he received his
professional certification, and wonders if his plunge into alcohol, which
lost him everything, might not have been his way of proving that he
didn't deserve the accreditation he had.

Perhaps the most publicized case of the adoptee as impostor was that
of Daniel N. Permutter, a federal prosecutor and assistant U.S. attorney,
whose job was to convict criminals—until he managed to get himself
convicted. He was sentenced to a three-year prison term for stealing
drugs and cash from the U.S. attorney's office in New York City.

During a television interview, Permutter told how he tried to make up
to his parents for the drug behavior of his adopted brother: "I remember
when I first started to perform well academically, and just thinking this is
a fraud, that someday they'll find out that I'm not intelligent, that I can't
do this well." When asked why he felt that way, he replied: "I can't tell
you. I just never felt that it was real."

When his marriage to his college instructor, ten years his senior, ended
in divorce, he began seeing prostitutes: "It wasn't for the sexual act; it
was a compulsive thing that made me feel like I wasn't myself, affirming
my own doubts about myself, that I wasn't this great, golden boy, but
instead was just some, you know, john, who would go to a prostitute."

Speaking of the time when he was acting as federal prosecutor, stealing money from the safe to afford more drugs, Perlmutter revealed the
split in his self: "There was a real dual existence of the prosecutor, the
kid in the Brooks Brothers suits with a clean-cut look, and then the kid
who goes—the evil guy who goes to the prostitutes and does coke and
steals."[8]

Perlmutter did not understand why he had the need to lead a dual
existence, or that one part of him was living out the dark side of his fantasies, his negative identity. In his own way, he had returned to what he
perceived was his true source: a prostitute mother in a world of drugs.

The Need for Control

Control is another key issue for adoptees, who, from the time they are
born, are moved about without any say in their fate and forced to live by
the strictures of a contract they never signed. As children, they feel con-

trolled by adoptive parents who cannot or will not tell them what they need to know. Gratitude is the unspoken currency they are expected to pay. Once they move out of the adoptive home, they are determined never to go into emotional debt again.

I remember the man who stressed how much he loved his adoptive parents, only to blurt out later in the conversation: "Adoption—I hate it. The lack of control. I had no control when I was dumped and no control over who picked me up." Despite having a Ph.D. and law degree, he changes jobs every few months and disappears periodically from his marriage. Like so many adoptees, he takes control by not letting himself be controlled by any situation or person.

This need for control can give one fear of flying, since someone else is at the controls. It can also make one into a pack rat, not throwing anything out because it would be like giving up part of oneself. "They've taken everything else away," says one pack rat, "but you can control this." Another pack rat, who is both an adoptee and a birth mother, says wryly: "You can take my mother and my kid, but not this paper bag. I might need it."

ADOPTEE AS PARENT

When I was a journalist in Japan and Vietnam, I yearned to take home every Amerasian child I saw in the orphanages or on the streets. I could visualize being an adoptive parent because it was the only kind of parenting that I knew, but my husband, who knew the other kind, convinced me that the timing was wrong and that we should wait until we had our own.

Eventually, we did have two children, but I know it was not mere chance that made me imagine adopting before I could imagine giving birth. The secrecy around an adoptee's birth makes the subject seem taboo; and since pregnancy puts an adopted woman in touch with the very mysteries that she has tried to block out, it is threatening to venture into this forbidden turf. Besides, if you don't feel real, how can you do anything as real as give birth to a real child? And if you don't know whose genes you carry, how do you know what you will pass on to your child?

I remember my alarm as a teenager when a young adopted woman in my hometown in Ohio gave birth to a deformed baby. It was as if she had confirmed my deep suspicion that a monster might already be lurking within me. Male adoptees carry these dark fears, too. One man spoke of deciding early not to marry because he might pass his birth mother's "defectiveness" on to his child. Another man dreamed that he was disgorging a large blob on an umbilical cord. It was a monster, but attached like a baby. As an adoptee, he had given unnatural birth to his unnatural monster self.

One reason adoptees fear they will not be good parents is because they were not parented by the woman who gave birth to them. The adoptee also worries about the adoptive mother: Will she feel bad seeing her child pregnant when she may never have been pregnant herself? A twenty-nine-year-old woman recalls going from high to low during pregnancy: "I felt great about being pregnant. There's a new life in process. But then my thoughts would go to my birth mom. How big was she with me? Then Mom. She's never had this experience. I think I felt like I was being pregnant for all three of us. Somewhat connected to my birth mom. Yet disconnected from Mom. I was in labor for about six and a half hours. Then it hit me. They put my baby in my arms. I was crying—crying for both my mothers. Not just me."

The adoptee as parent is in a double bind: one has fierce intensity (this is my only blood relative) and great insecurity (someone else could raise the child better than I can). Having been overprotected by their adoptive parents and disempowered by society, adoptees know more about being the eternal child than about being a mother or father. They may be more comfortable in the role of child than as a parental figure with their child. One woman spoke of retreating into never-never land with her children: "The emotional side of me has not matured, so I don't like leaving home. I avoid my peers. I'm better with my children. I like the playground. I know my children won't reject me."

No one romanticizes blood relationships more than a person who has never known them. When you finally hold your first blood relative, you cannot help asking the inevitable question: "How could any woman give up her child?" It is as if you are holding your abandoned self in your arms. While you nurture your baby, you have a chance to nurture your own baby within. All of the missing connection one felt with one's adoptive parents, all of the fantasies one has about the blood tie, one places onto this child, much like a survivor parent might place on the child who is born after the Holocaust the burden of making up for those who died in it. Adoptees, who do not know what disaster they have survived, look to their children to make up for all the blood relatives who are lost to them and to give meaning to their lives.

Becoming a parent raises issues of authority and self-esteem, the very issues that adoptees have been struggling with. They want to be a friend to their child, to be liked, but having been deprived of authority as children themselves, they have a hard time being authoritative. Afraid of alienating their children, they may be too permissive with them. They cannot bear anger, for they have repressed their own. They want everything and everyone to be happy, just as their parents wanted them to be.

Adoptees are often amazed to find themselves parenting much like their adoptive parents, who also experienced loss, questions of authenticity, and doubts about their parenting ability. Their insecurity may make them overly protective and possessive, as so many adoptive parents are, and their fear of separation may make them violate boundaries, just as their parents did.

Paradoxically, their insecurities can cause adoptees to distance themselves from their children. One woman admitted that she felt she was raising her husband's two children rather than her own, that she was just a caregiver, not a mother. Another, who also turned the children over to their father, believes that she had an inability to feel, as if some part of her were split off and she was not totally present. Now she realizes that her unresolved adoption issues kept her from bonding with her children: "If we adoptees become parents before we come to terms with our adoption and the loss of our birth parents, we are walking into rough waters and could easily drown."

One adopted man took a job out of town shortly after his wife gave birth, thereby avoiding a commitment to raising his children. Not until his wife threatened to leave did he find work closer to home, and make the discovery that he enjoyed being a father.

The subliminal message an adoptee gives to the child is: "I may be your parent, but I am really your playmate. Love me, and don't abandon me. You are my child, but I don't know whose child I am."

On the positive side, the adoptee parent, being exquisitely sensitive to the insecurities of a young child, tries to give her children the sense of rootedness she did not have (not through the failing of the adoptive parents, but because of the existential condition of being adopted). Without being aware of it, the adoptee gives inordinate stress to the blood tie, so much so that my ten-year-old son, shrewd about so many other things, thought that there was something special about being related to me by blood.

There are some adoptees, like Lee, who decide not to have children. "I really had no choice," she says. "I felt I would be a terrible mother. I had no history. As I see it, a child who has no mother can mother no child." Lee can say this while acknowledging that her adoptive mother was every bit a mother: "But there was this absent, ambiguous mother I couldn't ask about. It was like I developed a dual personality: I had a mother and grew up, but inside me was the frozen child who didn't know who her mother was. It was that frozen child who made the decision not to have children."

Even though adoptees know that they could have been an abortion, some choose abortion over having a baby. Something holds them back from becoming a mother. One woman said: "I was one of those adoptees who never progressed from being an 'adopted child.' I was stuck there in my child at the deepest level."

Another, who was told her mother had died in childbirth, has had twelve abortions. She never wanted children because, as she explains: "I was never born myself. I was afraid of dying in childbirth like she supposedly did."

THE GAY SELF

An adoptee's child may be the only blood relative he or she will ever see, and so it should not surprise us that gay adoptees speak of the sorrow of losing not only their past family but their future one. Alex, a divorced man with three daughters, said that he had such a horrible feeling of being alone all his life that he longed to have children of his own. When alcohol and drugs didn't relieve his pain, he determined to marry just to have children: "I was selfish. My need for connection overrode being gay. I got married for that reason. I needed that. A few years ago I came out, and I'm with another man now. But I'm glad that I have my daughters."

Conversely, one's very lack of connection to the past can deter adoptees from wanting children. Ruth, a lesbian adoptee activist, believes that her lack of knowledge about what she would pass on to her own children resulted in a feeling that reproduction was impossible for her. "This probably did not make me gay," she says, "but it could have led me away from one of the reasons men and women marry: to have children."

For some time now I have noticed an inordinate number of gay or bisexual people in the adoption movement, especially among the men. I began to wonder if this reflected the general adoptee population. Or is it that gay people are more sensitive to their feelings and social injustice and so would be attracted to a movement concerned with adoptee rights, such as open records?

I've also wondered what effect adoption, with its legacy of secrecy and disempowerment, has on a child's psychosexual development. Recent studies have emphasized a genetic basis for homosexuality, or stressed the importance of neuroendocrine factors, with the assumption that one's sexuality is fixed from birth.[9] All of this may be true for some people, but can we discount the others whose sexual orientation might be influenced by traumatic psychosocial factors such as one finds in adoption?

I first started thinking of this question some years ago when I received a call from a woman who said that she was at an AA meeting with five people who discovered they had three things in common: they were recovering alcoholics, they were gay, and they were adopted. They wanted to talk with me about which was their main identity. Until then they had been working on their problems with addiction and coming out, without ever considering their adoption issues. We met informally for several months, and they came to the insight that adoption had played a more crucial role in their sense of self than they had realized. So much so that of those three identities, they saw being adopted as the central one.

Over the years I have asked gay adoptees if they think there is a connection between being adopted and being gay. It will probably not be a question that engages them until they feel more accepted by society. "What is the value if there were some correlation between adoption and homosexuality?" a lesbian adoptee activist asked me. "I think the important issue is the ability to love. The gender of our lovers is less important, or would be less important, if we lived in a sane society that didn't harbor intense homophobia of gay love and its sexual expression."

I found that the more crucial questions for them now are what it is like to grow up adopted and gay, and which identity one comes to terms with first. "Being a lesbian and an adoptee affects all of who I am and how I view the world," one woman told a workshop on gay-adoptee issues. "It was only by coming to terms with being a lesbian that I was able to come to terms with being an adoptee. It's been an ongoing process of hiding and revealing my identity." An older woman, of a generation before gay rights, spoke of having had to come to terms with her adoption before she could feel safe enough to come out as a lesbian.

Still, I noticed that the question of whether one would have been a homosexual if one were not adopted comes up in indirect ways. A woman who spoke of feeling "displaced" rather than "placed" in her family wondered if becoming a lesbian was a way to connect to someone who is similar to her physically, as well as a way to equalize power in relationships. She felt "one down" in her adopted family. "Each person has her own fundamental reason for being homosexual," another woman said. "I think for me it is a love of women that motivates me. Not hatred of men or because horrible things happened to me. My ways of being connected to women enable me to connect to the mother I never had. But I don't think I'm a lesbian only because I was separated from my mother."

A male adoptee in the group expressed his belief that adoption is the ultimate "emasculation" experience. As a boy he had felt there was something sinful about the fact that he was not the "real" son but the "illegitimate" one. His father was abroad on business most of the time while he was growing up, and his adoptive mother was seductive with him. "How can you trust a woman?" he asked. "I had horrible fears of sex. I thought of birth as being sinful. Sleeping with women was sinful. I wanted to feel whole, and being with another man makes me feel whole. It has to do with nurturing. I'm attracted to younger, innocent men who remind me of myself between twenty and thirty. Or to strong, virile, masculine men, who are protective."

What it comes down to is that people who are both adopted and gay feel they carry a double stigma. "Adoptees feel fundamentally wrong, bad, different, a mistake," a woman explained. "Lesbians feel that way too. But it's possible to have a sense of wholeness about this. That's where I'm journeying."

FEAR OF HOMELESSNESS

Whether heterosexual or homosexual, many adoptees carry through life a sense of dislocation, a sense of being the outsider, a sense of orphanhood. The adoption papers are their passport, but their true home is lost to them. They have been in exile ever since being cut off from their origins, and they fear they will end up in exile. Having experienced total loss once, they fear they could experience it again. They can never be certain of what a secure home is.

If it is true that homelessness is an "archetypal state of transiency,"[10] adoptees have always been transients. They have a sense of being on the road even when they have a place to return to at night. They don't have the same relationship to things that other people have. As children, they may have stolen money to buy their friends' love with presents. That's all they wanted money for. Material possessions slip through their fingers. They are not destined for authentic heirlooms that will connect them to their ancestors. The disconnection they have experienced has made them devalue the things that others hoard and treasure.

Homelessness is abandonment with a different spelling. Even as they appear to be tucked safely into their adoptive homes, adoptees fear that homelessness lies in wait like a grave at the end of the road. One woman remembers crying whenever her parents drove past the cemetery where they had a plot. She feared they would die and leave her homeless again. Another, a divorced lawyer with no children, fears that when her adoptive father dies, she will be totally alone. The adoption tie, which saved her as a baby, will be cut with his death, and she will find herself falling through dark space into the void again.

YEARNING FOR CONNECTION

"Adoptees are like mythic heroes—orphaned, motherless, sent out into the world alone," says Walter, an artist who, at thirty-three, doesn't call any one place home. "And people can sense that. They're always saying to me, 'You're new around these parts, aren't you?'"

It seems that an adoptee's disconnectedness forms a distinct aura around him that people notice but cannot recognize. It is the aura of the abandoned mythic hero, whose primal loss and supernatural powers the adoptee still identifies with. The adoptee holds on to his mythic side as a protective shield against the terrible aloneness he feels. A defense, perhaps, but one that has become an integral part of his psychic reality—and unreality.

"Adoptees are glaziers of the cosmic mystery," an adopted man says. "They are prophets. Not everyone given the assignment of prophecy completes the assignment, but if you are successful you have something to tell for the journey. This is the problem life presented you. You have the opportunity to tell others about it." Another man confides, "I feel that everything that happened was intended. I feel the hand of God is moving me along for a purpose and is watching over me. I was put here to do good things. To try to make a better world." An adopted woman says, "I feel there is someone or something out there that is protecting me. I actually saw it manifest itself twice as small fluffy clouds over my bed when I was in trouble."

Adoptees are also perceived by others as being part of a divine plan. "Adopted people are a special breed," according to a scholar of Cabala. "Every soul has a purpose. Adoptees are beautiful souls. Old souls. They have a special fate—a special karma—to redesign the earth."[11]

It seems that something unnatural happens to children when they lose their parents, no matter how they lose them or how quickly after that they are adopted. They become something different, both wonderful and fearsome. They are accorded a special status. Things that we are attracted to, but fear, we endow with special powers. Perhaps this is the fascination that all cultures have with adopted children. They live out everyone's fantasy of abandonment. To placate the fates, we make them divine.

But who wants to be divine at the cost of abandonment and disconnection? Adoptees would trade their mythic connection to divinity for a connection to the human condition that has been denied them. And so, some set out on the first stage of the hero's journey, back through time, to that point, to that place, to that home that was never a home, where they were once connected.

PART II

The Self in Search

She is the mother from whom I sprung.
. . . Such being my lineage, never more can
I prove false to it, or spare to search
out the secret of my birth.
—SOPHOCLES, *OEDIPUS REX*

When a man decides, like Oedipus, to carry
the inquiry into what he is as far as it can
go, he discovers himself to be enigmatic,
without consistency, without any domain of
his own or any fixed point of attachment,
with no defined essence, oscillating between
being the equal of the gods and the equal of
nothing at all. His real greatness consists
in the very thing that expresses his
enigmatic nature: his questioning.
—JEAN-PAUL VERNANT, *MYTH AND TRAGEDY IN
ANCIENT GREECE*

10

The Call to Self

Where are you from? asked the man
     at the border.
From the world.
Where are you going?
Home.
But where is home?
I don't know.
—JANUSZ KORCZAK, *KING MATT ON THE DESERT ISLAND*

ONE MUST HAVE A HOME IN ORDER NOT TO NEED it, according to Jean Amery, a Holocaust survivor, for whom exile meant homelessness.[1] Just as he tried to examine the meaning of loss of home and mother tongue, I, as an adopted person, am trying to examine the meaning of loss of home and mother.

If we believe, as Amery did, that exile is a loss of biological and psychological identity, then adoptees have been in exile since their separation from the mother. The original birth certificate—that universal passport that connects everyone to his or her origins—is lost to them. From the time of Oedipus, adopted children have wandered through strange lands trying to recover that legendary place other people call Home—the place they started out from.

The word *home* is virtually impossible to translate into other tongues, we are told by the classicist Bartlett Giamatti.[2] It is not a concept, not a place, but a state of mind where self-definition starts. It is origins. We can see the search for Home as a universal quest, but for the adopted person it is also a literal one. It is a quest for the beginning of one's narrative; for the lost mother; for unconditional love; for meaning; for the recovery of lost time; for a coherent sense of self; for security; for form and structure; for grounding and centering.

The search for Home reflects the adoptee's need for biological, historical, and human connectedness. It is close to a religious search because it is an attempt to connect to forces larger than oneself.

The very idea of search and reunion is empowering, and, as the trauma specialist Judith Herman tells us, empowerment and reconnection are the core experiences of recovery.[3] Healing begins when adoptees take control of their lives by making the decision to search, but we will see in the course of this chapter how difficult it is to overcome internalized taboos as one sets out on this forbidden journey toward self.

There was a time, not too long ago, when many professionals believed that only maladjusted adoptees had a need to search for their origins. The implication was that good (and loyal) adoptees did not search. Now therapists are beginning to understand that there are primal strivings behind the adoptee's need to reconnect in some way with the birth family. A team of psychiatrists in Argentina has gone so far as to posit that the need to experience human connectedness through knowing about and seeing one's family of origin may have innate origins.[4]

The Argentine psychiatrists were amazed at how easily some of the "disappeared" children, who had been adopted by the military families responsible for murdering their mothers in the late 1970s, had been able to adjust when returned to their original families years later. The doctors decided that there must have been communication between the fetus and its mother that the baby had split off but not lost. The prebirth knowledge was "as if locked into a shell—in a protected nucleus capable of evolution at a later, safer time."[5] Reunion (or restitution, as they call it) permeated the protective cloak of the shell, so that the child felt an innate sense of familiarity with the mother's surviving family members.

As we have seen, American psychologists working in prenatal studies have come to similar conclusions. They speculate that the fetus has stored away cellular knowledge of its mother, which can be retrieved. Adoptees in search are trying to do just that: retrieve that lost connection, even though they know that their families, unlike those of the kidnapped Argentine children, gave them up voluntarily. They hope that a place has been reserved for them in the family unconscious, just as in the Argentine families—that they were relinquished legally, but not psychologically. But how can they know whether or not their mother and father or other members of their clan have kept that psychological connection and will be there to welcome them?

FEAR OF KNOWING

I am often asked why some adoptees search and others don't. What is the difference between them? A Zen answer might be that inside every searcher is a nonsearcher, and inside every nonsearcher is a searcher. The difference between those who search and those who don't lies in how they formed their defensive structures as children: how much they denied, repressed, and split off.

An adopted man tells me: "All people are brothers. Who cares who your parents are?" He admits that he was curious about where he came from when he was little, but he isn't anymore. He does not know that he is a searcher who has stopped searching. From the moment they are separated from their birth mothers, all adoptees are consciously or unconsciously in search of some place, perched somewhere between conception and birth, that could be called Home. Each time an adopted child wonders whose tummy she was in, what her mother looked like, why she was given up; each time he has a fantasy or a dream, looks on the street for someone who looks like him, the adoptee has taken a small step on the journey toward Home.

The adoptee may have run away as a child—acted out. That is a form of searching. He or she may have experimented with living at a friend's house or joined a cult. All of this is search behavior before things happen in life that make one turn toward or away from the possibility of a literal search.

Lee, a divinity school student who didn't start to search until after her divorce, said she never felt she deserved the information. "Everyone wanted my adoption to be a secret," she explained, "so it didn't seem right to disturb my mother's secret. It was like I was thinking, Good girls don't search."

A woman who tried to search off and on over the years without success said she gave it up because it was too painful: "I think it's too late to forge any kind of relationship, and anyway, it would never make up for what I've missed, what I've been robbed of."

Another woman admitted: "One side of me is afraid of what I'll find. That I won't be good enough. That she won't like me. But another side doesn't want to give her the satisfaction of my finding her. She gave me up, so she doesn't deserve to know where I am, who I am, and what I'm doing. Isn't that awful?"

And another, who gave up in her teens when the adoption agency would not give her information, said: "I've had a lot of emotional upset in my life and view searching as something that would be a disruption I don't need to seek out. My real mother would be infinitely less interesting than my fantasy mother. By now she would be in her seventies or eighties and probably in need of some care—that is, if she wanted to have a relationship at all. The last thing I want is to be emotionally, financially, or medically responsible for a mother who abandoned me when I was helpless."

Nonsearchers have a fine nose for scenting the possible psychic chaos waiting to be unleashed should they drop their guard. Ross, who didn't search until he turned forty, spoke of his "fear of knowing" being more powerful than his need to know, a fear that fueled his "fierce loyalty" when asked as an adolescent whether he would want to meet his "real" parents. A woman who also waited to search until her forties said, "I had an underlying feeling that if I knew where I came from, I would be annihilated."

Since the self's quest is always toward nurturance and growth and away from death-related qualities of disintegration, it is not surprising that an adoptee would turn away from the threat to the self that the very idea of search carries with it.

Still, the fact that an adoptee is not in search one year does not mean that he or she will not be in search the next. To mention the search to most nonsearchers is like banging on a door in the middle of the night and rousing the sleeper within. In *Lost and Found*, I placed adoptees in the tradition of fabled sleepers—Snow White in her glass coffin, Sleeping Beauty in her bower—and compared their decision to search to waking up from the Great Sleep. It was another way of saying that adoptees decide to search after they are in touch with the unconscious, when they have access to the feelings they have stashed away. Freud called it the "return of the repressed."[6] The dissociation, which has worn thin in places, like the ozone layer, no longer protects them from the ultraviolet rays of reality.

CROSSING THE FIRST THRESHOLD

Some adoptees get their "wake-up call" on "Oprah" or "Donahue." Others are jolted out of sleep by an unexpected life crisis and find themselves suddenly falling through a trapdoor in the self into the dark pit of the unconscious. Everything that was neatly arranged and nailed down in their psyche comes undone and flies through the trapdoor with them. They are caught in a gravitational pull toward an alternate reality: the very Ghost Kingdom they had so painstakingly split off. They could disappear entirely.

It is terrifying, this moment you realize you are going to cross a threshold from which you may never return. I know because it happened to me. I never intended to search for my mother. As an adult, I was sleeping soundly. I might be sleeping still if a relative, newly married into the family, had not mentioned hearing that my birth parents had been killed in a car crash. The trapdoor fell open. I had never heard this version of how they died.

All my psychological structures began rattling about, as if suddenly unhinged. Only the truth about what had happened to those parents could restore a sense of order. Yet, for all my courage as a correspondent in Vietnam, I did not dare cross the threshold of the adoption agency to ask how my parents had died. My husband did the deed for me—and discovered that the social worker had no record that either one of them was dead. My birth mother had been very much alive at the time of my relinquishment. Even more amazing, my husband was given her name.

I wanted to know about this mother, so miraculously resurrected, but was terrified by the idea of searching for her. I felt guilty at the very thought. "Who, me? Search?" I asked myself in disbelief, even as one foot was poised for the first step. "I would never search. Never!" But each *never* brought me closer to the realization that I would. For months I alternated between feeling like a traitor to my adoptive parents and feeling sheer terror that I might disappear if I entered this forbidden terrain. I hovered between wanting to forget the whole thing and wanting to learn as much as I could about my natural family.

It was a slow, laborious process, this awakening of much that had lain repressed in me. In this way I learned that the decision to search is not made in one impulsive moment, but is arrived at over a period of time as the self gradually evolves from one level of consciousness to another. I learned that when one is in touch with one's need to search, one has already changed from the person disconnected from the past into the one moving toward connection.

Having crossed the first threshold of the unconscious, one is pushed along by forces beyond one's control. Searching, as Marguerite Duras says of writing, is a matter of deciphering something already there, something you've done in the sleep of your life, in its organic fulmination, unbeknownst to you.

Glen

Glen, a teacher in his early thirties, crossed the threshold from a non-searcher into a "reluctant" searcher after reading *Lost and Found*. Just formulating a letter to me about why an adoptee didn't have the right to disturb a birth mother's life catapulted him to a new level of consciousness where adoption "reared its faceless head." He admitted he had burned with such a desire to see his mother when he was in high school that he fantasized about dressing up as a UPS man and going to her door: "Here, Mother, here is your package." In college he buried this need so deeply that he no longer had access to it. Even now that he had actually decided to search, he was filled with ambivalence because he felt close to his adoptive parents and to his younger brother, their natural son.

"I know search is selfish—for myself," he told me. "But I want to get it out of the way before marrying. It is an emotional burden, an obstacle, but it is a matter of achieving reality. I get the sense that if I don't, I will always be stuck in childlike ways of looking at the world. Attacking this issue is one way I can really grow up. It bothers me that I can't control the outcome but I can control my choice to search."

Rachel

When Rachel was in her early twenties and came across a magazine article about a woman who found her birth mother, she felt as if someone had suggested that nuclear war might be desirable.

"I had to bury this thought of 'the birth mother' almost immediately," she said. "For one terrifying second, I actually pictured her: she had no discernible features, but was like a creature from some dark netherworld who threatened to devour me by the mere fact of her existence. The biological connection between us was a kind of riptide psychic umbilical cord, which I dimly sensed had the power to drag me down into some murky depths.

That mini-internal earthquake was one of the first times I began to form a mental image of my birth mother as a human or semihuman being. She was evil; she had given me away. It was also the first time I consciously realized one can search. That which I had always thought was off-limits, completely untouchable, had entered the realm of the real, the possible, with a huge terrifying jolt."

A few years later, alone and ill in a hotel room, Rachel felt another internal jolt, but this one was comforting. "There are people out there to whom I am related by blood," she thought. "My people." She felt an "irresistible, magnetic attraction to this unknown tribe," and resolved to locate them.

Falling through the trapdoor of the self into the unconscious often happens when an adoptive parent dies or a relationship breaks down, making the adoptee feel disconnected once again. The primal terror of cosmic homelessness penetrates the unconscious, making a small dent here, a larger one there, until it breaks through the defenses.

Diane

Diane, a thirty-seven-year-old businesswoman, spent her life trying to be normal because "being adopted makes you feel so *different*." Something in her "snapped" when her fiancé said in anger: "You are so *different*!" She broke the engagement and fell into such a deep depression that she was unable to stop crying, even at work. Consulting a therapist for the first time in her life, she confessed that she was adopted. When he asked what she was going to do about it, she replied, "Nothing. It means nothing to me."

The therapist had just treated a birth mother who searched for her daughter, and was aware that adoptees often deny their feelings. He encouraged Diane to join an adoption support group. She did, but she didn't begin to search until she had reassured her adoptive parents: "Adoption is not the problem. It is the *before* that's the problem. The relinquishment, not the adoption."

Carol

At the age of thirty-nine, Carol, who was divorced, childless, and without a meaningful relationship, began to sense that something in her was dying. "My reaching forward to search was my last effort to save myself," she recalls. "I didn't know what I wanted to find, what my finding would bring me, or even if it would save me. I only knew that my life was inauthentic and that I must find my own truth. If I was going to die, it should be in response to that truth, my true facts. I didn't want to die along with the troubled actor pretending to be me, the result of some gross misunderstanding."

Search can also be triggered by a momentous event, such as when one's baby, or even a friend's baby, is born. It puts adoptees in touch with the mystery of their own birth.

Susan

When Susan dropped out of college after one year and went to New York to try her luck in theater, she felt real and rooted. It was the place of her birth. She had fantasies of becoming so famous that her mother would see her on TV talk shows. "I would say I was born in Manhattan and my mother's name was Louise Davis. If she is out there, please contact me."

But not until she was twenty-six, and peering through the window of a hospital nursery trying to locate her friend's newborn, was Susan in touch with her need to search actively for her mother: "When my friend came into the nursery, she gave a quick glance around and said: 'There he is.' That was her child. She knew. And I thought—I have to know. No more questions."

GREAT EXPECTATIONS

> Her mother saw her and stopped playing.
> She turned and dazzled Dorothy with her smile.
> She was so young and pretty and she reached out
> to hold her. Dorothy ran.
> "Dorothy. Where has my little girl been?"
> Dorothy began to cry and fell into her
> mother's arms and was held. "Oh, Mama," she said.
> "I had a terrible dream! Daddy was gone and you
> were dead, and I had to go away, and I never saw
> you ever again!"
> —GEOFF RYMAN, *WAS*

Adoptees are not clear what they are searching for when they first begin. They say that they just want to find medical information, or the reason they were given up, or someone who looks like them. Or they say they want to know their family history, to look into the eyes of someone of the same blood, to say thanks for giving birth to them. Having been out of touch with their feelings for so long, it is hard for adoptees to know what it is that is driving them forward.

Adoptees may deny that they expect to find anyone special in their birth mother, but unconsciously everyone hopes to discover a soul mate—someone strong and independent who will reach out with unconditional love. At the moment of beholding her, they expect to be instantly transformed into the whole self they were meant to be. As one man expressed it: "I want to make the outside me like the inside me so I can live as one instead of two."

Glen is determined to stay realistic: "I'm smart enough to know that after I find my birth mother, I still may not be able to balance my checkbook. I don't want to get obsessed. I worry that people will think it's not normal. I may not be able to control how far I get involved in this. I don't hold any conscious anger—but a longing."

THE HERO'S JOURNEY

When adoptees set out on the search, they are answering what Joseph Campbell describes as The Call: the first stage of the mythic journey in which the hero ventures forth from the familiar world into the unknown. According to Campbell, one is "following one's bliss."[7] For one adoptee, who "went out the gate with his tail on fire," this meant "alternating between feeling that he was a knight in armor riding a horse back through a great tunnel of darkness and feeling like an innocent child looking for a trail that was twenty years old."

The journey is the adoptee's heroic attempt to bring together the split parts of the self. It is an authentic way of being born again. It is an act of will; a new dimension of experience. It is the quest for the intrinsic nature one was born with before it got twisted out of shape by secrecy and disavowal. It is a way of modifying the past, of living out the script that might have been. It is a way of taking control of one's own destiny, of seizing power. It is a way of finding oneself.

Yet we must not forget Campbell's warning that the hero's journey, for all its glory and liberation, is on the razor's edge. The hero will have to go into a dark forest where he will be confronted with a series of trials that challenge his courage and ingenuity. The hero can never let down his guard: the glorious road to transformation and growth is strewn with death encounters and survivorlike experiences.

The adoptee's journey can be a time of chaos as well as wonder. There are no safe parameters. No way of staying in control. As they stagger through a dark no-man's land between two states of being—the born and the unborn—adoptees are elated one moment, devastated the next. In following their prenatal bliss, they must read carefully along the rim of an abyss that separates the material reality of the Adoption Kingdom from the misty nothingness of the Ghost Kingdom. They are moving not only toward the original mother but also toward the original trauma. Unexpressed grief and anger lie in ambush.

The Peril

We can see the adoptee on the journey home much as Mircea Eliade saw Ulysses, as the "trapped voyager."[8] Ulysses was on a voyage toward the center, toward Ithaca, which Eliade says was toward himself. He was a fine navigator, but destiny in the form of the trials of initiation he had to overcome forced him to keep postponing his return home. With every questionable move he made, he risked losing himself.

Adoptees face this risk too, trapped as they are by the taboos and guilt and divided loyalties that destiny, under the mandate of the closed adoption system, has inflicted on them. The journey toward self is draining, overwhelming, and lonely. And fraught with perils.

Adoptees are in peril because they are breaking the taboos around the birth mother. Just as primitive people believed that they would drop dead if they made contact with a tabooed object, so adoptees fear they could be annihilated by contact with the tabooed mother.

Adoptees are in peril because they are searching for an internal fantasy of the mother as much as for the external reality. They could lose the fantasy mother who is more real, and in some ways more important, to them than the real woman whom they seek.

Adoptees are in peril because by losing their fantasies of the birth mother, they could lose the center beam in the structure of the adopted self. These fantasies, like the adoptee, have developed over the years, but, like the adoptee, they are still split. The birth mother is still the archetypal Good Mother who offers unconditional love, but she is also the Terrible Mother, the devourer, the witch, the castrator. "She could crush me like a tin can," said a male adoptee, who turned back from his search. "She could destroy all the love I've had from others in my life—my wife, my children."

Adoptees are in peril because they could lose their own magical self that was fused with the birth mother. They could lose the self myth that the biographer Leon Edel tells us is the truest part of an individual. The myth gives us force, direction, and sustenance. Without their self myth, adoptees could become ordinary mortals, subject to nature's laws of aging and dying.

Adoptees are in peril because they could bring down the walls of the adoptive family system, like Jason brought down the walls of the temple. It is terrifying power. The adoptee wonders: "Do I dare disturb the universe?"

Adoptees are in peril because they could lose their adoptive parents, who were their only protectors and providers. One man turned back when he sensed that the search was putting a painful distance between him and the parents whose approval he had always sought. A woman stopped searching when she dreamed that her adoptive parents and birth parents had become the same, and both were abandoning her.

Adoptees are in peril because they could lose the self that grew up adopted. And no matter how fragile it might be—artificial, riddled with holes, patched, and fragmented—it is the only self they have ever known.

Adoptees are in peril because the search uncovers their psychic split, beneath which lies the threat of fragmentation and disintegration, which they have spent a lifetime trying to ward off.

THE PINOCCHIO SYNDROME

A male adoptee paints a portrait of a fragmented Pinocchio, and writes beneath it:

Am I some life-like toy?
Foundling, changeling, bundle of joy
Waiting to become a real person,
Child of wood-splintered heart.

Adoptees sometimes identify with Pinocchio, the wooden puppet who came to life only to be flooded with emotions he didn't know how to handle because he had never been able to feel before. As feelings quicken in them, adoptees experience a euphoria that they describe as a real high. They say things like: "I'm becoming real, I'm materializing, I exist."

But once they have opened themselves to feelings that had been split off before, adoptees are in touch with the loneliness that has always been there. This loneliness, the hole inside that cannot be filled, connects them to the baby falling through a dark universe after separation from the mother, as well as to the forbidden potential "true" self that now begins stirring. A male adoptee described it as "dropping into a black hole that I couldn't see out of and didn't know where the sides or bottom were."

Formerly disavowed feelings of grief, rage, fear, and abandonment can cause adoptees to have extreme mood swings, alternating between feeling ecstatic and depressed, alive and dead. One woman spoke of having physical reactions to her emotional states: back and chest pains and a variety of illnesses: "I even had suicidal thoughts—not that I was going to take an active role in ending my life, but simply that I lost my normally strong desire to live—wishing for death by apathy. This feeling was brought about by the recognition that at some level it was true that my birth mother didn't want me in her life. I didn't count. My needs as a person had been sacrificed to the needs of my adoptive parents with the pretense that I didn't have a family. Why, therefore, did I need to live? Who would care? Who would miss me?"

As frightening and intense as these mood swings are, the emotional chaos adoptees experience is a positive sign that they have managed to reconnect to those feelings that had been lost to them. It is a necessary stage before true healing can begin.

Mel

Mel, a music critic in his early forties, began searching after reading a book about adoptees who had been reunited with their birth mothers. His fantasies ranged from finding a concert pianist in Carnegie Hall to finding a bag lady in Penn Station. (He suspected the latter.)

"The adoption system incapacitates you," he told me. "I've been hobbling around not knowing anything. At least my life is more honest now." Three months into the search, he became terrified when he felt he was falling apart. He attended an EST weekend, but found it "confrontational and challenging" rather than comforting and consoling. The EST message was that one should get out, do what is difficult, and change quickly.

Mel knew intuitively that he had to go slowly because there was not a functional self waiting in the wings to replace the old one. Though he never felt that the Artificial Self fully represented him, he was afraid to jettison it for the fog and fantasy of the Forbidden Self that was more at home in the Ghost Kingdom. By abandoning his former self, he would run the risk of annihilation.

Mel vacillated between questioning what he was about to do—What am I unleashing? What if I hate her? What if I find out I come from bad stock?—and assuring himself that he had a right to know who gave birth to him. But with all of his wavering, he never doubted that he would complete the search.

Susan

Susan had already contacted one woman who proved to be the wrong person. Now she was trying again. "It's unreal," she said. "I never thought I would really do it. Sometimes I wake up and think this searching is a nightmare. It seems real and yet not real." For the next six months she isolated herself. She broke up with her boyfriend, went to movies alone, and avoided her friends. She returned to her former eating addiction, and struggled to limit her binges to popcorn and carrot sticks.

THE LADY OR THE TIGER?

Part of the danger of the search is that adoptees don't know who or what is out there waiting for them. They are like the handsome but poor warrior who had the audacity to fall in love with a princess in the short story "The Lady or the Tiger?"[9] The princess's father, a semibarbaric king, was outraged and ordered the young man to go into a special arena where he had to choose between two doors. Behind one was a beautiful lady (not the princess), who would immediately become his bride; behind the other was a fierce tiger, who would immediately devour him. (The reader is not told which door the young man chooses.)

When I counsel adoptees in search, I use this story as a metaphor. For the adoptee is like the warrior confronted with two such doors. Behind one is the beautiful mother, who waits with unconditional love; behind the other is a dangerous, sphinxlike creature in the form of a tiger who waits to annihilate him.

Yet the adoptee's fate is much more enigmatic. Whichever door he knocks on, he will find that the beautiful lady is also part tiger (the terrible, devouring mother) and that the fierce tiger is also part lady (the idealized, nurturing mother). With either choice, the adoptee will have to tame the tiger in the mother and accept the mother with all of her dark sides.

As we will see, the lady behind the door is not a goddess, but an ordinary woman with the virtues and devouring passions of all human mothers; and the tiger is not a ferocious beast, but a traumatized woman who gave up her cub and is trying to fend off the pain.

Most adoptees know intuitively that they are not up to taming tigers. They laid down their arms at an early age as a survival tactic to avoid abandonment by the adoptive parents. And yet they also know that they need to be strong to get through life. At the age of thirty, Walter still remembers the suit of armor and sword that he dreamed about at the age of six, and how he tried desperately to hold on to them when he felt himself waking so that he could be armed to face the day.

Howard: "I'm a Survivor"

Howard wore two hats: he was an adoptee who knew he was vulnerable to failure and rejection, and an adoptive father, which made him a legitimate (rather than an illegitimate) member of the establishment, like his own adoptive father, to whom he was close. For several years Howard was even president of an adoptive parent group and spoke out publicly against the right of adoptees to search. But when his younger sister went back to the Jewish adoption agency for "nonidentifying" information (which means some description of the birth parents and their families, but no names), he felt his rigid self-system cracking. As the older brother, he had always been the one to initiate things. If his sister was going to search, then so was he. Off he went to the adoption agency, this time in the role of helpless babe, which is what the adoptee is invariably reduced to in such visits.

Howard already knew that he was born in New York. Now he learned that his mother had been working there as an au pair after World War II, when she met his non-Jewish father, who was in the navy. As a child, during the war, his mother had been sent by train to London with other Jewish children from Eastern Europe. Her parents were killed in Auschwitz. "That makes me a second-generation survivor," he said. "But I'm a survivor in more than one sense. As adoptees we don't know what and who we lost. Our family was wiped out; we lost everyone."

Howard showed personal courage in his sudden turnabout from militant nonsearcher to cautious searcher. "My wife said our adoptive parent group felt I was letting everyone down. I had been the hero, the adoptee who didn't have to search," he told me. Still, it took him the next six years to absorb what he had learned and to take the necessary steps to locate his mother: "I wondered, since she lost everyone, what would it mean to find her son, or have her son find her? Wouldn't that be important to her? I know that people who have been through the Holocaust carry an open wound. I didn't think I could heal her wounds, but I could help."

When he learned that his mother resided in London, he wrote her a short letter, explaining who he was and assuring her that he didn't want anything special from her (even though he suspected he did).

"I was afraid to open her reply," he told me. "This woman who gave birth to me was writing to me. But it turned out to be a wonderful letter from a wonderful woman. She's a widow with a son and married daughter, who's a therapist like me. She was glad I found her. She'd lit a mourning candle for me every year on my birthday because she thought I'd died in Vietnam. I called her a month later. 'This is your son Howard,' I said. She said she named me Eli. We talked for two hours. It was an incredible conversation. Now we write constantly. She says she worries she might offend me. That I'll disappear."

Howard made pronouncements like "I feel claimed!" and "I can feel her love filling the empty space inside me," but he admitted that he still didn't have the psychic strength to go to London to meet his mother.

Instead he made a plan to become a "warrior" with impregnable defenses. "In this country we create sports heroes, but they are only paper tigers," he explained. "We've lost touch with the real heroes in our society—the handicapped, the elderly, those who do things that are really difficult for them." The unspoken hero, of course, is the adoptee who dares to search.

The first step of Howard's plan was to go back into therapy. "I needed to believe I was not going to betray my adoptive parents, that it was okay to split love and to have other feelings." Then he began training for the marathon. "I built up my body to be physically ready for the deep journey I was going on. I wanted to be in good shape. There's a spiritual preparation. I always feel alone. The one who takes care of me is me. I worried that I'd go crazy or have some disaster befall me. I'm very careful. I can't forget that as babies we experienced being thrown over a cliff. A descent downwards. We were lucky to be saved by being adopted. But we experienced falling."

Howard ran the marathon that year. "If I said to myself I couldn't do it, I couldn't. If I had negative thoughts, it wouldn't work. The last two miles I felt my leg buckle. I beat it. Then I kept walking. And finished the marathon."

THE CROSSROADS

All searchers come to the same Crossroads of Identity where Oedipus arrived so many centuries ago. It has not changed. The three roads still intersect.

One of the roads will take the searchers back to where they started, the Adoption Kingdom, at which point they return to the category of nonsearchers. One road leads to Limbo Land, where they can pitch tents and reside indefinitely, never knowing whether they are more afraid that their mother will *not* see them or that she *will*.

The third road leads forward, toward the Ghost Kingdom, for those who dare to cross over. The same outlandish Sphinx waits, but with a new riddle: Who goes there?

Who, indeed? The searcher does not know who it is who goes there. "Who am I?" is the very riddle that has brought him to this spot. He asks the Sphinx to let him cross over to find the answer.

Crossing Over

Crossing over means building a bridge between the material world one has lived in and the shadowy Ghost Kingdom one has fantasized about. It is a fearsome rite of passage, for one is moving away from the adoptive parents as one moves toward the birth parents. One lays a new plank over the abyss with each step one takes. One proceeds with fear and trembling that one could get stuck in the middle, able neither to turn back nor to reach the other side. There are no safe parameters in this no-man's land between two states of being, the born and the unborn.

What compels adoptees forward is that they are coming in sight of what Henry James called "the great good place."[10] They are going to be born again. But this time they will be in control, and will do it right. They are moving toward the birth father as well as the mother, toward the whole birth clan, toward the lost baby, toward that fragment of the self that waits to be reattached. Like astronauts on a dangerous mission, they defy gravity as they reach out into dark space.

Howard: "You fear you'll lose control"

For the next year Howard talked about booking a flight to London to meet his mother. And then one day he did—for three weeks that summer. "Going to London to meet my mother will be like going to Mecca," he declared. "One of the great adventures of my life, along with going to Colombia to adopt my daughter."

He admitted he had waited this long because he was afraid she might judge him (a not uncommon fear for both adoptees and birth mothers). "I needed to hear her say, 'We shouldn't judge each other. Is it all right if I'm just a plain person?'"

Two months before the flight, Howard put his warrior self back into therapy. "This is not a dress rehearsal," he said. "This is my life. And I'm dealing with so much loss now. I'm getting a divorce, I'm still not over my adoptive father's death, and I've moved in temporarily with my chronically depressed adoptive mother. I haven't told her about my search because I know she can't deal with it. And I'm upset because my birth mother just wrote that she can't introduce me to her friends with 'This is my *first* son.'"

One month before the flight, Howard was fretting over the insensitivity of a new therapist he had consulted to shore up his warrior resolve to get on the plane. "She had no insight into what I needed from her. She said I should not be focusing on myself but the two children I am leaving behind in my divorce. 'You were left,' she told me. 'So you are reenacting your betrayal. You are probably going to try to think of a way to leave therapy.' She was right about that. I sure did. I didn't need her to tell me that divorce is a betrayal for children. I know that it is a double betrayal if the children are adopted."

Howard also knew why he still might be resisting going to Mecca.

"You fear you'll lose control," he told me. "You'd be in a relationship that is not like with a friend or lover. You could escape from those. But with your birth mother—that's your beginning."

Susan: "Will I feel crossed over?"

Toward the end of her search, while she waited for her mother's response to her letter, Susan was fascinated to hear that a friend had met his birth mother. "He's crossed over," she said. "He did it. He's not one of us anymore. He's one of them." Then she brooded: "I wonder, will I feel crossed over?"

THE REGRESSED SELF

For the adoptee returning to the beginning of time, time curves back on itself. The adoptee regresses as time regresses. One is on a "pilgrimage back to the womb," as one adoptee put it, moving toward one's mother. Actually one is moving toward two mothers: the fantasy mother, frozen in time, whom one has internalized, and the actual mother, whose life has moved on without her child in the real world.

And all the while the adoptee regresses, he or she is becoming two people: the ambivalent adult who returns and the needy baby who was left behind. As one woman said: "I feel like two people: the child in me wants one thing—to kill her. It has a lot of rage and anger. But the adult wants to be rational and unemotional."

Susan: "I feel myself slipping away"

"I feel I am becoming invisible" is the way Susan described this very scary period. "I am in the process of being born. A baby. I need someone to take care of me. I could be an alien from another planet. I never felt attached, but when my mother holds my letter, it will be that connection. She will look at my handwriting, see my signature, just as she saw me as a baby. I feel myself slipping away from my adoptive parents and slipping back through the umbilical cord to where I should have been. Detached from everything. Waiting for the call to link me with my mother. I feel powerless. I can't control when this will happen."

Mel: "I was born and dumped"

Mel felt flooded with emotions that had been bottled up. "A lot of anger—she deserted me. I was born and dumped." Yet other emotions were "pushing and pulling" him. He felt a desire to suckle, to be cradled. "I am crying a lot, but feel there is some growth. I've never felt emotions in my whole life. Whatever emotions I had before were not authentic. I had no real feelings."

Rachel: "I'm in the womb"

Rachel had a dream while waiting for her mother's response to her letter: "I was in a fetal position in a womb, but I had my adult body. The outside walls of the womb were bright red and pink stained glass. I thought: 'It's really great. I'm full grown, but I'm in the womb.'"

Alice: "I want my Mommy"

Alice, whose search was stalled because her mother may have used a false name, found herself alternating between "age zero and age forty-six" as she was once again confronted with separation and loss. "One minute I'm in the womb crying and holding on to my doll, and the next I feel like a wounded woman who fails at all ultimate love relationships."

During this period, she clung to her therapist. "I feel like a baby cut off, unconnected, raw inside, curled up in a fetal coil," she wrote me. "The cord is bleeding, leaving a huge ache inside my tiny body. I want my Mommy. I want to be connected. I want to be."

11

Alternate Reality

The world was haunted. It needed to be
haunted. The Land of Was was cradled in the
arms of Now like a child.
—GEOFF RYMAN, *WAS*

THE EMOTIONS OF SEARCH FLOW INTO THOSE OF
reunion like a river into the sea. One contacts the birth mother and
crosses over, but one does not instantly feel born or transformed. One is
still subject to the same old tumultuous mood swings, the same old
doubts and fears. Like Alice who has gone intrepidly through the Looking Glass, one is on the other side; but one is still Alice, capable of alternately shrinking in size and stretching to a larger-than-life replica of herself.

Once across, one enters an alternate reality—the world that might
have been had one not left one's original self behind and continued on
without it. One summons ghosts that have gone on to their own des-
tinies. One is faced with making sense of the bewildering array of new
characters that materialize. The old reality no longer holds. It is, as one
adoptee described it, like being in a white space in which the adoptive
family and the birth family cancel each other out. One's identity is obliterated. Nothing will ever be the same again.

We will see how difficult it is for the most loving of adoptees and birth

mothers to make their way back to each other. The separation, unresolved grief, and secrecy have traumatized them both. And the closed
adoption system has made them taboo to each other. No matter how
positive the reunion, there is a psychological price paid by both parties in
the process. As the poet Anna Akhmatova said in another context, there
is no glue to put lives together at the place they have been cut off.

I have come across reunions that have ended after one meeting and
others that are still holding fast, despite ups and downs, after ten years or
more. They run the gamut from the adoptee being welcomed "home" by
the birth mother and her family to the rare cases where the adoptee is
denied any contact. In the majority of reunions, mother and child reconnect for a short period until it becomes clear that they will deepen the
relationship, maintain a cordial friendship, or disconnect. I have seen
adoptive families and birth families blend into an extended family for the
sake of the adoptee, just as I have seen the two families orbit separately
around the adoptee, without ever interacting. But in all of these scenarios, even the seemingly negative ones, the adoptee feels a sense of
grounding and renewal.

No matter who adoptees find—the All-Loving Mother, who flings
open the door; the Mother from Hell, who bars the way; the Ambivalent
Mother, who swings back and forth; the Mother who Married Father—
they will learn that the mother who left them behind has done her own
kind of splitting to survive. Her response will be influenced by how she
dealt with the shame and humiliation of her pregnancy; the pain of losing
the innocence of youth; her feelings about the father; and the trauma of
giving up her child. It will also be influenced by how much denial she has
done for emotional survival, the secrets she has kept, the guilt she has
felt, and the new life she has made.

The birth mother may have some resistance to reunion if she felt abandoned by the birth father; if she has rewritten her history; or if she has
changed her perception of herself from the fallen woman to the church-
going den mother and doesn't want to be thrown back to that earlier self.
The adoptee who returns is both the beloved lost baby for whom the
mother once pined and the dangerous enemy who wreaked havoc on her
life once and could do it again. The mother cannot embrace one without
confronting the other.

This is true for the adoptee, too. Although the adoptee's adult psyche is
bound up with the lost mother as profoundly as the fetus's archaic psyche
was bound up with her in utero, the mother is perceived as both goddess

and witch, representing both life and death. The adoptee cannot embrace one without confronting the other. Mother and child cannot help but react to the psychological fallout of their traumas. "All my anguish is because of you" is an unspoken message that lies between them.

Reunioning, as it is called, is still so relatively new that it will be a long time before we can chart all of its fevers.[1] Yet already we can see that there are stages of reunion just as there are stages of the search.

THE INFANCY STAGE

During the first meeting with the birth mother, the adoptee may feel "numb" or in an "intoxicated trance." This is understandable when we remember the dual nature of what is going on: the adoptee is both the adult meeting the mother in the Land of Now and the baby meeting the mother in the Land of Was. It is a primal moment in which one is reexperiencing the Big Bang of one's birth. There is one's original mother shining with all the brilliance of a supernova before it is destined to fade. For that wondrous moment one is one's original self—pure, authentic, and real.

"The first time she held me in an embrace, I knew this was Mama," said one woman. "Like a primitive knowledge. It blew me away. I felt totally vulnerable, like a naked child in the woods being sniffed by a wolf."

Another woman remembers asking her mother to go to the refrigerator, take out a yogurt, and feed her by hand. "I couldn't eat properly without her. I needed her mothering." Yet another adoptee recalls being filled with grief and rage as she watched her mother play with her infant daughter's toes, nuzzle her hair, and sing little songs that she had sung to the children she kept. "This was supposed to be me," she said. "I wanted to be in her lap having her play with my piggies and touch my hair. There I was an infant in a thirty-two-year-old woman's body wanting to crawl into a fifty-five-year old woman's lap and say, 'Just rock me.'"

The birth mother is also usually regressed by the time of reunion. Once again she is the young woman whose body was with child—a child whose reappearance may fill her with such physical longing that her breasts begin to hurt. There is a freshness to the perceptions of both mother and child during this initial coming together, a euphoria that some liken to a honeymoon period.

Yet there is a primal undercurrent to these heightened feelings. The relationship has a tentative quality. Adoptees speak of "walking on eggs," of being afraid to say or do the wrong thing. "One false move, and I get rejected again—for life." Often this requires not saying what one really thinks, a throwback to the Artificial Self's strategy of trying to please the adoptive parents.

Susan: "I've crossed over!"

Some adoptees describe feeling "spaced out" during this initial stage of reunion. Susan was shaking with excitement when she received a phone call from her mother, who was now living in Paris. "I've crossed over!" she told me. "Her voice was just like mine. She was sobbing tears of joy that my letter had started a healing process. She said it was a miracle I'd come back, and she loved me. But she was worried about my adoptive parents."

For the first time Susan did not feel alone. "I'm not floating like an empty balloon now. Before, if you stuck me with a pin, I'd pop. Now I'm solid, connected to all the walls. I'm whole." Still, though she thought she had overcome her food addiction, Susan went on an eating binge. She spent her evenings at the Overeaters support group before flying off to Paris for three weeks to meet her mother. She was petrified on the way over: "I couldn't fathom landing. I felt like I was entering a dream, but it was going to be a real dream."

Her mother was weeping when she met the plane: "My baby, my baby daughter," she kept repeating as she took one of Susan's hands and her half-sister took the other. "I felt like a little girl, and yet like a woman. I look like my mother, and we talk the same quick way. We spent some time crying together. I asked her what it was like when I was in her stomach."

Susan was aware that she was on guard at first, not letting too much in or out. "I was afraid of my anger, which made me slightly standoffish. I thought I wanted to be held, but each time she really touched me, I felt myself stiffen. I didn't feel a 'magical bond.' It was reality—and reality was just plain weird." But she watched with envy as her mother and half-sister rubbed each other's feet. "I felt like the left-behind child. I wanted to scream, but I had to act happy. It was so unfair. But I'm really good at closing off emotions."

Mel: "I felt a bond"

Mel was thrilled to hear his mother's voice on the phone. "My adoptive parents had shrill voices like birds in a tree, but she has a soft, musical voice like my own. I've heard that voice before, I thought. It was as smooth as a river bottom—the voice I'd heard in the womb. That was an immediate bond. I felt I was home."

His mother agreed to Mel's plan to come to Georgia to visit her, but she tried to back out of the reunion when he phoned on arrival. She said she wasn't feeling well. He called the neighbor whose telephone his mother used, and the woman suggested he just come to her house at 8:30 the next morning.

The neighbor's living room was full of the local men about to go hunting when Mel arrived in a jaunty sports jacket. They thought he was an insurance agent. The neighbor rang his mother's bell and asked her to come over; she had a surprise for her. Mel already knew that life had been hard for his mother, and that she was on welfare, but he was not prepared for what he saw. The woman who seemed to "flow" into the room wore a blonde wig aslant on her head and two or three housecoats piled one on top of the other. Still, he felt drawn to her; he had the distinct feeling that she had "maintained her soul."

"I said, 'Hi. I'm glad to see you.' I gave her a hug. She asked: 'Who are you?' She didn't mention that she had given up a boy a year after me, but I think she was wondering which one I was.

"It was awkward at first because everyone sat around listening. We talked for two hours. Two men went off hunting in the middle. I told her I knew that she had been raised in an orphanage because her mother was in and out of institutions, and that her father had committed suicide. I even knew she had sung in a choir as a girl. She said I knew more about her life than she did. I noticed she made large gestures with her hands the way I did when she spoke. Before I left she gave me a music box with terrible music. I gave her a copy of one of my books so she'd know I was legitimate. We drank bad coffee."

Back home, Mel kept thinking, "It's real." He knew he was lucky not to have been raised by this mother, but he still found himself wanting to see her again. "There's some connection there," he said. "I felt a bond."

Trish: "I got fantasy hell"

Trish didn't learn until the night before she was to meet her mother and father in the social worker's office that they had married two years after giving her up and had three more children. This scenario didn't fit in with Trish's fantasy of her mother as a self-sufficient, self-assured career woman whom she had named Elizabeth Eagan.

"I thought of Elizabeth Eagan as my other half," Trish said. "She was supposed to come back and fill the space she had left. That was the woman I wanted to meet as I walked into the agency. Instead, I got fantasy hell. Bertha, sitting there wearing a kelly-green print blouse, white pants, white sandals, and no makeup. It was the white purse that really bugged me. I thought, 'You are so wrong for me, this is a bad match. I don't condone white purses. And you're not supposed to be married.'"

Trish's father looked as "frozen and scared" as her mother, who had been his high school sweetheart. The three of them engaged in nervous chatter, but all the while Trish was thinking: Where's Elizabeth Eagan? Where's my mother? "I was having trouble recognizing my parents—my 'people'—or myself in them. All I could see were the suburban trappings of their lives."

Trish's mother had told the social worker that her daughter was not to know their last names or address. Over the next few months, she was distant and cold, pulling back when Trish tried to touch her or hold her hand. She did not invite Trish home—only twenty minutes away—to meet her three full siblings.

"I experienced her behavior as a stinging betrayal," Trish said. "I was still not able to perceive her life as separate from my own. In the profoundest sense, I had expected to find my 'other half,' the sacrificed self whose recovery would at last provide closure to the unfathomable nature of my being."

Even though her mother told her that they could never reclaim the bonding they had lost, Trish fell back into her old pattern of putting her own emotional agenda last. She made excuses for why her mother was withholding her other children along with her love. "I swallowed it. Big gulps of pain, confusion, and anger went down like medicine, just as they had with my other mother before."

Only the secret visits of Trish's father, who was able to express his pain, loss, and joy, kept her from falling apart when, four months into reunion, Trish's mother suggested that they not meet again. Trish was struggling with this when a few weeks later she got a call from her birth father that he wanted to bring her mother over. She refused, afraid she would be hurt again. "Please trust me. We have to come down," he pleaded.

"So I let them come down," Trish recalled, "and it was just like my mother was in labor. My father carried her through the door, placed her on the couch, and went to the kitchen to make tea. At first she didn't notice me hovering there. Then I walked over to the couch, and curled up on her stomach and was this baby again. She looked at me, recognized me, and cried: 'You're my baby, I love you.' And it was as if she had just had this baby."

After that, Trish's mother invited her to their home to meet her full siblings. Their relationship was "calm and joyous" for the next year, until Trish's need to keep bringing up the past caused her mother to pull back again.

Howard: "I came all this way to see you"

Although the male warrior in Howard had felt strong enough to board the plane to London, the adoptee in him felt completely vulnerable as he disembarked. He knew at a glance that the dour woman waiting for him at the airport was not the "all-loving mother" he had communicated with for the past year.

"Why are you wearing black pants when you said you'd be wearing a suit?" she snapped. "How would I have recognized you? And why did you send me such terrible pictures? You're much better-looking."

During the two weeks he stayed at her house, Howard experienced his birth mother's rigidity and bitterness. He found her "hard, like granite." This was not a mother who was going to take him in her arms and comfort him. She informed him the first day that he was the result of a date rape: "Having you ruined my life." She gave her second son the name she had given him, Eli. "I abused him because of you."

"I wanted to abort you," she said. "I waited too long. Then someone offered to buy you." Howard felt he would rather she had assaulted him than say that. "Do you like women?" she wanted to know another time. "I taught my daughter not to let a man touch her."

Howard learned that early in her marriage, his mother had confided in her husband, who could not understand how she could have given up her own child. He told her not to tell anyone. "And so my whole life is a lie because of you," she said. Somehow Howard managed to respond: "You are the liar, not me. I told everyone about you."

Howard began touring the city on his own to escape her verbal abuse. She was cordial and smiling only when her other son was present. "You are weak, not like him," she declared. And one night when he apologized for upsetting her by coming in late, she came back with, "A strong man would never apologize to a woman." For the first time he stood up to her. "I haven't seen you in forty-one years," he said. "I came all this way to meet you. In my country, it's polite to say one is sorry."

Only his siblings, whom he resembled, made the experience bearable. Although they had a different father, they shared his green eyes, light hair, and large build. "You are our brother," Eli told him. "Don't worry about Mother." His sister was warm and introspective. She explained that their father had been the heart of the family.

Sarah: "Where had I returned from?"

"Electric" was the way Sarah described her reunion. "If my hair could have stood on end, it would have." Like many adoptees, she had first thought of searching in college, but went no further once she got her nonidentifying information. Seven years later, it took an abortion and an emotional crisis to make her recognize "the need to find something about myself that I could call my own. And so I looked for my past." The search went quickly because she had her adoption papers and the luck to encounter two elderly women in her mother's hometown who knew her mother's family. "Bing, bing, bing"—and she was talking to her mother on the phone.

Sarah still remembers her febrile emotions during that first meeting: "I had to sleep in the *same bed* as my birth mother the first night we met. She'd arrived late from Maine to pick me up and we couldn't make it back up there the same evening. So to a motel we all went—me, my birth mother, my birth grandmother, and my birth aunt. The ladies.

"I needed a drink but the motel bar was closed. We didn't talk about anything emotional, just about the people we'd meet, the bars we'd hit, the family I'd become a part of. There were no hugs, but a lot of just leaning against one another, hands on shoulders, looking into mirrors a lot. I didn't have her hands."

But Sarah was relieved to see that she did share her mother's height:

five feet, eleven inches. She had towered over her adoptive parents and felt a lack of a "genetic guide" to learn how to move her body gracefully. "I took my attitude from my adoptive family, but not my walk," she said. "And there was Mother strolling through the motel room with shoulders back, long legs appearing from beneath a nightgown that was made too short by those legs, eyes fixed forward with an air of confidence, arms crooked at the elbow ever so slightly—my mother, doing so effortlessly what I had spent my life working at." Having also spent her life trying to emulate an adoptive mother who was always perfectly groomed, Sarah was glad to find that her birth mother didn't like skirts, formal dresses, or heels either, and neither did her grandmother or aunt.

"I didn't sleep well that night. I was too keyed up. I lay in the bed next to her, dozing, not thinking, and yearning for a drink. I did sleep finally, but it was not restful. When I woke, she was still there. They were all there, my grandmother, aunt, and mother, laughing a little self-consciously. And then we were on the road again, still comparing similar body parts."

All through the ride, Sarah wanted to cry out, "My mother! Kiss me, hold me, cradle me. Why did you go to bed with him? Where was I conceived? I don't want to be your grown daughter—I want to be your baby. Were you a good girl back then, gone astray? Let me light that cigarette for you. Jesus, don't touch me! Damn, why won't you touch me?"

Sarah met "a mess of relatives" and felt she was on display. "I could have been a mass murderer for all they knew or cared, just that I had returned." And then she asked the question that haunts all adoptees: "But where had I gone? Where did I return from? What was I returning to?"

CHAOS REVISITED

Soon after reunion, or later in a delayed reaction, adoptees experience a resurgence of the emotional chaos they had during the search. Once again all the unleashed emotions come crashing through their defenses. Especially grief and anger.

Whatever the nature of the reunion with the birth mother, the adoptee inevitably feels grief for the years they have lost together. Just watching her mother interact in her family with the children she raised can fill the adoptee with anguish for what might have been. There is grief for having been let go, for feeling that one is outside the immediate circle, for not feeling the immediate connection one expected, and for still feeling alone. There is so much grief that one often feels like Alice swimming in a Sea of Tears, the very ocean of tears that has been dammed up inside until now.

But scary as it is that, having started, one will never be able to stop, weeping brings rewards as well as relief. It can create "a river around the boat that carries your soul-life," according to the Jungian analyst Clarissa Pinkola Estés. "Tears lift your boat off the rocks, off dry ground, carrying it downriver to someplace new, someplace better."[2]

At the same time, one can also be overwhelmed with free-floating anger, such as one woman felt when her mother spoke of marrying two years after she had relinquished her. "Oh, you were able to fall in love and go on with your life instead of grieving over me," she thought indignantly. For a moment she wasn't even sure that she hadn't said it out loud, and was relieved to see that her mother hadn't noticed her change in mood. Some adoptees want to shout: "Where were you when I needed you? How could you have dumped me?"

Even though adoptees understand that the woman who gave birth to them was unable to raise them and did the best she could by arranging an adoption, a part of them will *never* understand. Whatever the mother's story—she was too young, she was too poor, her parents made her do it, her social worker pressured her—adoptees know that the mother was not strong enough to hold on. She let go. Not only she, but the whole clan let go. *They let go.*

Sometimes adoptees' anger finds other targets: the adoption system for holding their identity hostage, the social workers for treating them condescendingly when they asked for identifying information, the adoptive parents for colluding in the closed system, and even themselves for passively going along with the secrecy.

Again, we must remember that no matter how painful these waves of grief and anger are, they are part of the ongoing process of mourning that comes with reclaiming one's lost emotions and integrating them into the self. Adoptees find it hard to believe at the time, but the chaos carries healing in its wake.

Mel: "I was changing"

Mel would not allow himself to use words like "disappointed" after he met his birth mother, but reunion did not give him the sustained connection that he longed for. His mother, who had been unmothered herself, had "lost her focus" long before he met her. She would not, or could not, tell him who his father was. She did not answer his letters. He went through long periods of depression in which he found himself weeping uncontrollably. Even though he had no illusion that he would have been better off with her, he couldn't seem to separate from her.

"At first I was too depressed to work," he recalls. "I felt alone again. I clung to my therapist like a child to a mother. I used to say that knowing where I came from was not important to me. Now I knew it was. I was changing and I wanted to change my life—completely. I'd never had enough courage to end my marriage, but now I asked my wife for a divorce. Fortunately, we had no children. I found it hard to be with people. I didn't want to share who I was those last forty years, and I was not yet the person I wanted to be."

Still, Mel is happy he searched. "I'm in touch with my emotions now," he says. "I'd rather be despairing than a rock—a dead self." It is not unusual for an adoptee to want to jettison the old Artificial Self that he feels no longer represents him. Jean-Paul Sartre caught this transitional state in his biography describing Genet's self in flux: "One is still what one is going to cease to be and already what one is going to become."[3]

Susan: Elation and Depletion

Returning home on the plane, Susan felt a "true explosion of reality," as if she were flying back out of the clouds both literally and figuratively. "I thought: 'So that's it.' I felt disengaged from the whole experience. I was drained and yet stuffed with the feelings I had kept in the whole time. I realized that I had a mother and father back in the States—they were the ones who had shared my life experiences."

These feelings of elation and depletion continued after she arrived back in the apartment she was sharing with her new boyfriend. She felt frustrated that she couldn't work through her feelings with her birth mother because of the distance between them. Her anger finally erupted a few months later when she received a loving letter from her birth father asking her to come to Italy to meet him. "Then it hit me—why the hell should I be so sweet to them and they get off the hook so damn easily? I felt like a doormat. I wanted to tell them: Oh sure, it's OK that I am your flesh and blood, which for most people means taking responsibility. But for all your incredible love for your child, you still managed to leave me behind and confuse my whole existence."

Susan felt guilty that she was being ungrateful, especially when she was aware that many adoptees either can't find their parents or are turned away, but she also felt justified at feeling angry and betrayed. She slept a lot and found it hard to concentrate. "I got sort of depressed and felt drained most of the time. I realized that I had wanted to hurt my mother when we met. To say: 'Ha-ha, I'm so great (even though I know I'm not), you should have kept me.'"

THE TERRIBLE TWOS

We are reminded at each stage of reunion that adoptees are not having a rational experience, but are being carried away by nonrational passions. Primitive feelings and needs storm the defenses, and more often than not are in charge. Regressed adoptees want to relive that early period with the fantasy mother before the separation, and then to progress slowly like a growing child to the place in the life cycle where they are now. But the mother may not be emotionally available or may not want to linger too long in that early traumatic space. It is too painful. She may want to return quickly to the life she has so painstakingly put together, where she has other things to do than to reparent an adult child.

Trish: Pushing/Pulling

Trish, like so many other adoptees, was aware that she was being a prickly baby—giving one moment, taking the next. Either cuddling or raging. "Pushing/pulling" is the way she described it. Pulling the birth mother to you one moment, pushing her away the next, like an infant who doesn't know what it wants.

Although Trish continually tried to confront her mother with her feelings, her mother was not available. She would have had to deal with her own trauma before she could deal with Trish's. The more Trish demanded an honest appraisal of their relationship, the more her mother retreated; and the more her mother retreated, the more angry and frustrated Trish became.

Trish lingered for over a year in "the terrible twos," as she struggled to deal with her ambivalence and grief. "I was the worst toddler, constantly testing out. I could hear myself like a two-year-old that says 'I love you/I hate you/I love you/I hate you!' But I couldn't stop."

GROWING UP FAST FORWARD

At some point adoptees have to accept their birth mother's limitations and take some responsibility for reparenting themselves. This often means growing up fast forward, sometimes jumping directly from the terrible twos to the terrible sixteens—which resemble each other in their pushing/pulling. "There is a need to feel secure, and then a need to break from this security and be independent," said Robin, who "fell in love" with the birth mother who found her two years ago. Not until she felt secure in the knowledge that her birth mother's arms were long enough to embrace her "for a lifetime" could she dare move to the terrible sixteens and express her anger at having been left, as well as at everyday annoyances. "When I'd become cool, critical, and sarcastic, she'd say I should tell her outright what bothers me. But teenagers don't do that."

It is often hard to move fast forward without the help of a spouse, friends, a support group, or a therapist. One may need a combination of all of them.

Howard: "You can't pick your mother"

Howard had to reparent himself from the moment he met his mother. He felt debilitated for some time after his return from London. When he saw the videotape his brother had taken of his departure, he thought he looked like a man of seventy. "I have to process all this like a death," he told me. "It's like a postpartum depression. Anticlimactic. You have a fantasy of a perfect mother, but need a real one. She proves to be not perfect, or perfectly horrible. You want to be rescued, or you find out she's so horrible you don't want to live. What else is new? Life is what is presented to you. You can't pick your mother—either the biological one or the adopted one."

Only gradually could Howard forgive his birth mother by reminding himself that she was, after all, a survivor—a shattered person. "Her parents died in Auschwitz, while my parents were here for me," he said. "And her husband had just died. She was depressed. I can't criticize her. It would be like blaming the victim. That was the way she was. I revived her trauma, like ripping stitches off a wound."

But there are positive sides. He always wanted a brother, and now he has one who is in some ways like a double: he has the same large body, the name Howard was originally given, and the life Howard would have had. And he has a sister who also writes loving letters claiming him as a brother.

CLINGING TO THE WITHERED BREAST

Even when the birth mother is fully available at first, it is hard for adoptees to get all the physical and emotional nurturance they seek. Ideally, the mother would encourage adoptees to regress for as many months or years as they might need to regain their trust. During that time, she would in effect reparent them, holding and indulging their baby selves on demand and making herself available by phone or mail whenever summoned by the toddler or adolescent self.

Unfortunately, it is usually impossible to expect that a birth mother can stop her life to give unconditional love and attention to her adult child, who is in constant fear that she will disappear again. In the few cases I know of where this is happening, both adoptee and birth mother have sought therapy to work out their own needs while trying to attend to the needs of the other. They are able to see reunion as a process that may be frustrating at times but that has an eventual goal: the development of a relationship between mother and adult child based on trust.

Adoptees who cannot have the continual touching and holding of a preverbal relationship with the mother will seek to claim her in other ways, such as trying to possess every bit of information about her life during their nine months together and after. But no matter how much the birth mother reveals about the past, adoptees are often insatiable—as if there is something the mother is withholding, something essential for their well-being. As if they are addicted to searching for ways to break down the mother's resistance. As if they need one more drop of milk to slake their thirst.

When this goes on for too long, a birth mother may establish boundaries by refusing to talk about the past—"a brutal weaning," one man called it. "She wanted me to stand up, fly right, be independent."

Trish: "I was inquisitive, overbearing, verbose"

Trish knew that her mother resented her endless questions and her constant need to dig up the past that her mother had so neatly buried.

"There I was—inquisitive, overbearing, verbose, yearning, prodding, dramatic, pompous, vulnerable: the pain of her experience incarnate. My questions proved to be too specific, directed at issues that were long buried in sacred ground. I was forcing my parents to articulate their feelings even though it was obvious they'd shunned introspection ever since giving me up. I tapped into the subconscious stream running through the family. It was potent. I knew my mother was also thinking, 'I love you/I hate you!' And 'I wish I never had you.'"

It is not unusual for birth parents who marry after giving up their child to try to behave as if the birth never happened, much in the manner of Holocaust survivors who try to shed the traumatic past. The grief, pain, guilt, and shame are too great to bear. No matter what their joy, birth parents cannot help but feel exposed and even resentful toward the lost child for coming back with the discarded entrails of the past. Unfortunately, the child cannot return empty-handed.

"Where were you all those years?" Trish would rage at her mother in an effort to make her see the hurt, wounded child within. She knew it was a risk, confronting her mother with her pain, but she had to take it. Rather than attempting to comfort her daughter, Trish's mother—"a performance artist in anger"—became furious in return. She wanted to know why Trish couldn't just accept "what was there." Her father, caught in the middle, tried to preserve harmony in his marriage. "You've got to put your feelings in the closet," he advised Trish. "Let's put what happened behind us."

"He was saying I should go back into hiding like they did after they gave me up," Trish said. "But there was no way I could do that again. If I had grown up with them, I would have done this fighting, bickering, and confronting in adolescence. It would have been natural then. It wasn't now that I was an adult." During this period, Trish had a dream that her mother had a hysterectomy. "It was as if once her womb was removed—the center of our conflict—we could go on as friends."

Sarah: "I have a lingering sadness"

Sarah's mother did not know how to respond to the intensity of her daughter's letters, which Sarah now realizes were "overkill." From the beginning, her mother revealed an ambivalence that is common in those who are found and have not yet processed their feelings.

"I don't know what you want me to be, how you want me to perceive you," her mother wrote. "I am afraid of alienating you before I get a chance to know you. I feel guilty because I can't love you like I think I should. I need you to love your parents so that I don't have to feel pressured into committing too soon. I definitely do not want you to suddenly drop out of sight and lose you again, but I don't know if it's a motherly or a possessive feeling."

Sarah's birth mother was struggling with a dilemma that has plagued so many other birth mothers: Am I a mother or a friend? "I am not treating you like one of my kids," she wrote in an early letter. "More like a young friend. It's impossible to make a close, intimate, no-holds-barred friendship with one's own child." (The writer Lorraine Dusky has argued that it is as wrong to diminish the relationship to "friendship," without the bond of blood, as it would be to suggest that adoptive parents are no more than temporary caretakers. "We are more than friends but less than mother and child who were always together," she concludes.)[4]

Sarah was told that her birth father had died, but she sensed that her mother had secrets that she did not want disturbed. Her letters were filled with cryptic allusions that would remain unsolved mysteries: "I don't want you to love me too much because I have my faults, idiosyncrasies, and past—well, just passed pasts. I don't want you to feel cheated. I know I'll let you down."

Like many adoptees, Sarah wonders how far she has a right to probe. "How do you find out about your past if it is so tightly woven with someone else's anger, misery, and frustration?" she asks. One of her mother's letters seemed to answer that question. "I treasure my aloneness, oneness, and every one of my neuroses and would rather withdraw than change," she wrote. "I'm afraid of changing and finding out that I don't like my life. I like it the way it is and if I don't, let it lie for a while."

Sarah felt like rolling up into a ball and crying like a "newborn" when she read that. Her mother seemed to be opening and closing her arms at the same time, an emotional distancing that didn't change over the next decade as Sarah married and became a mother herself. "I think it was a relief to my mother that I found a husband who would absorb some of my pent-up emotions regarding—everything," Sarah says. "But I have a lingering sadness that whatever mother/daughter relationship we might have had was over and done with when I married—locked in granite—never to mature any further. It was like we grew up apart."

Although her mother writes often, shares books, and speaks to her by phone once a month, Sarah never feels satisfied. She has learned that an ongoing relationship carries with it the baggage of ongoing pain: "Each contact touches that wound that can never completely heal."

We can see the adoptees' desperate clinging to the withered breast as a need to stay in the child mode with the mother until they feel secure enough to move on to a more mature stage in their relationship, which means feeling secure enough to separate without anxiety. They cling even when they are deeply ambivalent about the mother, and recognize the irrationality of their need. As one woman expressed it: "I was inescapably drawn to her and repelled by her. In her presence I didn't like her. In her absence I longed for her."

TWO MOTHERS AND NONE

We could say that the reclaimed birth mother has risen as if from the dead, for her absence had made her as if dead to the child. Still, her reappearance in the adoptee's life does not necessarily undo the loss that was created by her absence. The phantom mother has been flushed out and then fleshed out, yet this actual birth mother with whom one has had no prior relationship cannot fulfill the promise of the fantasy mother.

"Once the elation of the reunion was over, I realized I had built a fantasy on the fantasy of my birth mother," one woman said. "When I was able to look critically at the reality of who she really is, I tried to back off, to go back to the way I was before my search. But of course I couldn't do that. You can't go back. I am a different person now, even if I don't know yet who that person is."

To witness the letdown that many adoptees experience after reunions of any kind is to realize the critical importance of fantasy in the early structuring of the self. When this structure is shaken or toppled, the whole self is threatened. The adoptee's survival strategies were built on that fantasy mother. To dismantle the fantasy is to dismantle the self.

It is yet another paradoxical situation: one set out to find the missing mother in order to find the missing part of the self, but in the process one loses the fantasies that were a vital part of the self. One is faced with a loss of dimensions that parallel the original loss, for the fantasies were the link not only to the "motherself" but to the magical, omnipotent part of the self that made one unique.

At some point adoptees realize that they cannot fully be their birth mother's child any more than they were fully their adoptive mother's child. "I can't go back to my original mother or to my adoptive mother," one woman explained. "There is no place to go. I have to go with me."

Trish: "All of us are lost to each other"

Trish, who found the very real Bertha instead of the fantasy Elizabeth Eagan, felt a sense of psychic harm that she attributed to losing her fantasy mother. She was aware of grieving even more deeply than before the "primordial loss of self and motherself."

Trish's attempt to integrate the loss with her newfound realities was also difficult and painful for both her mothers. Her adoptive mother, an emotionally unstable woman still reeling from her own feelings of abandonment after a divorce, attempted suicide soon after Trish's reunion. "You have your own family now, you don't need me," she said. Trish has tried to reassure her, while keeping some distance to protect herself.

"It is a very bizarre feeling to have no mother," she says. "To be a different person to my adoptive mother, to be a new daughter to my birth mother, and to have no connection with either mother. All of us are lost to each other at this point in my reunion. The irony of having two mothers while simultaneously having neither is not lost on me. In fact, this is probably the pea that gives me no rest."

Sarah: "Biologically she is my mother"

Sarah still feels motherless even though she can count the many mothers she has amassed over the years: her various nannies (who made up a veritable "Mother Rental Service"), her adoptive mother, her mother-in-law, and now her birth mother. None of them can give her the kind of love she craved as a child and still craves: that unconditional love that adoptees imagine comes like a CARE package attached to the umbilical cord.

Sarah's relationship to her adoptive mother, who had three sons (and two infants who died) before adopting her, had been especially stormy during Sarah's rebellious adolescence. "My mother was very much behind the search from the beginning because I'm certain she believed that I couldn't get any more nuts if I knew her than if I didn't. Our relationship was at an all-time low, and the search was her way of slipping back into my life on some positive level. But actually everything became strained after my reunion. I'm certain I just threw onto her all my mixed up feelings without ever saying anything, but just in my behavior."

Over time, Sarah began to feel closer to her adoptive mother than she had before reunion. "The search made me realize that I will never be the daughter that she has always wanted. But I finally also realized that I could respect her and even love her if I didn't always look at what I wasn't in her eyes. Instead, I had to turn around and look at myself, feel good about what was going on inside of me. Then, no matter what she said or implied, I would be safe from any criticisms. I could walk away proud."

The first visit that Sarah's birth mother made to her home—ten years into their reunion—was to be the last. Throughout her stay, Sarah felt a physical barrier between them even as she felt a physical pull. "We couldn't figure out how to touch one another. While in the kitchen going for coffee or just passing through, we would maneuver around like two ships avoiding collision or lock into a hug for an instant of emotional relief."

The moment her mother entered the house, Sarah felt herself regressing as she had during their initial meeting in the motel ten years before. "I still felt that nagging compulsion to crawl up into her lap as a child would and, like a child, cling onto her neck, smell her motherly smell, and bury my childlike head into her bosom as she gently rocks me back and forth. And with an embarrassed flush I would recall this yearning as I looked into her face, trying to listen to what she was saying, but feeling the taboo of how I felt deep down in my soul. So, in our casualness, our joking and laughter, and especially during those long moments of just looking at one another without apparent detection, drinking in the other's existence, a definition of our relationship was being established— but with a list of qualifications a mile long."

The qualifications? "Biologically I am her daughter, but I didn't grow up in her world and so we don't share the same past. Mystically, however, we found that there were so many similarities between us: our wants and needs, our likes and dislikes, our perceptions. I cry to think how much alike we might have been had I remained with her after my birth, and how different her life would have been had I not been given up. But I know my development was a by-product of the history she gave me genetically and the environment afforded to me by my adoptive family."

Before she left, Sarah's mother said, cryptically, "This is probably the last time I'll ever come here." And with a mixture of relief and despair, Sarah realized that she would have to come to terms with her feelings about "this stranger I call Mom." But after her mother was gone, Sarah had an acute anxiety attack. "It was horrendous saying goodbye. For the first time I was thrown back into an abandonment feeling. I couldn't stop crying. I felt like an infant reacting to separation from its mother."

Sarah has found some peace by realizing that the reunion gave her a present, a future, and finally a past. "That trio by definition is enough to make one 'whole,'" she says. "I was whole in the sense that I had all the pieces—it just took years to get the emotional mortar to fit it all together into a unit. I stopped feeling tormented when I accepted that I would be motherless, and in so doing, I stopped yearning for that biological love."

EMOTIONAL OVERLOAD

Emotions become overwhelming at some point in most reunions. Whether this happens early or late, adoptees feel they have no choice but to withdraw for a while, to take time out to regroup their psychic forces.

This decision for time out is not always a conscious one. In *Lost and Found* I wrote about the emotional turmoil many adoptees, including myself, experienced after reunion, a reaction that can be accompanied by immobilizing depression for varying lengths of time. I was so overwhelmed with anxiety and guilt after meeting my mother that I fell through the trapdoor of the self, down to what felt like rock bottom. It must have been the place where my infant self had landed after being dropped. For the next two months, I withdrew from everything around me, staying very still, until I could regain the psychic energy to climb back up into the outside world again.

Now I know that the self has to undergo a certain amount of breakdown in order to reemerge in its new shape. It is equivalent to the spiritual death and rebirth experience. For many years I did not feel strong enough to contact my mother. During that time I was unconsciously realigning the structures of my old self. By the time I felt safe enough to return to her, it was too late. She could not risk being hurt again. We spoke by phone many times after that, but we were never able to find the way back to each other.

Trish: "I had to withdraw"

Trish knew she had to take time out when her birth mother expressed her anger by becoming jealous of Trish's closeness to her twelve-year-old sister, Lori. She reacted as if Trish were a rival for the child's affections, and asked her not to come to the house. "You're like a birth mother coming back to reclaim Lori," her father told her. "Your mother feels like the adoptive mother in this situation."

"I've had to withdraw from mothers in general to be able to work everything through," Trish says. "My birth mother and I are taking time away from each other because it's not possible to communicate now. The coming together was one part of it, but this part is separate—it's about me. I have to work through that I'm thirty, in the middle of my life, and yet there is a part of me that is still nine years old, thinking about Elizabeth Eagan, this fantasy mother. It's hard to be thirty, a mother, a wife, and nine at the same time."

Adoptees may also feel the need to pull back if an adoptive parent is applying pressure for them to end the relationship with the birth mother, or if the birth mother is applying pressure to intensify the relationship before the adoptee is ready. "I want to feel normal for a while," one adoptee said. Others want to "protect" themselves.

STAGES OF RESOLUTION

"Refable-izing" the Birth Mother

There comes a time in reunion when adoptees accept that they will never have the fantasy mother whose breasts flow eternally with milk and honey. They do not give her up completely, any more than they give up their sense of uniqueness, but rather they retreat from the Here and Now back to the Ghost Kingdom with as much of her intact as they can manage. Refable-izing the birth mother is a way of holding on to what they need.

Sarah: "I had no place to put her"

"Just think of me as your fairy godmother, someone who can be what you want her to be, when you want her to be," Sarah's mother told her early in their reunion, after hinting that there were things she was not proud of in her life.

Sarah realized that to be a "fairy godmother" relieved her birth mother of commitment to the real world in which they lived, and protected her from her daughter's constant probing into a past that she did not want uncovered. Sarah also noticed that as she and her birth mother grew apart over the years, they "refable-ized" each other. Her mother was becoming the "phantasm" she was before they met.

"I naturally wanted to think of my birth mother as a part of my life, but because I had no place to put her, emotionally speaking (she didn't come with a set of directions), I had to formulate the place, and that's how she became fable-ized."

Sarah allows herself to yearn for that fantasy mother while tolerating the elusiveness of her materialized mother. She might not be invited to family gatherings, but she takes satisfaction in the special tie she has created with her mother.

Connection/Disconnection/Reconnection

The desire for connection drives adoptees to search, but even after a satisfying reunion, they may at times feel the desire to disconnect for a while. As we have seen, it is not easy for either party in reunion to hold on to a relationship that occasionally packs the voltage of an exposed electrical wire.

Jack, thirty-five years old and two years into a good reunion, still suffers when his mother does not answer his phone calls for two weeks. "I get desperate," he says. "It's like I need a fix, and only talking to her will take away the pain. Just connecting with her is so soothing, even though I know she's a silly, narcissistic woman." Yet he is tempted to break off each time his mother disappears on him. "It's too much power for her to have," he says. "She's there and not there. I really think it would be easier not to have contact than to go through these feelings of abandonment and rejection again."

Ten years after looking her daughter up, Lorraine Dusky describes the complexity of reunion from the birth mother's point of view: "When she is here for an extended visit, guilt still clouds our bond; guilt that I surrendered her to adoption; guilt that I didn't/couldn't/wouldn't raise her; guilt that I can't be a better parent today. And she plays to this guilt. In rational moments she can understand why I surrendered her for adoption

. . . but logic doesn't always win over feelings, and at times the guilt she's laid on me (and I have plenty of guilt of my own) has been exhausting."[5]

Dusky hung in there, but some birth mothers, like some adoptees, break off the relationship because of emotional exhaustion. Sometimes the birth mother displaces her anger—at her own mother, at the agency, at the birth father—onto the adoptee and refuses to see him or her again. Sometimes the adoptee displaces his anger—at the closed adoption system, at the adoptive parents, at his fate—onto the birth mother.

An adoptee may end the relationship when the mother persists in keeping the adoptee's existence a secret from the rest of her family, or blows hot and cold, depending on her mood. "The first time my mother cut me off four years ago, I felt sorry for her and was cooperative," one woman said. "This time I've just had it and will tolerate no more. I grew up."

Adoptees may also break off with the birth mother if she becomes too emotionally demanding, and uses the relationship to work through her own needs. In such situations there may be a role reversal, with the adoptee expected to hold the birth mother's pain and to supply the unconditional love that the birth mother never had from her own mother.

It is not unusual for an adoptee to break off the relationship if the spouse resents the emotions being spent on the birth mother. Ross, a young businessman who was initially thrilled to find his mother, married the following year. Soon he began to complain about his mother's "constant" calls, letters, and gifts, and her resentment toward his adoptive parents. "I cut off contact because it became clear to me over time that I did not want to maintain a relationship," he says. "And quite frankly, her persistence frightens us, especially since we have a new baby."

In such cases, the adoptee retreats back into the Artificial Self, splitting off the birth mother once again in order to avoid the emotional turmoil that including her in his life would cause. In situations where the spouse welcomes the birth mother into the new family, it is possible for her to become a part of the adoptee's life and even a grandmother to his child.

Michael: "The confetti's on the floor"

A relationship may break down over issues of trust and betrayal when the adoptee goes in search of the birth father. If the birth mother has not resolved her anger at the father, it can get projected onto the adoptee. "You got what you wanted from us, now you can go to the other side," one birth mother told her daughter. "There is no other side, Ma, they are both me," the adoptee replied.

"We are betrayers of our adoptive parents when we search for our birth mother, and betrayers of our birth mother when we search for our birth father," concludes Michael, who is finally in a good marriage after his Don Juan years.

At their first meeting, Michael's mother had extended her arms and whispered "I've got my baby back," as she rocked him back and forth. And Michael felt himself regressing into the "earliest, most archaic cellar of my soul" even as he tried to hold on to his adult, rational self. A year into their reunion, his mother became so angry when he asked about his father that he went from being *her* son to *his* son. "I became an extension of him," Michael says. "She would say how much I look like him, speak like him, and how much she hates him. I have to admit there are times I regret having found her. If I can stay adultified, I have sympathy for her. But if I never see her again, it's fine with me. The excitement is over, the confetti's on the floor, it's like three in the morning—I danced all night, I'm sobering up. A dose of heavy reality is smacking me in the head." And then he adds, "I'm not really sorry I searched. I'm reclaiming a piece of me whose absence had caused a fracture of the self."

Sarah: "It's over for now"

A long reunion that goes in spirals but does not develop in depth may eventually cave in under the weight of its own ambivalence and distrust.

In the year following her mother's visit, Sarah dealt in therapy with some sexually abusive behavior on the part of her two older brothers, who were her adoptive parents' natural sons. Hoping to share this with her birth mother, she went to visit with her husband and young children. It proved to be a disastrous encounter. Far from wanting to console her daughter, Sarah's mother retreated into alcohol.

"She couldn't handle it," Sarah said. "I knew from her sister that she had been abused by her stepfather, and her daughters had been abused by her second husband. She has never dealt with it, and did not want to unearth it with me now. I realized after a few days that trying to communicate with her was like beating a dead horse. She had lost her childhood, her child, and her self-respect. She was a survivor who had built walls around herself. I had everything from her that she could give. And so I cut our visit short. 'You don't have to worry about me anymore,' I told her. 'We know where we are if we need each other. And so let's be kind to each other now as we say goodbye.'"

Her mother looked relieved, but Sarah didn't really believe it was goodbye until she didn't receive the usual birthday card from her. "It's over for now, maybe forever, I don't know," Sarah told me. "The truth is our relationship wasn't going anywhere. We had never talked about it; we just let it amble on by itself. For now I'm glad to be free of it. It was a burden. I'm happy as a peach."

Trish: "I try to keep some connection"

Trish has been working through her grief of losing her birth mother after finding her, and is struggling to find some meaning in her reunion. "I realize that projecting your fantasies onto your birth mother is a real trap for adoptees," she says. "I didn't see her for who she really was, but what I imagined her to be. I wasn't present in the moment. It was like a hallucination—finally some physical body had a correlation to a birth mother. But now, in order to be present in my life, I try to keep some connection. I send cards and Christmas and birthday presents, even though I'm not sure the younger children get them." The last time she phoned her birth parents' house and her mother asked why she was calling, Trish replied: "I want to know how everyone is doing. We don't have to spend time together, but you're people to me now. You'll never disappear for me. I'll always acknowledge your existence."

Howard: "You have to work on the relationship"

A year after Howard's disturbing reunion with his birth mother, she came, along with his brother and sister, to the States to visit him. She was a changed woman, her bitterness having dropped away with the secrecy and the guilt that had weighed her down. They were able to talk about her experiences in the Holocaust and the negative effects of her keeping secrets. Howard was changed too. He was back in his marriage with his wife and children, and philosophical about everything he had been through with his mother. He hadn't let go of the relationship, but had kept up a dialogue in letters and phone calls.

We can see that it is not so much being in reunion as being in a reunion process that is important. If the birth mother is not available to reparent the child, or the child is not available to be reparented, the relationship may not develop. One birth mother, who is in a close reunion with her daughter, said that the most important thing they did was to keep talking through and around the withdrawals, angers, and hurts. Without that processing, relationships such as Sarah's and Trish's can get mired down or self-destruct.

Yet, even when a relationship seems terminated, there is still a connection, just as a connection remained when the mother and child were separated from each other originally. Sometimes a relationship that appears over one year springs to life a few years later as mother and adult child grow individually and are ready to come together again. Ross hasn't fully closed the door on his mother: he offered to provide her periodically with news about himself and his family. And though Michael admits it's "not rational" because his mother keeps blowing hot and cold, he keeps calling her. "It's like I'm filling in holes, and can't stop until the rupture is repaired," he says. "Anyway, how does one disconnect when the baby in you is still crying out, 'Please need me'?"

One doesn't disconnect as long as the abandoned baby still needs a "fix." And even when that moment comes, one doesn't fully disconnect. "The connection once made is always there," says Sarah. "Even when you're not in contact with each other."

Reconnecting Through Siblings and Grandparents

When the relationship with their birth parents breaks down, it is not uncommon for adoptees to get emotional sustenance from their half or full siblings, with whom they form close friendships. They may also develop a strong bond with birth grandparents.

Trish takes her son to see her maternal grandmother occasionally, but she is especially close to her paternal grandparents, who had offered to take her before she was put up for adoption. "I'm a lot like them temperamentally," she says. "They are a real support. They love me unconditionally." Trish doesn't know how much her grandparents share about her with their children, but she senses they are able to relieve their own guilt and sense of loss over what happened. She can tell that the communication channels that had been blocked in the family are coming open, and unfinished emotional family business is finally being worked through.

IN LIMBO

There are some adoptees who find themselves in limbo, an arid stretch where the relationship seems permanently on hold. They are neither in reunion nor not in reunion. They are as if stuck in the birth canal.

Limbo is a place where things can go either way. Ambivalence rules. Your mother puts off meeting with you, but holds out some possibility for the future. Or your mother refuses to meet you, but does not block your relationship with her parents and extended family. Or you manage to meet your siblings without your mother knowing. Or your mother sends out mixed signals, affectionate one time and hostile another, so that you do not know where you stand with her.

Sometimes adoptees fear that they will spend their lives in limbo. Sometimes they do. But sometimes things take a turn for the better just when they have given up hope.

SHUFFLING THE STAGES

Not all reunions develop in the same way. Some begin with intensity and then peter out, while others that start slowly may get stronger through the years. Many factors can influence this process, especially geographical distance and the emotional availability of mother and adult child.

One learns that a reunion keeps shifting over time. Just when you think you have seized it, it changes shape and transforms into something else. Some adoptees are able to grow up fast forward on their own, while others need to merge with the birth mother for a year or two in order to be able to separate later. It's the birth mother's task to help the adoptee "push off" from her when she is ready—to let go, as all mothers have to do when it's time for their children to separate. The weaning requires, as one birth mother put it, "a delicate balance."

Maud: "The adoptee is in the middle"

For the first few years of her reunion, it looked like Maud was never going to get weaned. When I first met her, she and her mother were like Siamese twins: they couldn't let go of each other, even holding hands across the table during our two-hour interview. Any kind of separation became so intolerable that Maud divorced her young husband and moved from one coast to the other to live with her mother and her family. She changed her name to the one she had at birth. She and her mother traveled to Europe to meet all the relatives there. They went to rebirthing sessions together, attended adoption conferences, led workshops. They even looked for the birth father, with whom Maud now has a good relationship.

Then, after three years of being reparented by her mother, Maud fell in love with a fellow artist. She realized that she was finally ready to separate from her mother and start a family of her own. Her mother, not yet ready, was inconsolable when Maud moved out. It was as if she had lost her baby again. She felt angry and used, an emotion not uncommon to birth mothers who are unable to let go when the adoptee is ready to separate.

Maud tried to be considerate, but she held firm about going on with her own life. "My mother has her own internal work to do alone," she explained. "It's hard for an adoptee and birth mother to reach the same point at the same time."

Meanwhile, Maud has reconciled with her adoptive parents from whom she became estranged while living with her birth mother. Her parents had felt betrayed at first, but after going into marital counseling and patching up their own relationship, they softened in their attitude toward the reunion. Maud accepted their overtures and is planning to visit them with her boyfriend. From the outside, it may look as if her reunion has tipped like a seesaw back to her adoptive parents' side, but she's still close to her two half-sisters and confident that her birth mother will pull herself together soon. "The adoptee is in the middle," she said. "Both sides are you."

It was necessary for Maud, as for many adoptees, to fuse intensely with her birth mother in order to find and then free herself. "I'm happy for once," she says. "I'm not controlled by adoption stuff anymore—I have it under control. We're always going to have scars, but some adoptees and birth mothers don't let go. They get stuck in adoption issues and keep repeating the same stories. It takes work to free oneself. I needed to go to the depths—and I did. It's an ongoing story."

It is just that. When I last talked to Maud she'd had a baby, and her relationship with her birth mother was back on track.

We have looked at some of the stages and complexities in the reunion process when the adoptee crosses over from one reality to another. We've seen how time becomes collapsed in reunion, so that mother and child have to relive in a few months or a few years a life cycle that should take twenty to thirty years. Nonadoptive parents and their children test their emotions and work out their grievances as they go along, but adoptees and birth parents, with no history to fall back on, have to begin from the beginning.

In the next chapter, we will follow some of the tragic twists and turns the reunion scenario can take due to the trauma that mother and child have experienced in the closed adoption system.

12

The Painted Bird

The problem with telling a child he's a bastard
is that it is a negative identity.
Shakespeare's bastards are full of rage
because no one trusts them.
—ERIK ERIKSON

"I WOULD LIKE TO FOUND AN ORGANIZATION called ARNO, an acronym for There Are No Bastards," the poet Muriel Rukeyser told me toward the end of her life. "Its purpose would be to take the word *bastard* out of the English language." Muriel had been brave enough to keep the child she bore as an unmarried woman at a time when illegitimate children were considered "bastards," born of sin. Her impulse to start ARNO reflected the deep pain she felt at the way she knew society viewed her son.[1] "I bastard mother / Promise you / There are many ways to be born," she wrote in one of her poems, as if she could lessen the taint for her child.[2]

The word *bastard* is still alive and well, as evidenced by Woody Allen's use of the word for his son conceived out of wedlock with Mia Farrow, as well as for her many adopted children. He meant it in a "joking" way, he said.[3] Some joke. Even those adoptees who were never called "bastard" are familiar with its dark resonance. The knowledge of having arrived illegitimately into the world is buried deep in the adoptee's unconscious, waiting to be tapped.

Patricia Storace tapped into it in her poem "Illegitimacy":

Hence the stigma of the illegitimate
in whom father and mother
are left coupling forever
so the child appears,
as it were, impaired,
conclusive proof of the social fear
that love outlasts lovers, and is eternal.
We bastards know it.[4]

THE BASTARD MOMENT

Stan tapped into what adoptees call the "Bastard Moment" when he did a guided imagery exercise in a men's workshop. "We were to imagine ourselves in our mother's wombs, floating in the warmth of the amniotic fluids, preparing to be born. The next instruction took me totally by surprise: we were asked to begin thinking about who was in the waiting room preparing for our arrival. The image of an empty waiting room and my birth mother's agonizing decision to give me up while growing me bombarded me with the incredible separation and immediate experience of abandonment." Stan began to think of his mother's loss of self-esteem in dealing with an "illegitimate" pregnancy in the 1940s, and of his own initial experience in life: rejection and loss.

Polly tapped into the Bastard Moment when she fell into a sudden depression while planning a picnic to celebrate her thirty-ninth birthday. Her birth had not been a cause for celebration at the time, she thought, so why should it be now? Ten years after finding her mother, her existence was still a secret to most of her mother's friends. "My mother was ashamed while pregnant, ashamed while giving birth, and was obviously still ashamed," Polly said. "I wondered if I was entitled to be happy on the day that was a hardship and trauma for my mother. I wasn't welcomed into the world, so why was I here? Was I entitled to be alive?"

Polly's therapist suggested that she go through with the picnic as planned because it meant a lot to her husband and other family members who loved her. At the same time, he advised her not to try to hide the pain that was surfacing now. She should speak openly about her conflicted emotions with the friends who came, tell them about her feelings as an adoptee and how much their friendship means to her. She did just that, and her guests were very moved and supportive. A few even wept. Polly felt something lift inside her, as if she had affirmed her right to be alive. Maybe she wasn't supposed to be here, but she was. And she was going to make the most of her life. She called it an "aha" experience.

One knows one has experienced the Bastard Moment when "illegitimacy" becomes a painful feeling instead of an abstract concept. When the euphemisms of adoption are torn away and one is confronted with the shameful social reality of one's birth. When one is not certain one is entitled to exist. These moments are made even more incomprehensible when a birth mother both denies her child's existence and yet wants her present at special occasions.

Some adoptees experience the Bastard Moment for the first time when the birth mother does not introduce them to the rest of her family. This happened to me when my mother refused to tell her next born, my half-brother, about me. "Wait until he finishes graduate school," she said. And after that: "Wait until he gets settled in his profession." As if knowing about me would unsettle him. Curiously, years later, when her niece was getting married, my mother felt obliged to invite me and my husband to the wedding—with the proviso that we would assume other names and identities. I couldn't agree to those conditions, which meant I did not get to meet my brother and other members of her extended family. Looking back on it now, I regret that I turned down such an opportunity, that I didn't understand that meeting everyone incognito could have been a step toward meeting them openly in the future—the only step that my mother was able to offer at that period of her life. But at the time, I was immobilized by the shameful power of the Bastard Moment, which threatened to extinguish the legitimate identity I had as a woman, wife, mother, and writer.

Some male adoptees become infuriated when they experience the Bastard Moment. "She's been treating me like a bastard," said a man whose mother kept their relationship a secret from her other children. "It happened forty-two years ago, what do you want from me?" she snapped once while he was trying to tell her how he felt. "It's ruined my life, your life—let's just forget everything." When he asked her if she didn't want to see him anymore, she softened: "Well, I'll see you. Oh, don't listen to me. I don't know what I'm talking about."

One adoptee spoke of experiencing the Bastard Moment when her mother asked her to sit alone in the back of the auditorium at her brother's high school graduation. Others tell of being asked to hide in another room when neighbors drop by. One was told to keep out of sight at a family funeral—"like this dead man would know I was there with my birth mother."

Adoptees experience these Bastard Moments as ugly and demeaning. "It makes you feel dirty, like a dirty little secret, as if your mother is ashamed you exist," a woman said. Adoptees have grown up on the legitimate side of the tracks, so to speak, but such moments throw them back into the shadow world of their shameful origins.

"I have to keep telling myself that there is a difference between being ashamed of someone's existence and being ashamed of the person herself," said the woman who felt like a dirty little secret. "I know she's not ashamed of me as a person. Frankly, I am the best product she ever put out and she knows it."

THE DEAD MOTHER

One can experience the Bastard Moment even when one's mother has died. I thought of this when I received a tearful phone call from Jean, who, after twenty years of searching, found that her mother was deceased. Her mother's seventy-five-year-old brother invited her to visit him in another state, but said he would not introduce her to his friends as his unmarried sister's daughter. "My sister's past was private and should be respected," he told Jean when she protested that honesty was an important part of her life. He couldn't understand that Jean felt demeaned as a person by the very idea of being introduced as someone she wasn't.

Jean realized that although her adoption had rewritten her social history by making her legal, it could not rewrite the psychological past. "Once we stray into that other realm, where we came from, we become, once again, illegitimate," she said. "I was aware that on some level this kind, gentle man regarded me as the bastard child who had brought disgrace to his beloved sister and, by extension, his whole family, forty-six years ago. I felt reduced to the status of the helpless infant I was then."

While going through old letters her uncle gave her—letters that her mother had received from her own mother—Jean saw that two weeks before her birth, her grandmother was fussing over what color the drapes and sofa in her home would be. The day of her birth, her grandmother wrote the obstetrician how happy her daughter must be that "it is over." And a month later, her grandmother, a staunch Christian Scientist, wrote advising her daughter: "If you feel weak or find it hard to sit—deny it—right in the face of it. If you stay with it, the pain and fatigue will vanish when you aren't looking." In the seven years of letters after that, there was no mention of her birth or what her mother went through. It was as if the baby had indeed vanished. There was one consolation. Although her uncle remained adamant about not introducing her to his friends as his sister's daughter, he did say as she was leaving: "I want you to know that if your mother had lived, she would have loved you very much, and she would have been very proud of you."

Jean would have liked to have heard this from her mother, who was thirty-two when she gave birth and fifty when she died of cancer; she never married or had any other children. It was as if her emotional life had stopped with the relinquishment of her child. In an attempt to learn whether her mother had confided her feelings to anyone, Jean searched for the women who knew her during her pregnancy. They described her as outgoing, popular, a good friend, and a wonderful singer and pianist, but they all agreed she was a very private person. She never mentioned the baby or what she was going to do. When she went away for a few weeks and returned no longer pregnant, no one said anything. They hadn't wanted to pry.

Jean's mother was discreet in death, as in life. She was cremated by her mother, and so there is no grave. Jean has only such mementos as her mother's passport, her high school diploma, a tiny telephone address book, some job applications, and family photographs. She is struggling to find her mother through all the silence. If she could know whether her mother had seen her at birth, had held her, had loved her, she feels she would know whether she is entitled to exist and entitled to love herself.

It helps Jean to have photographs of her mother, along with a letter briefly describing her life. For the first three months, she carried these pictures to work in her briefcase every day. "I was almost afraid to be parted from them, as if they were my only visible link to her," she said.

When I first met Tony, a shy man in his mid-twenties, at an adoption conference, he was carrying a large, framed high school picture of his deceased mother. In workshops, his mother's picture sat on the table in front of him, staring out at us, a shy, lopsided smile forming at the lips. It was uncanny, because they were Tony's lips and smile: her face was his face, her eyes, his eyes. There she was reincarnated in Tony. Her life had been hard and she died young. One day she just gave up, crawled into bed, and didn't get out. She died on Tony's twenty-fifth birthday.

For almost a year after he discovered he had missed his mother in this life, Tony was crazed, almost mute. He lived as a recluse or, rather, lived alone with his mother's picture. The two of them, together at last. It is a sign of his rebirth that he has been able to bring himself, and her, to the conference, and to introduce her to all of us. She is preserved in the picture as the young mother of his dreams, untouched by suffering over the years. To people who tell him it's too bad that he didn't get to meet his mom, he gives their lopsided smile and replies: "It's allowed me to keep my fantasy going."

There are many ways to commune with a dead mother. By giving her life within you, you are giving life to yourself. Some adoptees do this by becoming part of her family and visiting her grave. One man, on learning that his mother had been cremated, found the warehouse where her unclaimed ashes were stored. "She now has a resting place here with me, where she will remain forever," he says. A woman told me of lying across her mother's grave, "wanting to dig in the earth and touch and feel her bones." Another woman, on finding out that her mother had been buried only the day before, persuaded the caretaker at the cemetery to have the casket dug up and opened so that she could see her mother's face and say goodbye.

Robert Childs, a Jungian therapist who runs dream workshops for adoptees, said, "I met my mother in my dreams." And another man, who believes in life after death, declared: "After all, it will be the first time I can meet my mother."

"Can one be reborn if one's mother is dead?" I am often asked. My answer is yes, but only after you have gone through a painful grieving process, which is not unlike a death and rebirth. It is a difficult process, for this is not the recognized loss of a mother that brings sympathy and comfort from family and friends. Even those who have seen their mother only a few times are overwhelmed by the impact of their grief. This dead mother was the woman who gave you life. Your body, born from hers, feels wrenched by its disintegration, even programmed by it. I did not hear of my mother's death until four months after it occurred. It was the end of a dark fairy tale in which we could not rescue each other, or ourselves. She took her grief and her loss and her secrets with her, just as she took some part of that child she had held on to, and who continues to hold on to her.

THE REJECTED SELF

One quiet afternoon Ramakrishna beheld a beautiful woman ascend from the Ganges and approach the grove in which he was meditating. He perceived that she was about to give birth to a child. In a moment the babe was born, and she gently nursed it. Presently, however, she assumed a horrible aspect, took the infant in her now ugly jaws and crushed it, chewed it. Swallowing it, she returned again to the Ganges, where she disappeared.
—THE GOSPEL OF SRI RAMAKRISHNA

My seventeen-year-old mother tried to keep me when I was born, and it was only when she failed that she turned away in order to preserve herself. But there are some women with untimely pregnancies who never accept the reality of what is happening to their bodies.

"A birth mother must make the baby into a nonperson to give it up," Erik Erikson once told me when we were discussing the complexities of reunion. "Having done so, she will have a hard time when that nonperson comes back looking for her." I thought of this when a birth mother confided to me: "I cut off my feelings when I was pregnant. She was not really mine. Her conception was her death for me."

It can feel like death to an adoptee when the birth mother refuses a meeting, as if only she can sanction the reality of his life.

"It is not you the birth mother is rejecting, but her former self," I tell adoptees in counseling. This concept helps them understand the birth mother's behavior, but it does not take away the deep pain of rejection that the child within feels. For all adoptees, whether or not they are pro-choice, harbor the knowledge that they could have been aborted. And adoptees who are turned away by their birth mothers often feel as if they have been, as if they have absorbed the infanticidal fantasies of the woman who unwillingly carried them. They were aborted after they were born rather than after they were conceived. They may know that the unwanted offspring of married parents carry the same dark insight, but they still believe that they are not entitled to be alive because they did not come into the world in a legitimate way.

Some prenatalists believe the unborn child is aware of the mother's emotional stress and ambivalence: that wanted fetuses will experience feelings of pleasure and well-being, and unwanted fetuses will experience fear of death. Luis Feder, who has studied what he calls "preconceptive ambivalence" in women, reports that the adopted child is traumatized by his unconscious perception that he was unwanted by his "rejecting, filicidal, foeticidal" mother.[5]

An actress, on learning that her mother had considered having an abortion, understood why she was born two months ahead of time: "I was aware of it in the womb and wanted to get out of there. I think it's why I've always felt like a blob. Not in my socially civilized self, but in the deepest part of myself. If I keep going back, I get to the fuzzy, moving, undulating heartbeat with nothing around it. There is just a heartbeat."

Alice, who suspects that her mother gave a false name to the hospital, has always had the feeling that she was unwanted: "Sometimes I wish she had chosen an abortion. And in a way she did. What she really aborted was my own person, the seeds of my identity. I carry a dead self like a heavy emptiness inside my body. A self which curls up and cries at night, still wanting to be held, touched, like only a hurting infant can be gently held. The cord was severed, and I began. But I guess I'm still waiting to be born the real way, like other babies get born."

A mother who has aborted her child emotionally has buried the experience, and will not enter into a reunion of any kind. She has split off that defeated, humiliated part of herself and refuses to reconnect with it, which means she cannot reconnect with her child. She has also split off the woman who was in love with the birth father and the woman who would have mothered their child. She lives in the present and will not look back. As the Polish saying goes: she cut off her past like a fish's tail. She is protecting the self she has reconstructed over the years, what I call her "postsurrender self."

It is devastating for adoptees when the mother who has lived in their fantasies will not acknowledge their existence. A woman who heard from a birth aunt that her mother "hated her from the moment she was conceived" was overwhelmed for months with feelings of "grief, rage, depression, and loneliness."

The danger for adoptees is that even though they have seized power by going on the search, they have given the natural mother unnatural power over them: the power to give them a proper birth or, if she chooses, to keep them unborn.

Rachel

Rachel had no reason to suspect that her mother would refuse to meet her. Her search had turned up an attractive newspaper photograph from the days when her mother had been a movie critic in Montreal, and articles about her present activities in local politics there. She seemed to be a mirror image of everything that Rachel hoped to be. But Rachel's letter to her was answered by her mother's friend: "Your mother read only the first paragraph. She doesn't want to see you or to correspond. I'm sorry." After a brief exchange of letters with this intermediary, Rachel received this final note: "To no avail. Not a realistic hope."

But Rachel was not ready to give up. She took a trip to Hungary, from where her birth family originated, and began studying Hungarian. Determined to see her mother's face, if only from a distance, she made an overnight trip to Montreal. Walking through the lobby of her mother's office building, she spotted a notice that her mother would preside at a community meeting the following week. She decided to return to Montreal for that meeting. It was scary; with this decision, she was taking control of her life out of her mother's hands.

When she found herself seated in a circle in a small basement room with only twenty-five other people, most of whom knew one another, Rachel felt she was "outside of time." Her mother, who looked nothing like the winsome newspaper photograph, was short and stocky, with a weathered face devoid of makeup. Only her nose and close, deep-set eyes looked familiar. Rachel became embarrassed for her mother when she began officiating over the meeting like a harsh schoolmarm who doesn't care that she is alienating everyone by her intimidating remarks.

"I wasn't prepared for someone so tough," Rachel said. "I kept thinking: How could I come from her? She gave the impression of a woman who was without a soul, a woman who was dead inside. If you put a stethoscope to her heart, you would hear nothing. I left without daring to go up to her. I knew I wouldn't be able to tug at her heartstrings. There are none left."

Rachel was depressed for months after that. "I thought searching would take me back to that place we shared, but the years have passed and she's in a completely different place. She has split off from her feeling self. In an almost vampiric sense, I think she drew her power from the blood of her daughter, the one she so ruthlessly sacrificed and continues to sacrifice. And she was flinging it in people's faces. 'Condemn me, hate me, cast me out—I don't care!'"

Still, Rachel felt more solid. Seeing her mother had somehow strengthened her, as if some invisible transfusion occurred during that meeting. "I have seized a bit of my history, grasped what was my right," she said. "Seeing her in person made her real. Not an imaginary construction I was musing on unconsciously all my life. It's a relief to know. Now I can stop fantasizing."

One year later, however, Rachel was still fantasizing—this time that her mother would relent and agree to meet her. And she was still in pain. For though she felt empowered by seeing her mother, she needed to come to some resolution with her. "I need to say to her: 'Here I am. I exist.' It would allow me to break through the limbo she's assigned me to."

One night, on impulse, Rachel picked up the phone and was startled to hear her mother's high-pitched "hello," rather than the machine's usual terse announcement: "If you want to talk to me, you'll have to leave a message." Rachel quickly identified herself. "I have questions I want to ask you," she said.

"Don't you understand I don't want to have anything to do with you?" her mother replied sharply.

"I am a human being," Rachel stated.

"So am I," her mother declared, slamming down the receiver.

After that, Rachel spoke of herself as an emotional abortion. "It was my first confrontation with the contradiction that haunts me to this day: that the woman who gave me life just as surely killed me off." Still, she knew she was not dead. In fact, she felt more alive than ever. And that, too, was a contradiction. For as the adoptee gains ego strength in the process of searching, she becomes aware that she has an autonomous self that was strong enough to survive the original abandonment and is strong enough to survive this one.

Martin

One can end up feeling aborted even if one was initially welcomed by one's birth mother.

Martin, a twenty-five-year-old delivery man, took his birth mother by surprise one afternoon with a knock on her door, and was received warmly. They talked for a few hours, alternately weeping and rejoicing at the miracle of his return. He sent flowers and cards after that, with no response. A few weeks later, he received a letter from his mother explaining that her psychologist and minister had advised her not to see him again: it would upset her personally and be detrimental to her two young children.

I recognized the psychiatrist and minister as keepers of the establishment's perceived truths—one representing mental health, the other moral certitude. They were accomplices in keeping the adoptee aborted from the consciousness of his clan. They saw him not as the returned lost baby but as the returned dead, who seek vengeance. Rather than understanding the healing she would undergo in having her lost child back—the chance to be forgiven and to forgive herself—they, like the Grand Inquisitors of old, advised her to abort him yet again.

I recognized Martin's mother, too, one of thousands of women whose suffering is described by a poet who also surrendered her baby, as well as herself, to the harsh strictures of the closed adoption system:

> the shame and guilt built
> in the hospitals, prisons, agencies, churches
> in the hearts of bureaucrats, bosses
> social workers, parents, priests
>   tied our hands, stilled our voices
>   defiled our humanity, our love
>   We were buried
>   in ceremony, in darkness, in papers,
>   in the revenge of a dying city.[6]

Martin became almost crazed when his mother abandoned him once again. He couldn't believe that the receptive woman he had held in his arms and wept tears of joy with could become this cold, rejecting woman who refused any more communication. It was like having the great prize that you had dreamed of all your life torn away from you at the moment it became yours.

The first and only time I heard from Martin's mother, she had crossed some border in the mind where the adoptee moves from being the beloved to being the enemy, and becomes a threat to the birth mother's existence again. This potential is always there and, once it is triggered, the birth mother is flooded again with the "filicidal, foeticidal" feelings that Feder described. "He looks just like my dead brother whom I hated," she told me. "And he acts like him too."

"He's not your brother," I reminded her.

~~She couldn't hear me. Martin had become her~~ brother, put on earth to torment her. She had gone to court to get a restraining order to stop him from sending letters, books, and candy.

When I last heard from Martin, he was filled with rage. He was determined not to be banished again into the shadows. He had just sent another letter to the fantasy mother who had received him so lovingly that first day. He will probably not succeed in breaking through her resistance, but by entitling himself to do what he needs to feel alive—staying in contact with the woman who gave birth to him—he is saying "I exist." When he truly believes this, he will be able to move on.

Janet

Janet, a businesswoman in her early forties, had had a hard life with a domineering adoptive mother, two divorces, an alcohol addiction she was recovering from, and a tendency to fall in love with dependent men. And so she felt she was "being born" when she made the first phone call to her mother in upstate New York.

The woman who answered sounded breathless and energetic when she picked up the phone, explaining she'd just come in. But when Janet asked if her birth date meant anything to her, the woman's voice dropped to a hardly audible "no." She wanted to know how Janet got her maiden name and other information, while still denying that the date meant anything. She agreed to take Janet's phone number and let Janet write to her, though she said she couldn't see the purpose.

A birth mother who is taken by surprise on the telephone may at first deny who she is. It is a shock to have the child whom you have split off from your consciousness, as if dead, reappear in your life suddenly, without warning, as if resurrected. Then, too, how can you be sure that someone is not blackmailing you? With time, a well-documented letter may make the birth mother feel safe enough to respond positively.

Janet wrote a friendly letter, even though she felt upset by her mother's negative response. Why was she doing this? The anger that Janet had always felt toward her adoptive mother was now directed at her birth mother.

While she waited for her mother's answer, Janet fell back on another addiction: overeating. "I can't stop stuffing myself," she told me. "Even if I meet her, I know she won't be able to fill me up." When her mother did not reply after a few weeks, Janet made a second call.

"She's not here," said the woman who picked up the phone.

"I think she is," responded Janet testily.

"Not for you," said the woman. "She can't talk. Don't call anymore. My daughter is here."

Janet's "red flag went up": "I need to meet you," she said. "I have to go on with my life and get this over with. I'll call back tonight."

"My daughter might still be here."

"When is a good time?"

"Never—for you."

"Don't hang up," ordered Janet, as stubborn as her mother. "I'm try-ing to make it on your terms. But if you don't want to meet me, I'll come up there and contact the rest of your family—your sister and others."

"Leave my family alone. You are a terrible person!"

Too stunned to respond, Janet hung up. Then she picked up the phone and called back. This time her mother's husband answered. "Not now," he said when Janet asked for her mother. Before she had a chance to tell him that she was not a terrible person, that she just wanted to know her history, he hung up.

She waited a week and called again. This time her mother answered. "You are ruining my life," her mother said. "This is supposed to be dead. I didn't want to have you. I don't love you. It was the most painful part of my life. I've kept it a secret, but now my daughter knows."

When Janet asked her to answer just a few questions, she retorted, "You were lucky someone adopted you. You should see a priest. You're old enough to lead your own life."

"I don't want anything from you," Janet tried to assure her. "Just a chance to thank you for giving me life."

"I had no options," replied her mother. "If you have to know, I was drunk. So there it is." She admitted to having been an alcoholic, as Janet had been. Now she was happily married. "We're just plain folk," she said. "House people." And she ended the call with, "Leave me alone. I don't want to remember it. You're ruining my life. I want this to be dead."

The following month, acting as an intermediary, I called the mother and managed to convince her that Janet needed at least one meeting to resolve her personal identity. She agreed, on the condition that Janet would never contact her again. The reunion was set for the end of the summer in the lobby of a hotel in a town midway between their two homes.

Janet made a point of not showering or washing her hair before set-ting off by car with a friend, who was going along for emotional support.

She put on old slacks, a T-shirt, and sandals. "I didn't want to dress for her and be rejected."

The gray-haired woman waiting in the lobby with her husband had Janet's body build, even her teeth, but she was as formidable in person as on the phone. "I want you to know this is the only time we will meet," she said. "Don't write, or call, or contact my children. You can ask what you want now, but then you go back to your family and forget about all this."

"I just wanted to look at you," Janet said. "I wondered how I would feel."

"I don't feel a thing," said her mother.

Janet had prepared a list of questions: Do you get headaches? Is there arthritis in the family? Did you ever think of me? What was your pregnancy like? Her mother told her that when she discovered she was pregnant at the age of twenty-seven, after a blind date, the only people who knew were her mother, grandmother, and sister. Their priest made arrangements for her to hide in a Catholic maternity home in New York City.

Janet's mother sat ramrod-straight through all this. She got a little teary when talking about going into labor, but controlled herself. "It was an easy birth," she said. "I drank orange juice and castor oil to make you come early. When I returned home, my grandmother said, 'See, now you know what it's like.'"

"Did you name me?" Janet asked.

"I am seventy-two years old—how can I remember?" her mother snapped.

"Did you see me? Hold me?"

"Of course, we had to. They made us take care of the babies for two weeks."

"I'm sorry for you, but I'm not the enemy," Janet said. "I had nothing to do with it." Then she asked the question she had saved for last: "Who was my father?"

At first her mother refused to answer, but relented when her husband urged her to get the meeting over with. She scribbled it on a piece of paper, as if not daring to say it aloud, and handed it over with the comment, "He probably won't want to see you."

"Can I hug you?" Janet asked as they all stood up.

Her mother's "yes" was given grudgingly, but she stood there waiting for it. For one moment Janet held her mother's large body, so like her own, but then, unable to control her sobbing, she pulled away. Her mother walked off without looking back.

"I'll never know if she would have responded had I been able to hold on," Janet said. Like all adoptees, she still had the need to believe her mother felt some love for the unborn baby with whom she was once merged.

THE PAINTED BIRD

The adoptee who is not recognized by her birth mother is not unlike the painted bird in Jerzy Kosinski's novel of that name. Separated from its flock by a sadistic peasant, the brown bird is painted all over in brilliant colors and then released. It soars happy and free, pulled by "some instinctive force" toward its kin, who do not recognize it. The painted bird circles from one end of the flock to the other, vainly trying to assure the other birds that it is one of them. But, dazzled by its alien colors, they fly around it unconvinced, and then charge toward the intruder. The "changeling" is attacked from all sides, and shortly the "many-hued shape" loses its place in the sky, drops to the ground, and dies.[7]

The adoptee does not literally die, but lack of recognition by one's birth mother feels like a death threat—the threat of annihilation—which the adoptee must muster all her psychic forces to survive.

I am often asked whether I think a birth mother has the right to shut out the child she brought into the world. My answer: an unequivocal no. As for whether adoptees have the right to meet with the birth mother at least once to hear their life story: an unequivocal yes. As one birth mother said, "You can't relinquish all of the responsibilities for parent-hood just by relinquishing the child."

Does the child have a right to demand a relationship with the birth mother after she gives him the information he needs? No, the child does not have the right to intrude on the life the birth mother has made for herself after relinquishing him. Does the birth mother have a right to be part of the adoptee's life? No, the birth mother does not have a right to anything that the adoptee is not ready or willing to give.

It cannot be stressed enough that the original intent of adoption was to serve the best interest of the child, and the original intent of the sealed record was to conceal the child's illegitimate birth from the public, not to cut him off from his heritage. When adoptees, at any age, need to know their origins, those needs should supersede those of the other adults in the triad. No birth mother has the right to confidentiality from her child at the expense of her child's well-being. As the family therapist Randolph Severson points out: "All people who walk the face of the earth possess the inalienable right to know their history and to meet the man and woman from whom they drew breath."[8]

Yet, in reunion, we are faced with psychological rather than legal and moral dilemmas. Violent acts, such as having to give up a child unconditionally, can cause violent responses. The birth mother is as much a victim of the closed adoption system as is the adoptee, traumatized to such a degree that, even when it returns, she may not be able to recognize her own painted bird.

13

The Fathered/ Fatherless Self

Who is my father in this world, in this house,
At the spirit's base?
My father's father, his father's father, his—
Shadows like winds
Go back to a parent before thought, before speech,
At the head of the past.
—WALLACE STEVENS

Old man whose sperm swims in my veins
come back in love, come back in pain.
—TOI DERRICOTT

THE SEARCH FOR THE LOST FATHER RUNS THROUGH much of modern literature. The father may have disappeared for a myriad of reasons: divorce, illness, desertion, death. The child who grows up without the father who gave him life will feel abandoned and unprotected in the world. The poet Stanley Kunitz tells us that the son goes in search of the father to be reconciled in a healing embrace. In that act of love he restores his father's lost pride and manhood. Perhaps he also finds himself. This could be said for the daughter too, although, as Kunitz points out, "the song of daughters is different from that of sons."[1]

Little has been written about the birth father. Most adoptees blot out all thought of that ghostly figure—as if they were born by immaculate conception—until after they find the birth mother. Then they discover that, deep in their psyche, the lost father waits to be summoned.

If the reunion with the mother proves satisfying, the adoptee may have less emotional investment in the father. He is a more abstract concept, but the adoptee's anger toward him may be as deep or deeper than toward the mother. He is, after all, a double abandoner: he abandoned the mother as well as the child. Yet there is an attraction to this missing father; his absence puts him in the romantic tradition of the loner, just passing through and disappearing on his way to the next frontier. Unlike the law-abiding adoptive father, the birth father is part outlaw, hovering on the fringes of society.

Jung said the father encompasses the roles of creator, lawgiver, impregnator, and master. The adoptive father, who represents authority, power, and control, is not the impregnator, and may be perceived by the adoptee as asexual (infertile), henpecked (dominated, like the children, by his wife), and tied down (by the family), while the birth father, who lacks the adoptive father's virtues, is perceived as virile (he produced a child), macho (sexual), and a free spirit (he refused to be tied down). The birth father may surface in the male or female adoptee's fantasy as James Dean, a TV star, an astronaut, or a millionaire stockbroker willing to invest in his lost child—much as Daddy Warbucks opened his checkbook, as well as his heart, to Little Orphan Annie.

If the adoptee has been unacknowledged by the birth mother, or is disappointed in her, there is always a second chance with the birth father. Just as Athena sprang into being from the head of Zeus, so the adoptee may hope to achieve some kind of rebirth through the father. No matter the past, the irresponsible father can redeem himself if he will take up the coils of kinship that the mother dropped, if he will be midwife to his child's rebirth. He will in return find himself the recipient of the intense love and need that the adoptee had preserved for the birth mother.

The birth father's response to the adoptee will, as with the mother, depend on many factors: his relationship with the mother at the time of conception; his loyalty or disloyalty to her during pregnancy and delivery; his involvement in the adoption decision; whether or not he has kept the child a secret over the years; and whether he feels he is in a secure place in his present relationships.

FATHERS AND DAUGHTERS

I recognize my father in myself more than I ever have until now, and in a hundred ways. We are kin. I stem from that root: the

fierce dedication to work, the irrational rages, the compulsion to answer letters, the hatred and fear of worldliness, the love of animal pets, the absurd resentment of anything that interrupts the adamant routine that makes work possible.
—MAY SARTON

An adopted daughter who looks in the mirror hoping to see her birth mother's face has no way of knowing if it is her father who looks back at her. She is linked to her mother through fantasy and longing, but her father is lost in the void with no mooring. Many birth mothers make sure he stays lost by refusing to give the adoptee his name, as if the mere mention of it will make him, and the pain associated with him, materialize on the spot.

Rachel

Rachel's mother was an exception. Although she declined to meet with her, she did allow an intermediary to reveal the birth father's identity. Intrigued to learn that her father was a professor of literature, Rachel sent him a letter immediately, but did not get a reply. After a year had passed and she despaired of ever having a relationship with her mother, she left her name on her father's answering machine. He responded by leaving his name on hers a week later. Encouraged, she called his office again, and this time he picked up the phone. She thought he'd recognize her name from her letter, but he obviously hadn't. "How can I help you?" he asked.

The conversation went something like this:

"I'm calling to follow up the letter I sent you."

"What letter?"

"I sent it a year ago."

"Well, what did it say?"

"This is going to be dramatic—I was given up for adoption in Montreal."

"What year were you born?"

"1960."

"What day?"

"July 27."

"Oh, my God." He started laughing, and then said, "I feel like I owe you thirty years."

"I don't want anything from you, but I'm interested in my genetic background."

"We should meet."

"If I come to Montreal, will you have lunch with me?"

"Yes, lunch is a good place to start."

The words *to start* thrilled her, and made her relax. She told him about her mother's refusal to see her, and how she had observed her at the meeting.

"This is something out of a book," he said. "So what's it like to be adopted?"

What could she answer to such a sweeping question? She mumbled something about needing to know where she came from. He suggested they meet in a hotel lobby at noon the following Tuesday.

Rachel flew up the night before. On the plane she felt herself hating her thirty-year-old body: if only she could return as a young child. She arrived early, but he entered the lobby ten minutes late—with a fast stride like hers, puffing on his pipe, looking very much like the tall, intellectual father she'd dreamed of. She was too much in shock to say more than "hi."

After they were seated in the hotel restaurant, he said, "Let me look at you." And then, as if continuing the phone conversation: "So what's it like to grow up cut off from your biological roots?"

She found the question as disconcerting as it had been on the phone. "Very difficult," she replied. "Well, you know, when you're little you're expected to forget you have other parents, and you repress your feelings." She told him that she never felt like her adoptive parents, but all the time she wanted to cry out: "Hold me! Hug me!"

When she mentioned she was studying Hungarian, her father commented: "So you're learning it to get connected to your mother's heritage." After which they were somehow arguing about whether the Hungarian language had more cases than Finnish, and disagreeing on books and movies—making those irrelevant subjects the target for the conflicted emotions they didn't dare express. At the same time that Rachel was struggling to repress her anger, she was thinking: "Oh, this guy is my father. He loves books and movies like I do. He's throwing light on my genetic map. He's giving me permission to go into my real self." She felt overwhelmed by grief, anguish, and even bitterness at how much she had missed out on, even as she remembered that this was the man who decided to let her go into the world alone.

In order to focus their talk, Rachel abruptly changed the conversation by asking about his parents and their religion, which was different from that of her adoptive parents. Her father told her that he too was an only child, that his father had died young from heart disease, and that she looked like his mother. She was flattered until he informed her that this mother, though intelligent, was a self-absorbed, dependent woman, who phoned him constantly with various complaints. "I'm not good with hungry people," he said, a comment that would come back to haunt her.

She learned that her father and mother were just breaking up a three-year relationship when she was conceived. They decided that adoption was the best decision, but he had felt guilty and torn about "abandoning" a child. He saw her once right after the birth in the hospital nursery, and wondered over the years what her name was and whether she were alive. Both he and her mother married other people soon afterward, and both divorced—he after three children, she after one.

As he spoke, Rachel felt she was walking into an alternate reality that was inaccessible, just beneath the surface. "My identity was obliterated," she recalled. "My adoptive family and my birth family canceled each other out."

"Have you told your children about me?" she asked her father.

"No. Would you like to meet them?"

"Yes."

"Okay, then you will. I've got to think of a way to wedge you into my life."

He talked openly about his relationship to his children from his first marriage, but seemed ambivalent about setting a time for when Rachel could meet them. When she told him that her adoptive parents couldn't understand her because they weren't genetically related, he replied: "That can happen in any family." He seemed overwhelmed by the consequences of the decision that he and her mother had made to send her out to be raised by biological strangers.

Still, they'd laughed a lot that first meeting, and Rachel had even dared to ask whether he liked her. She got an affirmative reply, a kiss on the cheek, and a hug as they made plans to meet for lunch again the next day before she flew back home. She noticed the way he smelled of tobacco and after-shave lotion.

During the second meeting, however, her father seemed distracted and hid behind his pipe. He announced that he had only forty-five minutes, and admitted that he had mixed emotions about everything. He worried that she had high expectations and that he would disappoint her.

"I wanted to cry," Rachel recalls. "I was feeling abandoned. But I mumbled something about hoping we could have an ongoing relationship."

"I can tell you want a father," he said, moving from a filial into a professorial role. "Sometimes when natural parents and natural children meet, there is a desire to go back in time."

"It's kind of hard not to feel that way," Rachel confessed. She felt him slipping away from her. "Are you really going to tell your family about me?" she asked for the second time, hating herself for turning into a needy child she could not control.

"I feel a lot of hunger coming from you," he stated. "Hungry people have a difficult time with me." She saw something click in his eyes, as if he were thinking: "You look just like my hungry mother."

She felt devastated, especially since she'd always hated her emotional hunger, which she'd attributed to being cut off from her birth parents. "Do you dislike me because I remind you of your mother?" she heard herself asking. He fended off the question with: "Liking comes and goes in relationships. It's beside the point."

Before they parted, her father said he would tell his second wife and his children about her. He promised to send her some of his favorite Eastern European novels, but asked her not to call or write his office. He gave her a warm hug and said he would be in touch with her.

Rachel waited two months to hear from her father. Then she wrote to him. No answer. She left messages on his machine. No response. Finally, after four months, she sent an eighteen-page letter by Federal Express to his office. It was in the genre of Kafka's famous letter to his father, in which he tries to explain his sensibilities with the hope that his father will see him at last for the person he is. Now Rachel answered her father's question about how it feels to be cut off from one's roots—painful—and let him know how devastating it would be to be cut off once again. No reply.

She kept remembering how he had crossed his legs tightly when he said that hungry people found him difficult, and worried that her intensity had driven him away.

"You pay such a terrible price for becoming a real person," Rachel told me. "I thought I would be magically healed, and now I feel more alone than ever. I lost him my first thirty years, and now I've lost him for the second half of my life as well. All I wanted was to know what it's like to be loved by a person who happens to be my biological parent."

The white light of the alternate reality was fading, just as her father was fading back into the mist from which he had so briefly materialized. But her grief stayed with her. "I still love him despite everything, but in a sense he has died for me. It's so painful to know that he still lives—for others. I wake in the middle of the night shaking with anxiety over the plain cold fact: your birth father has abandoned you again."

At its most harrowing, the journey of reunion skirts the borders of life and death, threatening the tenuous hold that adoptees have on existence. The adoptee who is rebuffed by the birth parents must, and eventually does, find other ways to be born, but in the meantime she has to survive the emotional chaos.

"Being adopted is a nightmare," Rachel says. "My birth parents don't want to acknowledge my existence—they can't deal with me at all." She found that she had to struggle against her birth parents' denial of her identity in order to hold on to her own sense of being. "One part of me wants to give in, to match their spiritual negation of me with a real physical negation, like death."

Looking back over her life, which reunion forces people to do, Rachel, like other adoptees (including me), cannot understand how she could have stayed unconscious for so long. She feels not only that she has been betrayed but that she has been an accomplice in the betrayal. "My birth parents are behaving cruelly, and yet I cannot help but feel that I have actively consented in the erasure of my own identity," she says. "I committed the sin of allowing the past to completely slip through my own fingers. I allowed years, even decades, to go by, building my life on a rootless present. I acquiesced in the great compromise in order to belong to something, in order to become a pseudohuman being. When I met my birth father, the magnitude of this error hit me full in the face."

We can understand why Rachel and other adoptees might feel responsible for having compromised themselves, but are they? As we saw in chapter 4, the adopted child has little choice but to acquiesce to the non-negotiable mandate of the closed adoption system: thou must shut down psychologically and deny thy birth mother and thy birth father.

Still, the adult adoptee has other choices—for example, the choice *not* to shut down psychologically again. The choice to become a fighter, which in the psychiatrist Alexander Lowen's sense of the term means to become an individual who knows he has a right to be, a right to live, and a right to fulfillment. Rachel chose to live and to fight, which in her case meant to continue her life narrative as an assertive adult, not as a needy baby. With the help of her therapist, Rachel was able to deal with her anger and sense of helplessness, and even to forgive her father for the pain she felt. But she knew she had to confront him at least once to say that his behavior was not right.

A year after their meeting, Rachel flew to Montreal and, despite her nervousness, went to her father's office unannounced. He opened the door and stepped out. She recalls the moment she saw him again. "My father!" she thought with awe. He was embarrassed to see her; since he had a class, he suggested they meet for lunch the next day. She was determined not to regress as she had last time, and to make their encounter upbeat and positive.

"I know this is difficult," she told him as soon as they were seated, "but I think you should have gotten in touch with me. I understand that you had limited choices thirty years ago, but that's no reason to cut me off now."

Her father admitted his ambivalence, and even seemed relieved that he had a chance to resolve the situation in some way. "I know it was shabby of me," he said. "I've thought about it every day. My original intent was to integrate you into my family, but when I realized it was not possible I just procrastinated."

He looked so overwhelmed and guilty that she didn't press it. "I felt affection for him," she told me. "We were reserved with each other, but there was no verbal sparring like before. We were two people having lunch and getting to know each other. He talked about his work and asked questions about mine. This time I could accept him as a person with a large family that made conflicting demands on him. He said he still couldn't introduce me to his other children, but was willing to meet for lunch again whenever I returned to Montreal."

The father whom Rachel had first met, who seemed interested and committed, had reemerged. The next time she visited Montreal, he invited her to his home to meet his wife, a beautiful young woman who greeted her warmly. He showed her photo albums of his other children— all of whom she noticed looked something like her—and his mother. His wife observed how ironic it was that a child he didn't raise should be so like him in interests and talents. While driving her back to her hotel, Rachel's father said, "I'm sure coming here makes it more real for you."

She knew he meant it was more real for him, too. "You take care," he said as he dropped her off. And this time he wrapped his arms around her in a strong, fatherly hug.

"I feel I can get on with the rest of my life now," Rachel says. "Having a greater understanding of my father gives me a greater understanding of myself, and makes me feel more connected. This is not to say there isn't sadness over the years I could not know him, or still some hurt over the fact that he never got back in touch with me, but the benefits of getting to know him make up for everything." And then she added, "Sometimes when I was with him, I was so overcome with emotion I couldn't speak. I felt like Cordelia: 'My lips are silent, but my heart is full.'"

Janet

There are birth fathers who are more decisive than Rachel's, and who act as midwives for their child's rebirthing. These fathers are willing to acknowledge a child they may not have even known existed, and to take emotional responsibility for that child's adult well-being, even at the risk of their own emotional discomfort. They make the illegitimate child feel psychologically legitimate.

Janet found her father, a retired machinist, in Arizona one week after her mother gave her his name. He welcomed her in the first phone call: "There was a lot of beer there, but if you're my child, you are part of the family." He recalled that he paid some of her mother's expenses at the maternity home.

But her father was more reserved during Janet's second call, as if her revelation had sobered him up. He said she shouldn't rush down. "I wouldn't want you to be disappointed if there's some mistake," he explained, and suggested a DNA test—just to be sure. Janet made all the arrangements, paid for the tests, and waited nervously for the results. When they proved 99.7 percent positive, her father was his jovial self again on the phone. "Now I have three children," he declared, and invited her to visit him and his wife.

Janet flew out to her father's hometown and rented a car at the airport. She remembers how anxious she was as she pulled into his driveway.

"My father's wife walked out the front door and toward me with her arms open. As I cautiously moved into her circle of welcome, I looked over her shoulder to see him for the first time. He moved slowly, but with intent, and gently took his eldest daughter into his arms. Why did I feel like running? I was crying. To be held for the first time by a parent. To be safe. To be home. To be able to break, to melt, to be human. Could he possibly understand what that meant to me? Did it matter? As we embraced, he pushed back a bit to look at me. I saw for the first time my eyes, my nose, my hair. It was overwhelming. I was two months old, drowning in need, my miniature fingers and toes wiggling open and closed, exploring dark space. My infant sensory system screaming, 'This is my father. I'm OK now. He'll take care of me.'"

Later, Janet would learn from her half-sister and half-brother, who phoned from different parts of the country, that their father, a perfection-ist, had not been easy to grow up with. Her appearance had had the posi-tive effect of opening up other secrets in the family (a not uncommon fallout of reunions), and both their mother and father had become more candid with them. Janet wept when her father told her on the phone that he loved her, because she knew he had found it hard to say to his other children. When she admitted she was still suffering over her birth mother's rejection, he said, "Forget about her, you've still got us. You hold your head high, and we go on from here."

Kaitlin

Kaitlin, an artist in her late twenties, was in the unusual situation of finding her father first. She was very close to her adoptive parents and her two adopted siblings, but she always wanted to know about her other family.

"I used to think my father was Robert Redford because he was blond," she remembers. "But I'd paint my birth mother with a headless pregnant body. Or I'd paint a baby floating out in space with its broken umbilical cord trying to reattach to its mother's body. In my teen years, I used to sit in bars with my brother and cry. He'd cry, too, though he wasn't interested in searching."

Kaitlin's birth father, an investment banker in Boston, was stunned when he received a call from the social worker who told him that his daughter was looking for him. He said he had to think about things, then called back the next day to ask why Kaitlin was contacting him. He hadn't told his wife or children about her. Despite his concerns, he called Kaitlin that night to suggest that they meet on Valentine's Day, when he would be in New York on business.

She remembers how nervous she felt going to meet her father at Rockefeller Plaza. "As I approached, I saw a tall man in a trenchcoat who had my exact same eyes. I grew up with short parents, so this was the first time I had contact with anyone who looks like me. We hugged, and he suggested that we walk around. He thought I would be angry at him. That night he took me to an elegant supper club. I actually had the nerve to ask him to dance. It was strange to feel my father's body—I felt attracted in a certain way." (She laughs as she says this, and tosses it off.) "But he's more conservative than I am, and we argued about politics a good part of the evening. It was all very intense. He called me every day for a while after that, now only once a week."

Her birth father helped her locate her mother, and she flew south to that reunion barely ahead of the first snowstorm ever to hit that region. Her birth mother, who had been thrilled to hear her daughter's voice, said she would come to the airport on skis if necessary. It wasn't. They held on to each other in the terminal for ten minutes, tears streaming down their cheeks. They were delighted to discover that not only did they resemble each other but they had similar methods of painting and teaching. Kaitlin's mother, who did not marry until ten years after giving her up, adopted a son when she had trouble conceiving again. A few years later she gave birth to another son. Although her husband knew about Kaitlin, the children didn't, and so she put her up at a friend's house.

Kaitlin learned that her parents had known each other for six months, but her father was not ready to get married. He was the one who suggested adoption. "I felt I didn't have a right to keep you because I wasn't married, and you deserved a loving home with two parents," her mother said. "I held you tightly the few days we had together, trying to push all the love I could into you."

"I wanted to revert back for a second and feel that mother-daughter connection," Kaitlin says. "Once while we were sitting together in the backseat of the car, I put my head down on her stomach and tried to understand what the baby experienced. And that summer I went swimming with my father to get a better look at him. He has skinny legs like I do. I like to massage his feet. I have his intensity and my mother's personality. I felt I was falling in love with *both* of them. I needed to hug and touch them to understand the connection. I wonder how much more touching and sharing we have to do before we can part without an ache. We are doing things in reverse: we were separate and now we're coming together. You have to go through that. I figured that's part of it."

Another part, she discovered, was coping with the emotions she was feeling—sometimes ecstatic, sometimes scary. "I felt my reality was wiped out. Everything you know is pulled like a rug out from under you. I was just floating in the air while I tried to get rooted in this new reality. I couldn't concentrate. I questioned everything. I felt angry—angry that adoptees have to skulk around searching for information about themselves, angry at the sexism in adoption that doesn't support women keeping their babies, and angry at my birth father for not dealing with things in a different manner."

Kaitlin's birth father has continued the close relationship with her, despite the difficulties it causes in his home life. His sixteen-year-old son accepted his new sister right away, but the thirteen-year-old daughter was angry and refused to meet her. The turning point came when the younger one had a nightmare one night while Kaitlin was staying over. She came down to sleep with Kaitlin on the couch, and after that they became close friends.

The real problem is with Kaitlin's father's wife, who accepted her at first but then decided she was not ready to incorporate her into the family. "Maybe if you looked more like the kids," she explained it once. She even suggested that Kaitlin get a DNA test. The wife's negative response is not unlike that of other spouses who feel threatened by this unprecedented relationship with the adult adoptee, a reminder of someone their partner either loved or was involved with sexually.

"Can't you just have a relationship with him and not with the whole family?" the wife wanted to know.

"I'm not asking to be part of the family or to come on holidays," Kaitlin told her. "I have a family. But I do want a relationship with my sister and brother. I have some rights."

"No, you don't have any rights," her father's wife responded. "My friends ask why I let you in the house. Aren't you happy with what you have?" Kaitlin knew this woman was jealous of Kaitlin's intimacy with her father and was trying to say, How much more do you want?

A year into reunion, Kaitlin went to Indonesia for four months on a job assignment. It gave her the time and space to put things into perspective. When she returned, she moved back in with a boyfriend with whom she had broken up just before she began her search, and spoke of feeling grounded: "I knew I was missing something, and I was. I feel like a completed puzzle now. I can move on." She continues her warm relationship with her mother, and accepts that, for now, she can see her father only when he makes a special trip to New York.

FATHERS AND SONS

[Telemachus] and his father have almost nothing in common either in experience or outlook. Though they share a strong sense of belonging to each other, this is still an entirely *a priori* bond of feeling—a cherished hypothesis without any empirical proof as yet. For nearly twenty years each has thought and wondered about the other. Now, when their hopes and anxieties are to be put to the touchstone of reality, what will the result be—love or hate?
—W. B. STANFORD, *THE ULYSSES THEME*

The long lost Ulysses revealed himself to the son who had searched for him with: "I am that father whom your boyhood lacked / and suffered pain for lack of." Perhaps it is fear that they will not hear such words that keeps most adopted males from searching for the birth father. Fewer men than women search at all, and most also speak of wanting to find the mother first. It may be harder for men to confront the pain they have experienced or the fathers who abandoned both their mothers and them. They have more pride, more anger, more vulnerability. There is the stark question: Will it be love or hate?

Some men, also like the women, begin to think about the birth father only after failing to have a relationship with the birth mother. "I'd like to know who this guy is—what makes him tick," one man told me. Another said, "All of a sudden he's gaining prominence in my thoughts. I want him to rescue me. To make me feel better. To join me in hating her." Yet many years may pass before these men search for the birth father. Their male need is buried too deeply beneath their vanity and rage.

The poet Robert Bly, writing on men's need for a father, says that the father's birth gift cannot be quantified. "His gift contributes to the love of knowledge, love of action, and ways to honor the world of things."[2] It may be that the birth father's withholding of that gift is another one of the reasons male adoptees put off meeting him. The male adoptee may feel more betrayed by the father who has denied him his lineage and more loyalty to the father whose name he (unlike the female adoptee) has been entrusted to carry like a banner into the future. This missing father, whose body he may be growing into, whose baldness or alcoholism he may have inherited, whose image stares back at him in the mirror, this father left him to live or die under another man's protectorate and to learn how to be a man from men of another clan.

A boy who sees his father as more powerful and stronger than he, a figure to be admired, envied, and challenged, also depends upon him as a shield against dangers in the outside world. Does an adopted boy feel defenseless without his natural father as he grows up with another father more powerful and stronger than he? The adoptive father's unconscious anger and shame at not producing this child (even though a natural child may have been born to him after the adoption) may make him try to put down an adopted son: to pull out the supports rather than provide them, to be competitive with him, as if to prove his own manhood. The boy may have nowhere to be safe except with his mother, who herself is standing in for a woman who has deserted him.

We might ask if a son who has already been deserted by one father can stand up to the one who rescued him. Can he risk abandonment by the only father he knows? Might he not find it safer to be submissive, and not compete with this father or with other men out in the world?

Can the male adoptee think of a father not of his blood as his real father? Many do. But some feel like the man who said: "I had a father, but not the one I wanted." Or another, who felt he had two missing fathers: "I was my mother's project. My adoptive father did not feel a real connection because I was not of his bloodline." He remembers watching his adoptive father cry when his own father died, and thinking: "Didn't you know you'd lose him?"

Can the adoptive father regard a boy not of his seed as his real son? Again, many do. But Mark believes that men connect impregnating to manhood and fatherhood. He felt that his adoptive father was filled with unconscious rage—sometimes directed at him: "I couldn't help him realize the trance he wanted to be in to forget his infertility. He wanted me to be a miniature of him—powerful, a big shot, prominent, with lots of money. He wanted a super-competing, world-beating son. He robbed me of myself. I was afraid of him—his temper, his violence, his power. I invited it, hated it, wanted it."

What kind of attachment is there without the blood tie?

"We are ambivalently attached," Mark said. "I knew in my heart of hearts that this man was not really my father. I think he knew that this boy was not really his son. If he had raised his own son, who had his own temperament, they would have worked out a different equilibrium. If I was more like him, he could have tolerated my differences."

Erik Erikson once told me that an adoptive father may unconsciously treat a son as not descended from him and therefore opposite of his own kind. The father can feel hostility because the son doesn't have his sense of humor or other traits. "Genes enter into it," Erikson said, acknowledging the importance of genetics in creating closeness among family members.

Perhaps Erikson's own life as a half-adoptee who didn't know his real father made him sensitive to identity issues. His mother, a Danish Jew, never told Erik the true story of his origins, wanting him to believe that her husband, the pediatrician Theodor Homburger, was his father. As a boy growing up "blond, blue-eyed, and flagrantly tall" in Germany, Erik thought it strange that his father was short and dark. He was acutely aware that he was referred to as a *goy* in his father's temple, while to his schoolmates he was a *Jew*. He thought of himself as a "foundling."

During a psychohistory conference at my Cape Cod house in 1981, Erikson told me a "secret" that he had never spoken of before. It was an experience he had when he was eight, one that seemed to me not unlike the one that Oedipus had at the banquet when a drunken man suggested that he was not his father's son.

Erik was in the Black Forest watching an old peasant woman milking a cow, when she looked up and asked, "Do you know who your father is?"

He was taken by surprise. It was the first time anyone had said such a thing to him. He knew she must have noticed how different he looked from his father. Like Oedipus, he rushed to his mother to ask for the truth. He was given a half-truth. She admitted he had been adopted by Homburger, whom she married on the day Erik turned three. She spoke vaguely about having been abandoned by her former Danish-Jewish husband in Copenhagen while she was pregnant, and going to Germany to give birth. Sensing her discomfort, and responding to his own anxiety, Erikson submerged his need to know more about his father at that time. In his adolescence, he would hear rumors that his real father was not his mother's former husband, but rather a Danish aristocrat whose name her brothers had sworn never to reveal.

Erik, like many adoptees, expressed amazement at how well he had managed to cut off his early childhood memories. "Look here," he said, prefacing his words with a phrase he used when he wanted to emphasize a point, "I must have remembered *something* of the three years I spent alone with my mother before her marriage. I knew she had a sadness I could not understand." He was even then trying to unravel why his mother had not been able to tell him the true circumstances of his birth. Why she had given him yet another false father in naming her former husband. Why everyone in her extended family in Denmark kept the conspiracy of silence about the identity of his real father, so that he was never able to learn it. Something was rotten in the state of Denmark, something that drove his young pregnant mother into exile in another country to deliver her fatherless child.

"Did you ever try to find your father?" I once asked him.

"Not really," he admitted. Years before he had asked a relative who was traveling to Copenhagen to talk to a dying aunt, the last living person who knew his father's name. The aunt went into a coma just before the emissary entered her room, and with her died the possibility of Erikson's ever knowing who his father was.

"Why didn't you go there earlier yourself?" I wanted to know.

"Maybe I was too proud," he admitted, after a pause. And he added with the familiar nonsearcher's rationale: "If my father hadn't cared enough about me to want me then, why should I look him up now? If I went back to an aristocrat's home, maybe my father would think I wanted something." Erikson had no way of knowing that his father was an aristocrat, but I didn't question that.

"How could you *not* have searched for your father?" I asked, not willing to let him off the hook completely. "After all, you are the father of identity."

"No, I am the father of identity *problems,*" he responded playfully. Then he added, "But look here. Perhaps I thought it is better to keep one's fantasy. We create ourselves in a way. When I became an American citizen, I realized that I could take a name of my own choosing. I made myself Erik's son. It is better to be your own originator."

Ted

If the father of identity theory represses his need to know the father who abandoned him and his mother, we can understand why most adopted men fear rejection and repress theirs. Ted was an exception, in that he had always been obsessed with wanting to find his father—that father whom Robert Bly tells us "gives with his sperm a black overcoat around the soul, invisible in our nights."[3]

Ted was eighteen when he first wrote me from his home in a small Midwestern mining town after reading one of my books. He had been adopted at two weeks by a blue-collar family who had a natural son a few years later.

"They have always done everything they could for me materially," he confided, "but I've never felt that I belong to them or to their family. I resent being given a name and a family and relatives and being expected to accept it unquestioningly. This, to me, is sheer hypocrisy and injustice. I can't just go on with my life not knowing about my past, because nothing I do will have a firm foundation under it."

Ted had not searched yet for his birth father, but he had the "infinite longing" for him that Sherwood Anderson's fictional boy in *Winesburg, Ohio* has for the outside world. He expressed this yearning in a series of poems, one of which he titled with the Hebrew word for father, *Abba.*

> *The mirrors are draped but I can hardly tell the difference;*
> *they've always been opaque.*
> *How many times have I stared into dull grey eyes trying to*
>   *catch*
> *a glimpse of you, or at least a shadow, to no avail?*
> *I've rent my clothes above my heart, my imperfect heart,*
> *that I may have inherited from you.*
> *What more shall I do?*
> *I would sit shiva*
> *I would say kaddish*
> *I would light a candle once a year—*
> *if only I knew what name to carve upon the stone.*
> *But even if I knew the name, I'd be praying for myself*
> *as well as for you.*

I wondered about the Jewish imagery in his poem, because Ted had no information about his origins. His adoptive mother goes to the Southern Baptist church, and his adoptive father is not interested in religion. Ted explained that he began to identify with the Jewish people after reading some books on their history and the Holocaust. He was attracted to their long tradition and close-knit families, and could relate to their sense of being marginalized and singled out, because he was confused about his sexuality as well as his ethnic background. He suspected he might be gay because he wasn't interested in dating girls, and he thought he might be Jewish because some friends had remarked on his dark complexion.

When, at sixteen, Ted decided to convert, however, he became a Catholic. "I didn't know any Jewish people in our town," he explained. "My parents would have thought it really strange if I suddenly became a Jew."

Still, Ted held on to his belief that he had inherited his love of books and poetry from a Jewish father. He sought out older men as friends and, very tentatively, with great trepidation, he decided to search for his father. But in order to find him, he had to search for his mother first.

Ted's mother proved to be an adoptee who knew nothing about her own heritage, and showed surprise that he would want to know his. She was a divorcée living in a trailer park with her daughter, whom she identified as his full sibling. She said his father was her ex-husband, whom she was about to divorce when Ted was conceived. According to her, this man was a ne'er-do-well stonemason who had not helped support his daughter.

Ted called the ex-husband and was both relieved and shattered when he vehemently denied being his father. He tried to put him and the subject to rest in his poem "Memorial":

Since you have chosen to die alone,
I have only this to say
Father, there is no reprieve for such loss
The persistence of your memory and name.

For the next few years, Ted concentrated on his college courses. And then, feeling his father loss stirring again, he wrote the sister of his mother's ex-husband to ask how he could contact his half-siblings by his father's second marriage. He soon received an angry letter from the ex-husband, declaring again that he was not the father. He suggested Ted ask his mother about the man she was involved with before the divorce was finalized. He gave Ted the man's name. "My conscience is clear," he wrote. "This is my final statement on the subject. Have a good life."

Ted's mother denied that she had had a relationship with any other man. But Ted saw his life opening up again: he now had a second chance to find the father for whom he yearned.

Alan

There are a few men who search for their birth fathers because their relationship with their birth mothers is very satisfying; they seek completion in finding both halves of their heritage.

Alan, a thirty-eight-year-old editor, never thought about his father as a child, but wanted to meet his mother from the time he was told about his adoption at eight. He had been searching on and off for years, but it wasn't until she contacted the adoption agency that they were able to meet. "I was found, but I had been waiting," he says.

Alan likes to joke that his birth mother, Hannah, is an emotional clone. They have the same sense of humor, the same volatile temperament, and even the same phobias. He surprised himself by eagerly asking about his father during their first conversation. Hannah described a year-long, passionate romance with a professional gambler, who took off once she became pregnant.

It took Alan ten months to locate his father, who was still a professional gambler but still had not gambled on marriage and children. They met under the dim light of a lamppost in front of his father's house. Although Benny was no longer the tough, macho guy with the black leather jacket and slicked-back hair his mother had fallen for, Alan was struck by his charm and the resemblance between them: "I felt as if I were staring into a magic mirror, and saw my masculine reflection. He was about my height, with the same broad shoulders. I'd never thought about myself as having broad shoulders, but now I realized I did. Seeing him, I could appreciate my manhood for the first time."

As they sat at the kitchen table, Alan was moved by how attentive and nurturing his father was: the table was laid with bagels, cream cheese and lox, apples, and Scotch. Now he noticed that his father's mouth jutted out slightly like his, they had the identical curled lips, and they clasped their hands together in precisely the same position.

Benny said that he had used his underworld contacts to try to locate Alan soon after the adoption, but failed because Hannah had used her old married name on the documents, rather than his. "I knew you'd have to find me, but I gave up when you were twenty-five. It's a miracle you're back." As an old-time gambler, Benny said, "the odds were off the board."

Alan felt his heart sink as his father spoke nostalgically of his love affair with Hannah. He knew he might offend his father if he stood up for Hannah, the jilted lover, and himself, the abandoned baby, but he felt he had to.

"Why didn't you marry her? Why did you leave her in that position?"

His father paused before answering. "I'm no saint and I won't try to bullshit you on this," he replied. "Maybe I didn't do the right thing, but I just wasn't the kind of person to settle down and get married. It wouldn't have worked with me traveling all the time around the country."

Alan learned that he came from a long line of strong, healthy Russian Jews, many of whom lived to be a hundred. His eighty-eight-year-old grandfather was a World War II hero, who still gambled, drank occasionally, and had an eye for the ladies. With a large cigar dangling out of his mouth, he was often mistaken for George Burns on the streets of Miami Beach. Benny said that his father was now handing out cigars to all his friends, announcing that he was a grandfather for the first time.

When Alan got home that night, he placed a picture of himself between photographs of Benny and Hannah—the way they looked when he was conceived. "I stared at our three photos for hours and realized that there were no more missing parts to the puzzle—for the first time in my life I could stop searching."

Alan hears from Benny all the time: he calls whenever he sees a show about adoption on TV, and is irate that the records are sealed. He was willing to see Hannah again, but she is unforgiving. "I seem to have gotten the best of both of them," Alan says. "Her outgoing nature and his charm help me get newspaper interviews others can't get. Until I met my father, I didn't realize how tough I was when I challenged politicians and went after hard stories. Even though his lifestyle and interests are different from mine, just knowing him, I can appreciate my male identity for the first time. I used to be fearful because to die and not know where I came from would have felt as though I had never really lived in the first place. Now, no matter what happens, having solved this mystery, I feel real."

Having come to terms with the reality of his father has liberated Alan "from his trance of love and yearning, from his seductive loyalties," as Stanley Kunitz phrases his own deliverance of bondage to the father who committed suicide before he was born. He could now "embrace new loves to prepare himself for the fresh assaults of existence."

Alan found he was able to commit himself to marriage and to take new risks in his career. He was also able to improve his relationship with his practical adoptive father, who was always critical of his son's creative ambitions. "My father was shocked when he first learned about my search, even distant for a while, but he has more respect for me now that my identity is stronger. My reunion has freed him in a lot of ways: he can be more playful, and view me more as an adult."

14

The Found Adoptee

You've opened a door I have to go in.
—CHRISSY, A THIRTY-ONE-YEAR-OLD ADOPTEE

THERE ARE ADOPTEES WHO SAY THEY WILL NEVER search, but would not object to being found by their birth mother—it would mean she cared enough to look for them. They remain in a psychological holding pattern, passively leaving it up to fate to decide what happens. There are other adoptees who feel threatened by the idea of being found—it would take away their control over an issue they do not feel ready to deal with.

It is not easy for birth mothers to get up the courage to search; they have to get in touch with the feelings that they cut off at the time of surrender. They were told that if they loved the baby, they would give it up, that two parents were better than one. They were assured that they would forget and were encouraged to get on with their lives, as if they were robots and there were no such thing as the sacred mother-child bond. Many describe numbing themselves and keeping their relinquishment a secret. Not a few were so traumatized that they had no more children. If they sought therapy for depression, the chances were that the loss of a child was not seen as a core issue of their unhappiness. Yet, through therapy or with the help of understanding friends or spouses, many were able to get in touch with their grief and anger and their need to know what happened to their children.[1]

As with adoptees, it can be a life crisis that jolts a birth mother into another state of consciousness. Or it can be watching another mother reuniting with her child on TV that reconnects her to the loss of her child. Or she might come across a story in a magazine about adoptees who want to know their heritage but are afraid that their birth mothers will reject them.

Birth mothers also fear being rejected. They fear that the adoptee will be angry at being given up and refuse to see them; that they won't live up to the adoptee's expectations; that they will lose the adoptee for the second time. Yet, in spite of all their fears, some birth mothers are driven to seek out their children.

DEMETER AND PERSEPHONE

I see birth mothers who search as descended from the Greek mother goddess, Demeter, who never gave up trying to find her lost daughter, Persephone, whom she had conceived with Zeus.[2]

According to the Homeric myth, Persephone was picking flowers in a meadow when the earth opened up and she was abducted by the King of the Underworld in his golden chariot. Demeter had turned away for a moment and was not aware of what had happened. We are told that bitter pain seized her heart when she realized Persephone was gone. She sped like a wild bird over the firm land and the yielding sea, seeking her child. But no one would reveal where her daughter was.

Birth mothers who awaken to their grief realize that they were not aware of what was happening when they let their child disappear into the dark underworld of the adoption system. It was as if they had turned away. They accuse social workers, their parents, the adoptive parents, the closed system itself, of abducting their child. Because the lips of the record keepers are sealed, the child has vanished from the mother into the Land of the As If Dead.

For the first nine days of her search, Demeter wandered over the earth so crazed that she neither ate nor drank nor bathed. When, on the tenth day, she learned from Helios, the sun god, where her daughter was, she felt savage grief and anger. She sat down at the Navel of the World, the place where her daughter had been separated from her. Birth mothers sit at that place, too, the place where the umbilicus was cut. A part of them remains there, even as another part goes on with the motions of life.

Demeter could not cease her lament. She turned herself into an ancient crone beyond childbearing, and sat by the Maiden Well. Birth mothers sit there, too. Their youthful innocence disappears with the lost child. They become prematurely old.

Then Demeter, the bringer of seasons and goddess of crops, sat by the Laughless Rock and spread her barren feelings over the earth. For one year there was famine. The human race was threatened with extinction. Not until Zeus realized that there would be no one left to make offerings or sacrifices to the gods did he send an emissary to order the King of the Underworld to release Persephone.

The myth does not tell us whether Persephone felt abandoned by her mother, who had been powerless to save her from this fate. It does reveal that when she learned she was to be allowed to return to her mother, she accepted food from her husband for the first time—the seeds of the pomegranate. She did not know that those who eat of Hades' seeds must return three months of each year to the underworld. Demeter's joy at reunion with her daughter was bittersweet when she learned that her child could not completely return to her.

So, too, the birth mother's joy is bittersweet, tempered by the realization that she can never fully have her child back. The adoptee has been nourished by the love and culture of the adoptive home, and some part of her will always belong to that world. "When I saw my adult daughter acting so reserved with me, I knew I was not going to get my baby back," said one birth mother, expressing what many feel. "I felt a double grief that I would have to separate from this young woman as well as from the infant I never really had."

Unlike Demeter, some birth mothers may not be clear about what they are searching for. They may think that all they want is to know that the child is alive and well and to answer any questions he might have. They may say they hope to have a friendship with the child, but that they do not want to take the adoptive mother's place. Karla, a birth mother who searched for her son when he was eighteen, remembers feeling "excitement" when she made the decision. "Then there was the self-doubt. Was I good enough? Would he like me? Then anger at all the closed doors.

Fury at the bureaucrats who kept me from information about myself and my son. Then elation and a sense of empowerment when I found him."

When she reunites with her adult child, however, a birth mother is startled to find that she has also reunited with the younger self she left behind with her baby, as well as with the grief that she had buried. "Searching for and finding my son was the beginning of grieving that I had repressed for eighteen years," Karla says. Still, her expectations were high: that she would have an immediate bond with her son, would be invited into his adoptive family, and would be a part of his life. "I didn't expect to be a mother, just an intimate friend," she explains, "but I also didn't expect to be rejected by his adoptive parents, who were very threatened when I contacted them. I had such feelings of worthlessness when I communicated with them. And then depression when my son didn't want to meet me."

It is very difficult for adoptees to respond to a birth mother when their adoptive parents are threatened. They move into a protective mode—especially some boys, who have a hard time dealing with emotional conflict. Karla waited patiently for four years and was "euphoric" when her son wrote that he was ready to meet her. "He exceeded my fantasies, but he's kept himself at arm's length and not shared himself with me. He seems to have a loving and respectful relationship with his parents, though he says he is not too much like them. For the past three and a half years, it has been happiness and disappointment. I am happy that I know him and disappointed that he doesn't want more of a relationship."

As with many birth mothers, Karla finds herself full of maternal longing and "hungry" for more meetings with her son. Once she connects with the adoptee, a birth mother longs to hold her lost baby, to give it the hugs and kisses that were not possible before, to have an ongoing relationship—to be a mother.

FEAR OF BEING FOUND

How adoptees respond to being found can depend upon whether they are living on their own, their sense of guilt toward their adoptive parents, and how much they have disavowed their feelings about being adopted. "Had my mother found me before I had therapy, I would have turned her away," Robin says. "I would have been loyal to my adoptive mother and felt too guilty to have a relationship with my birth mother."

Winnicott might have been describing the fear of the nonsearcher when he wrote about the fear of "being found before one is there to be found."[3] Unlike the adoptee who evolves psychologically in the process of searching and is ready for reunion, the adoptee who is found by the birth mother is still in a deep sleep and may not be there to be found. One woman described being flooded with a range of feelings "from intense fear, anxiety, and dislocation, to an incredible curiosity." Under all of this is the adoptee's fear of not only being found but of being *found out*: when her mother recognizes her for the impostor she really is, her mother will reject her once again.

Found adoptees may need to retreat for a while, either to marshal their psychological defenses against possible annihilation that would follow such a rejection or to restructure them in a way that could include this alternate reality. They may, like Karla's son, leave the birth mother waiting weeks, months, even years, for their response. They need to feel they are in control of themselves and of whatever happens.

Frank

Some adoptees who are found may also need to protect the magical hero self they have created out of the mystery of their existence, without which they fear they would lose their sense of uniqueness.

Frank, a married businessman in his late twenties, believed he had a transcendental link to the universe: God had put him on earth for some plan and was watching over him. And so he panicked when he was informed by a court intermediary that his birth mother had requested to meet him. "Until then I enjoyed creating a mystery around myself," he said. "I was an actor in life and in our local theater. I could change my personality with each part. I could even change my body physically. When my birth mother contacted me, the mystery was laid open."

Frank let weeks go by before agreeing to meet her. "I'm a very private person. I had on my businessman's armor. I own two profitable corporations, and I wasn't sure what her intentions were. My adoptive parents were the greatest any child could have. I felt intruded upon."

During his first meeting with his mother, Frank was startled to see himself looking into a "genetic mirror" at someone who could have been his sister. But rather than stealing the monetary things he had worried about, he felt she was stealing his identity. "I didn't like being told I resembled other people. She said my eyes were like hers, my cheekbones were like someone else's. I wanted to say: 'These are my eyes and my nose. They're mine. I'm me. I want to stay me.'"

That night Frank cried as he had never cried before in his life. "My crying was like a baby who has just emerged from the womb and is spanked by the doctor. It cries because it is alive." The next day he was angry and scared. "Before I met my mother, I thought I had emerged out of nowhere. I felt close to God. Now I worried that God would think I no longer needed His help. He would think: 'Things are set straight for Frank now. He can fend for himself.' I felt kicked off a high horse. My frame of reference was gone. I was disappearing."

During the next year, however, Frank became very close to his mother. She had married twice, but he was her only child. They marveled over the many things they had in common, which included owning two dogs, the need to rescue stray animals, and a stubborn streak. Frank managed to revise his self myth, without giving up all the magic. "We were meant to be separated," he says now. "It was for the best. We could both grow and come together later. I realize I can still be unique. Nothing of that has changed. I'm still basically the same person. For twenty-seven years these things are engraved on you. I had a strong sense of self before— now I have a different sense of self."

WHERE WAS SHE?

Some found adoptees seem to melt like infants into their birth mother's arms, while others fend their mothers off. Some feel the miracle of her reappearance; others feel the anger they had repressed, especially when they realize she has gone on with her life without them.

One young woman, whose adoptive parents were dead, waited two years before agreeing to meet her birth mother, who had married the birth father. Initially, she felt happy to be found because she always wondered how a mother could give up a child and never think of her again; but she got confused when the intermediary declared that her "real" family had come to claim her. She wondered if they thought that her life until then had been a "masquerade." After that, she was overcome with anger that twenty-one years after giving her up, her birth mother dared to seek her out. She has met with her mother just once, but allows phone calls from her twice a month. She concedes that someday they might become friends, but not like mother and daughter. By controlling the situation, she manages to stay loyal to the memory of her adoptive parents.

Young adult adoptees who still live with their parents or are financially dependent on them often resist meeting the birth mother for fear of hurting their adoptive parents. Even if the adoptive relationship was stormy, they may still have the need to cling to the adoptive parents, who are more of a ballast for the adopted self than the ghostly figure who has just materialized. It feels safer to put everything on hold for a while until they feel equipped to handle the situation.

Some adoptees, especially young men, have difficulty letting go of their anger: it may build rather than recede over the years. Unlike female adoptees, who understand how one can get pregnant at the wrong time, males tend to take a more judgmental attitude that their mother didn't care enough to keep them. Marvin, who was approached by his birth mother in the schoolyard when he was sixteen, has refused to communicate with her for the past eight years, even though she continues to write him and send presents on his birthday. During this period, his birth mother spoke on the phone a few times with his adoptive mother, who sent her photographs and news of Marvin but could not convince him to meet with her. Marvin's adoptive father, who died recently, felt threatened by the idea of a reunion. It may be that Marvin is being as true to the close relationship he had with his father as to his anger, for he has not budged from his dug-in position.

Yet one detects a trace of ambivalence as he struggles to explain the resentment he harbors.

"I just don't know how to act towards someone who has no emotional or social bonds with me, yet who is tied very closely physically to me. She acts like she knows me, like I'm an old friend. Well, no, like I'm her son. And my head is saying 'I'm not your son. I'm my adoptive parents' son.' So take my feelings of social awkwardness and shyness, mix in the confusion of having two mothers, one who raised me but did not bear me, one who bore me but did not raise me, and then add in my inconsistent approach to life in general, and the end result is for me to deal with her by not dealing with her. I don't believe this is fair, but I feel it's the way it has to be. Trying to relate to her and to deal with her would take an enormous amount of energy for me, energy that I can't afford to give up. I rationalize it by thinking, 'She left my feelings and development to fate when she gave me up for adoption. By ignoring her, I'm just extending her original act of giving me up.'"

It is possible that the very act of struggling to articulate his feelings may help Marvin to gain a new perspective: to see that his birth mother was in a difficult position, that she did the best she could for him at the time, but that she never forgot him.

THE FOUND ADOLESCENT

There is a controversy in the adoption field over what is known as "minor search"—a situation where the birth mother, such as Marvin's, makes direct contact with a child who is under eighteen or gets in touch with the adoptive parents.

Birth mothers who contact the adoptive parents first run the risk of receiving a letter from the family lawyer that the child has no interest in her now and that she should disappear—or else. The threats are usually scare tactics to ward her off—What parents would want their child to learn they had put his mother in jail? Society has accepted that, despite sealed records, some birth mothers search for adult adoptees, but younger children have been considered out of bounds. Yet even this may be changing. In a case history of Ron, a twelve-year-old adopted boy, the child analyst Calvin Colarusso states his belief that meeting their biological parents, if they want to, can enhance the identity formation of older adopted children.

Ron

Ron had been referred to Colarusso at the age of ten because of difficulties in school, lack of motivation, and growing isolation from other children—some of the early symptomatology we have seen in adoption trauma. When, two years into therapy, Ron's adoptive parents were contacted by his birth mother, Colarusso, after much thought, advised them to go ahead with a reunion and admits his surprise at how well Ron reacted.

Despite his age, Ron understood his adoptive parents' concern. "My mom is worried that my birth mother will want to take me away. She won't. The Longs are the only family I have," he said. And another time: "I'm not going to jump up and say, 'Mom, let's go.' I'm sort of like a dog. I'm real loyal."

Ron was visibly moved when his birth mother told him that she had always loved him. She had married and had another son, but she assured him that she had never forgotten him. Colarusso noted that the boy's increased self-esteem was almost palpable. "It's amazing that we found each other," Ron said. "It's kind of like 'E.T., phone home.'"

Ron met with his birth mother twice a month for a few months, and then met her extended family. At first he denied an interest in knowing about his birth father, saying: "I'll find him someday and I'll give him hell for leaving my mom." Later, expressing sadness about not knowing "this guy who made me," he said, "There's a hole inside me that only he can fill."

Colarusso found that Ron showed an amazing ability to integrate "an awesome experience." When asked how he felt about having two mothers, the boy replied: "Fine. I'm really lucky to have such nice people for mothers."[4]

Paul

Paul had just turned fourteen and was beginning high school when his adoptive parents told him that his birth mother wanted to meet him. It wasn't easy for them—in fact, they had panicked when they received Linda's letter a few months before. "She'll be young and beautiful, and Paul will love her more than he loves me," was the first thought that Joan, the adoptive mother, had. Her husband, always the practical one, called their lawyer to ask, "Can she take him away from us?" Only after speaking to Linda's intermediary did they both feel comfortable enough to talk to her by phone. "When I heard her voice, I knew she was real," Joan says. After consulting their minister and the school psychologist, they decided that Paul had a right to know his mother had contacted them.

Paul, now twenty-seven, remembers bursting into tears when his parents sat him down in the living room and broke the news. "I never thought it would happen in my life," he says. He was also relieved because his parents looked so solemn, he was afraid they would say they were getting divorced or that his grandmother was seriously ill. Still, his first question was: "Does she want me back?" He was trying to understand whether this was "good" information or was going to cause problems for the family. His parents reassured him that she just wanted to meet him, but they felt a twinge when he said that he wanted to meet her, too. "I thought Linda did an extraordinary thing to find me," Paul says. "How could I not meet this person?"

A key advantage to reunion when the child is young is that the adoptive parents can be involved and stay involved. They become part of the reunion scenario and integrate the experience along with their child over the years. Joan made the arrangements for everyone to meet Linda for lunch at a hotel near the airport. "It's good to meet in a public place," Paul's grandmother said. "If she wants to steal him, there'll be people around."

The party that set out for the restaurant included Joan's best friend and Paul's younger adopted sister. Paul's father chose to let the women handle the situation. By chance, the women entered the restaurant's ladies' room just as Linda was coming out. Paul, who was waiting in the hall, recognized her, but felt very shy. They stood there awkwardly making small talk until Joan rescued them. She was relieved to see that Linda, though attractive, was not the long-haired, blonde princess she'd feared. Linda was under added stress because she was in the process of divorcing Paul's birth father, whom she had married a few years after the surrender and who felt she should wait to search until Paul was older. During lunch the two mothers did most of the talking. Later, Paul told Joan that Linda seemed like one of her younger friends from church.

When Paul's church group went camping up north near Linda's home, Paul asked to spend a week with her. "What happened?" Joan wanted to know when he returned. "Nothing." "What did you talk about?" "Things." "How do you feel?" "I feel good about it."

Paul visited Linda a few times over the years, and she came down to stay with them. "I had a special relationship with her," Paul says. "I told her things that I never confided to my mother or any other adult. She had information that no one else could give me, and she listened to me. She was interested in my accomplishments and troubles. But she didn't fit my definition of a mother. I never felt I had to answer to her, like I did to my parents, who were responsible for me."

Paul says he probably would not have looked up his birth father if a college professor had not asked his advice about looking up his birth son. "How will he feel about me?" he wanted to know. Learning that his professor was a birth father made his own father more real to Paul, and gave him the courage to make contact. His father, who had remarried and now had two young adopted children, received him warmly. But Linda, who had not resolved her anger at her former husband, saw Paul's action as a betrayal. She became increasingly critical of him, refused to attend his wedding, and sent a letter ending their relationship. "She rejected me once and she's rejecting me again," Paul says sadly. "But that's her choice and her anger. I can't cope with it now, but I hope she'll come around someday."

Asked how he feels about the whole experience, he says, "I'm really glad Linda found me when she did. I don't feel the anger and frustration of other adoptees I meet at adoption conferences. I've been able to resolve my feelings over the years, and I'm not hung up on adoption issues now."

Francesca

Not all young adoptees are as fortunate as Ron and Paul to have flexible adoptive parents and empathic professionals to support them. With their parents behind them, preadolescent children can integrate the experience of meeting their birth parents better than adolescents, who seem to have a more difficult time navigating the slippery slopes into the Ghost Kingdom. Because of their need to separate from parents in adolescence and to have increased autonomy, there is the danger that teenagers may try to resolve the confusing situation by splitting off the adoptive parents, just as they had previously split off the birth parents. They may, like Francesca, attempt to jump into a new *as if* self—to try to live the life that might have been.

Francesca, as she calls herself now, was named Mary Jo when she was adopted at six months. She was sixteen when she was approached by a man with grapes standing at the checkout counter in the supermarket where she worked. He smiled and said, "Hi, I'm your Dad." She remembers being angry, and thinking, "How dare he take away my choice!"

Francesca's father had planned this carefully with her mother, with whom he now had two young boys in a common-law marriage. They had initially contacted the adoptive parents, and retreated when they were rebuffed. But once they discovered that Francesca was living in a trailer home with her boyfriend and his mother, they decided to take action. They contacted the adoptive parents again to suggest that they all go into therapy, with no success. It was then the birth father took matters into his own hands and went to the supermarket.

Francesca shuttled back and forth between her adoptive home and the trailer home while she got to know her birth parents. She worried at first that they would interrupt her life, that she'd become different. "It's difficult to know what you are, what others think you are, what you think you are," she told me.

At the time she was found, Francesca looked much older than she was. She wore heavy makeup and expensive miniskirts that her adoptive father, who worked two jobs, bought her on their frequent shopping trips together. He favored her over his natural son and his passive wife, a waitress, whom he verbally abused. "I was the only thing she had," Francesca says of her adoptive mother. "I didn't want to become like her, always crying. I thought, 'Don't give me your problems. It's not my fault.'"

No one respected boundaries: her adoptive mother read her mail, went through her belongings, and listened in on her phone calls; her adoptive father came in and out of her room at will; she pawned her mother's favorite jewelry and took money from her father's safe.

Six months after she was found by her birth parents, Francesca asked if she could live with them for a week while she looked for an apartment. She stayed three years. It was rocky at first. Jealous of her brothers, she competed for her mother's attention and was seductive toward her father. She drank, kept late hours, and lied about her activities, just as she had in her other life. Her birth parents were patient and loving, but firm, as they tried to instill their values. After a year, she asked them to adopt her. It was then that they learned her adoptive father had been sexually abusive: he often came into her room naked in the middle of the night "to check on the heating." Francesca suffers from memory lapses and can't remember anything more.

When her adoptive father agreed to let the court terminate the adoption rather than face sexual charges, she became a legal member of her original family. She also became Francesca, discarding Mary Jo, her former self, just as she discarded her former family, her former friends, and her former life in order to become a completely new person. She copied everything about her birth mother: her casual dress style, the way she walked, the way she talked, the way she gestured. At an age when most girls are trying to separate from their mothers, Francesca was trying to merge with hers, as if she had never been separated. She wasn't completely successful, even though her new friends were not aware of her past. In her dreams her adoptive parents and birth parents become interchangeable, as do her new boyfriend and her old one. She still suffers from Mary Jo's low self-esteem and worries that her boyfriend will discover she is not who he thinks she is. She is studying home economics in college now, but knows that Mary Jo would be studying in a beauty school.

Sometimes Francesca finds herself signing her name with the same flourish that Mary Jo used. One Christmas Eve she secretly went back to her adoptive parents' home to pick up a present they had for Mary Jo. Another time, she tried to trick her adoptive father into paying her tuition, even though it was covered by a grant. She was unconsciously trying to reattach to her former life, but didn't know how. She was trying to reconnect to Mary Jo, the abandoned child within her, who cannot grow without her help, and whose low self-esteem she cannot shake.

Francesca sought therapy off and on while she finished college. She has her own apartment now, and is beginning to use makeup and to dress more like Mary Jo. She recently made a phone call to her adoptive brother and is beginning to feel she "owes" her adoptive parents something. She's not sure what.

"I jumped over the lake," Francesca says. "Now I have to build a bridge."

15

The Mark of Oedipus

At the back of the Oedipus saga there really stands the mysterious question of origin and the destiny of man, which Oedipus desires to solve, not intellectually, but by actually returning to the mother's womb.
—OTTO RANK

Birth, death, and incest all involve going back to the mother's womb.
—LEONARD SHENGOLD

SEVERAL YEARS AGO A MAN ASKED TO SPEAK WITH me privately after one of my talks. Seated at a nearby café, he told me that the son he and his wife had given up for adoption twenty-eight years earlier, before they married, had recently found them. His wife is now obsessed with the son, and he with her. They cannot keep their hands off each other. What should he, the husband and father, do? I was leaving town early the next morning. All I could think to suggest was that he tell his wife to be responsible, to act like a mother. And to seek some kind of counseling.

His wife called some months later to tell me that she and her husband had gone into therapy. She described the magnetic pull she had felt toward her son. As a professional woman, she had control of everything in her life—except this. She described the need she had felt to hold this lost baby, to caress him, even to take him to her breast. One thing had led to another on the last day of his first visit, until it seemed that to refuse him anything would be to reject him again. She still could not believe that she had crossed the incest barrier. "Part of it was the longing of a mother," she said, "and the other part the lust of the seventeen-year-old girl I had been."

She has not seen her son since she and her husband made his going into therapy a condition for continuing the relationship. He responded with ominous threats to their family. "How could I have been so carried away that I didn't pick up how unstable he was?" she asked. And then she answered her own question. "I believe it was primal, going back to that moment when the bond was severed. We were trying to reconnect."

THE INCEST TABOO

Since encountering this couple, I have heard many such anguished stories. Some male adoptees and their birth mothers relive the scenario of Oedipus and Jocasta, who, after being separated for years, are irresistibly attracted to each other. Some fathers and daughters find themselves in a similar scenario, as do mothers and daughters, and brothers and sisters—although only a few actually consummate their desire.[1] In adoption circles, this bewildering phenomenon is spoken about in whispers as "genetic sexual attraction."[2]

Is it genetic? If life is in the service of perpetuating our genes, as the sociobiologists tell us, do genes call out to genes when people discover the kin they've never known? Is it sexual? Or is it just the emotional need for connectedness that drives their behavior? Is it incest? Since birth parents, adoptees, and blood-related siblings are not legally related, are they breaking the incest taboo when they act on this attraction?

Taboo is an old Polynesian word that means "forbidden." The taboo against incest has existed from early times, as if primitive and ancient peoples recognized it as something both desirable and dangerous. Moral dread, horror, and shame were, and still are, associated with it. If we accept Freud's comparison of persons and things regarded as taboo with objects charged with electricity, we can get some insight into the dangerous magnetic field around the birth mother and father when they reappear in their children's lives.

Sons and Mothers

> My son was shaking fiercely, his heart pounding so hard I couldn't tell when I embraced him if it was his heart or mine.
> —A BIRTH MOTHER

The conditions said to be conducive to incest actually match those of adoption: a mother who has been absent during the child's formative years, the absence of a strong father, and a minimal age difference. Only a few cases of mother-son incest are reported in the psychological literature, and most of them describe disturbed mothers who abuse young children. The birth mothers and sons involved in genetic sexual attraction, however, are mutually consenting adults and, for the most part, of sound mind. Something is going on other than mental instability or lust. Something that is new in incest literature, if not in myth. How do we explain it?

I think we can begin to understand the libidinal pull that parents and children have toward each other if we see it on the far end of a continuum of repressed longing that has accrued over the years since separation and builds up during search and reunion. The touching and holding that they were denied with that separation can become eroticized when they return to each other emotionally regressed but in adult bodies. So powerful are their heightened feelings that some behave as if they are under a sorcerer's spell or lost, like Titania and Bottom in "A Midsummer Night's Dream."

Adoptees who experience this attraction are baffled by the uncontrollable passion that sweeps over them in reunion. A twenty-five-year-old man reported his alarm at having an erection while speaking with his mother for the first time on the phone. Mel, who had only one meeting with his mother, also spoke of feeling aroused when he first heard her voice on the phone. "I think of it like a form of masturbation, or auto-eroticism," he says. "It's like touching a part of yourself for the first time. Not literally, but symbolically—being in touch with yourself."

A thirty-year-old gay man spoke of "walking up to see my maker," as he met his birth mother in the very motel where he had been conceived. "She began to paw me like an animal. In the arms of my birth mother I began to shake. I wanted to fall asleep between her thighs, to have that physical connection. How do we negotiate?"

Another man in his thirties, who had recently found a mother only fifteen years older, called me in great agitation: "I've never felt anything like this before. She's the closest thing to me I've ever run across in my entire life. I feel an incredible bond with her. Do other people feel this way? I need to be near her, to be touched by her. To—it embarrasses me to say it—to suckle her. We laid next to each other for four nights fully clothed, but we haven't crossed any boundaries yet. I wish I could have married a woman like this. We're confused in our feelings. Tell me, is it normal?"

Unfortunately, it seems all too normal. One can only warn someone going through the experience to watch those boundaries and keep one's distance. As the psychiatrist Alexander Lowen noted: "An infant is fulfilled on the oral level, an adult on the genital level. Sucking on a teat is a nurturing act for a child, but a sexual act for a man."[3]

Some birth mothers are as caught in the gravitational pull as are the adoptees. They call it the "magnificent obsession." They describe feeling like adolescents getting ready for a date as they fuss over their makeup and clothes. Some express the wish to go away with their sons for a few months, just to hold them like babies in their arms. But they are aware of the complexities. As one woman asked, "How do you rebond to a twenty-year-old man who acts like his father, looks like your brother, and is your son?"

A birth mother remembers her shock when her twenty-three-year-old son asked if he could touch her breast during their first and only meeting. As she tried to pull away, his fingers around her breast reminded her of the way a baby holds its hands while nursing. Speaking softly but firmly, he said he "wanted to lie naked between her legs." Before she could respond, he pulled off his shirt and began tugging at hers.

"Blood is blood!" she screamed. "I'm your mother!"

He froze, and then fled the apartment. She has not heard from him since. We can see the regressed adoptee seeking to recapture that earlier state when he and his mother were still merged as one, seeking to return to his source of life and explore its mysteries.

Jung wrote of incest as the symbol of the desire of the infant to return to the lost paradise of the womb. "It is not the incestuous cohabitation that is desired, but rebirth."[4] Both adoptee and mother seem to respond to reunion as rebirthing. A mother, reunited with her son after thirty years, said: "It's like giving birth all over again—with the same nurturing love I felt toward all my babies when they were born—only much different. I want to hold him on my lap, touch him, give him a bottle, kiss him and make it all right, but he's a grown man—his needs and demands are more complicated. There are no simple answers—we are not dealing with skinned knees here, but big issues."

Another mother recalls her son starting to tremble when she sat on the couch next to him. "I want to consume you," he said. "Just suck you in. Sex is the way people do it, but that's not right for us. My need to consume you goes *beyond* sex." The mother understood what he was saying. "It's like we wanted to suck each other into our beings," she said. "I wanted to engulf him, to pull him back into my womb, and never let him go again. It wasn't a sexual, orgiastic longing. Sex would be over quickly, and it wouldn't solve the problem—just create another one."

Sex does create rather than solve problems, especially when a mother and her son bring into the relationship a need for love that they hope the other will fulfill.

A deeply depressed fifty-year-old divorcée told me about the affair she had just had with her twenty-seven-year-old son. Not too long after she found him, he divorced his wife and moved in with her. "The intensity of our love and attraction was overwhelming," she said. He looked like a combination of herself and his father, whom she had loved, and for one year he was alternately the baby at her breast and the lover in her bed. He had limited opportunities in his adoptive family, and she felt she was reparenting him with scuba diving, skiing, rock climbing, and tennis lessons. But as he moved forward quickly in the life cycle from the needy infant to the bratty adolescent, he began to rebel. He balked at doing his household duties. She, in turn, became the nagging mother, and their quarrels began.

"For months I put up with his anger and rage. He blamed me for abandoning him and for becoming his lover, as if it were all my fault." When he pulled a gun on her in one fray, she called the police. He moved out, and began dating attractive women closer to his age. She became "insanely" jealous. "I guess I feel I have no options like he does," she said. "I lived alone for years, but now I don't know how to live alone anymore. He admits he'll be jealous if I go out with anyone. He says he wants me to stay home and cook for him like a mother whenever he comes around."

It was a mother that her son wanted, and still wants. He is much like a pragmatic young man who once told me, "We did it, got it over with. Now we can go on with life." This birth mother, however, is not ready to go on. The baby and lover are still merged for her. It was not only a son that she wanted, and still wants, but a lover and the sense of being desirable that he restored to her. In such situations, a mother's own personal needs can keep her from acting appropriately with her child, just as the child can have another agenda along with craving for union. The son's need for penetrating the mother who gave him up can represent revenge and power as much as desire. Anger is mixed with love in reunion, much as joy is mixed with grief.

"Keep in mind that the Oedipal rival, the father, is absent," a therapist pointed out to me. "It makes the son's winning the mother an uncontested victory." An adopted man phrased it another way: "I'm going to play with the cosmic mother. Do spirit battle with the cosmic father." The victory is also made easy by the birth mother's wish to make up for the pain of what her surrender caused her son. She wants to give him anything he wants—the ultimate gift. As one birth mother said: "Just as she gave her body in creation, she gives her body now."

Daughters and Fathers

> "I don't feel toward you as if you were my daughter."
> "I don't feel as if you were my father."
> "What a tragedy. What are we going to do about it? I have met the woman of my life, the ideal, and it is my daughter. I cannot even kiss you as I would like to. I'm in love with my own daughter!"
> "Everything you feel, I feel."
> —ANAÏS NIN

> "Do you want to sit in the car and talk?" he asked when we left the bar on our first meeting.
> He put his arm around me and kissed me. I pulled away. "This is weird," I said.
> He smiled, pulled me back, rubbed my breast, kissed me on the mouth, and began kissing me all over my face.
> "What do you think of your old man?" he asked.
> "Handsome," I heard myself saying.
> "If we met, and didn't know, we might have married," he whispered.
> He reached for me again, but this time I got out of the car and slammed the door. It's been a year, and I still can't talk about it without crying. I'll never forgive him. And yet I know I want to see him again.
> —AN ADOPTED WOMAN

Fathers, like mothers, can be thrown back to the past when they meet the child they have not raised. The daughter returns with the youth the father has lost, and with the adoration and need that restores his old virility and pride. It is miraculous to see this younger version of the woman he once loved without the grief and recriminations that tore them apart, and to feel again the erotic energy that passed between them. The adopted woman who appears before a birth father in his likeness, or in the likeness of his former lover, or a combination of them both, is and is not his daughter, for she has been adopted and raised by another man. And he is and is not her father, for he abdicated that role before she was born. He will think he is holding a woman in his arms, but she will know it is the regressed baby who is claiming its father's unconditional love.

Nina, who is twenty-six, married, and the mother of an infant, called from another state to tell me that she was in love with her father. He is forty-two, married, with two teenage sons. She said they want to run away together to make up for all the years they've lost. "What should I do?" she asked.

Nina's mother, who wanted more time before meeting, sent the father's name instead. They had been married for a few years after giving Nina up and, as Nina was to learn from her father, had a brief affair a number of years after the divorce.

Nina's father declared his love for Nina in a bar the first night they met. He said he felt guilty that other people had taken on his responsibility. They drank a lot of beer and almost did "the act" in his van, but he stopped in time. She was angry that he stopped because she felt he was rejecting her again. "There's a little kid in me that cries 'Don't leave me' every time I'm with him," she said.

She took my suggestion that they meet only in the daytime and in public places. Sitting on park benches, they talked endlessly about their attraction to each other. "Maybe if we do it once, we'd get it out of our system," her father said. But no, they decided they'd want more.

One night Nina visited his home when his wife and children were away. They gravitated to the bedroom and once again came close to having sex. This time she wasn't angry when he stopped. By now they'd talked about the possible consequences: "We'd lose everyone, and probably each other, down the line."

And something else. She looks like her mother, who refused any contact with her after hearing from the father how attractive he found their daughter. When Nina asked him whether he'd go back to her mother if he could, and he admitted he would, she wanted to tell him to get lost. But she didn't. She couldn't let him go. "I could have sex with my birth father and not feel it is incest," she told me. "It would only be incest if I did it with my adoptive father or adopted brother."

Nina's personal definition of incest is understandable if we remember that social custom requires adopted children to act as though the adoptive parents are the real parents. If the blood-related parent returns, adoptees can rationalize their behavior on the grounds that society defines their adoptive parents as the real ones.

Nina had been sexually active when younger because it gave her the feeling of being loved. Now she was using physical holding as a way of feeling loved by her father. Were she not adopted, she might have learned that she could have her father's love without sexual proof, for these emotions are less about sex than about emotional need. I talked to her about how her father has to be helped to behave as a father and not use her as a way of recycling his past.

The last time I spoke to Nina, she felt her life was under control. She and her father have decided to cool it so that they can have a long relationship. She is being treated for an ulcer and has gone back to school. She hopes someday her mother will meet her. "I've gained my dad and his family even if I've lost what I never had—my mother," she said. "I'm trying to count my blessings and not dwell on my pain."

We could say that we are cradling our fantasies in our arms when we embrace the lost ones who are returned to us. The fantasies can be even more intense if the birth father is also an adoptee, as occasionally happens. Each has the adoptee's need for connection and unconditional love, and each has the illusion that the other will provide it.

At the age of thirty, Sharon, who is divorced, is suffering over the decision of whether or not to give up her job and move to a different part of the country to live with her birth father. "We're both composers and we're both adopted," she told me. "We'd compose together and be soul mates."

Sharon's father knew her mother in college, but they decided to give the baby up rather than marry. Remaining a bachelor, he roamed the country working in various professions. When she contacted him, he immediately invited her to visit. She went for a week, and then he followed her back to her home. "I am his only flesh-and-blood relative," she said. "He's had an adventurous life, but he's not well. He says I am his reason to live, the first woman who has taught him to love."

Sharon feels that she and her father have found the lost parts of themselves. "We're drawn by the electricity of the connection," she said. "It is an intense and pure love, unlike any other. I guard it like an angel secret. We have a pact: we will not consummate it. That would be shameful—a lashing out at the gods." But Sharon admitted she was not sure how long they could keep the pact if she makes the decision to join him.

Kaye never doubted that she would consummate her relationship with her father. While searching for him, she had a waking dream that when they met, he pulled her down on the couch and raped her. She wasn't frightened or repulsed. When he said, "This is why you feel the way you do," she understood that her strong sexual nature came from him. After she located him, she was not surprised to find that her father was sexually provocative on the phone, or that she felt herself becoming sexually aroused. She agreed to fly down to visit him alone, without her young son.

"I knew as I flew out to meet him that I needed certain psychological things, and that I couldn't stop myself from being completely trusting and vulnerable," Kaye said. "I knew, too, that in the first flush of excitement, he would have unconditional love for me. Just like with a new baby. That's why I wasn't afraid to trust him. I just hoped I could get in there, get what I needed—the psychological stuff, not the sexual stuff—and get out alive before the unconditional love faded."

During the first two days Kaye and her father took turns being seductive and encouraging, and then cautious and discouraging. "When it finally happened, it was entirely a mutual desire," she said. "It seemed natural that my search for self and my roots should take this extreme form. When I was with him, I was almost completely uninhibited. I was not afraid to say anything to him, or to touch him in any way. I had automatic trust. It was as though I was with myself."

Kaye would later feel "murderous rage" when her father refused to introduce her to his two grown daughters as he had promised, which meant she couldn't be a natural part of his family. In trying to analyze why her relationship with her father had become so sexual, she decided: opportunity; two minds thinking alike; physical closeness combined with unusual psychological excitement; and the fact that she was never a child growing up in his house. There was, on her part, she said, "a strong urge to reenact a certain scene in order to 'correct it.'"

But can that scene ever be reenacted or corrected, any more than the lost years they didn't share can be recovered? She could neither replace her mother in that moment of conception nor save her baby self from being sent out alone into the world. Kaye feels alternately depressed and resigned. "I got part of the prize anyway: strength, history, kinship, and my reflection in the mirror," she says. She got the sense of identity she was seeking, but the part of the prize that she and other adoptees who cross the incest barrier forgo is a natural relationship with that parent and the chance to become an accepted part of that parent's life.

The adoptee may have the illusion that she is recovering her father's love, but often she is little more than a conduit for all the birth father's unresolved feelings for the mother. The daughter steps into the sexually charged current that once existed between her parents as she fulfills her own needs in the Oedipal triangle. In some cases, the birth father has an affair with the mother behind the adoptee's back as well as his wife's back. It is not unknown for the birth father and birth mother to divorce their spouses and go off with each other.

Daughters and Mothers

Mothers and daughters can act with less risk on the physical need to claim each other. They can be relaxed about caressing in front of others and can sleep in the same room or bed without the fear or stigma of incest. Yet adopted women can also feel a physical craving to be reconnected with the mother. One woman spoke of wanting to see her mother's vagina as proof that she had been born: "I wanted to see where I began."

Jill, a lesbian adoptee in her early twenties, believes that all female adoptees are looking for a mother. Her fantasy mother was the "anchor" of her life: sometimes she was the Avon woman, sometimes the librarian, sometimes an actress on TV. She always attached herself to older women in her community, and was desolate when she found out that her birth mother had died in a car crash a year after relinquishing her. "I belong to the Dead Mothers' Club," she said. She acknowledges that she would have liked "to sleep with her mother, be part of her, connect and merge with her." She thinks her breast fixation is related to this, as well as her penchant for "fisting," which is inserting one's hand in the lover's vagina, going in as deep as one can—until it curls up next to the womb.

Theresa, who is also gay and in her twenties, says, "My emotional birth was when I met my mother and she didn't reject me. It was the first day I felt like a human being. Every other relationship I had fell off the face of the earth."

Theresa moved in with her mother, her mother's husband, and two younger half-siblings for a year. "In our honeymoon period, my mother put me to bed each night, read stories to me, and held me. We'd look at each other and be amazed. I recognized her smell, the feel of her body, the sound of her heart. When we touched, an electric current went through me. 'I can't hold you close enough,' my mother would say. 'I want you inside my womb again.' She made sexual overtures, but I wasn't attracted to her in that way. I was in a child mode. I wanted her to be my mother.

"We were careful with each other at first. Afraid we might break. I saw her as a savior in that early stage of reunion, not someone who was at fault. I didn't ask why she left me until I felt secure with her. Then my mother cried and I had to console her. I thought, Am I ever going to get comforted? I wanted to tell her to stop crying, and just put her arms around me and soothe me."

After that incident, Theresa could separate enough to move out of her mother's house and into the apartment of a young woman who shared her interests. Her mother was distraught: she was not ready to part with her baby. She distanced herself from Theresa for a while, divorced the husband whom she had married in the confusion of her relinquishment, and set up house with an adopted woman of Theresa's age. Now, five years later, she lives with another divorcée of her own generation, and both of them give Theresa motherly attention when she comes to visit.

Siblings

Adoptees who do not get emotional fulfillment from a reunion with the mother or father will often find it with a half- or full brother or sister. The sibling, being closer in age, resembles the fantasy parent, without the toll of time and without a history of abandonment and betrayal to cloud the relationship. Adoptees may see a mirror image of themselves in a sibling. One man said: "Intellectually and emotionally, we're stamped out of the same cookie cutter." A woman said: "When I met my brother, I saw my masculine self, the other side of my soul."

Erikson once observed that the person who comes from the same mother is attractive to one.[5] Not having grown up together, siblings separated by adoption often do not feel a strong incest barrier, but they are aware that they could be caught in an erotic riptide that could carry them off. When Mel was thinking of searching for his sister, whom he hoped would be his "other half," he worried that he would feel "uncontrollable sexuality" toward her. Siblings of the same sex can also feel this attraction. They, too, may have a need to examine each other's bodies, and to look for physical similarities. They, too, may have to fortify their boundaries.

John and his half-sister, on his birth father's side, consummated their relationship, even though both identify themselves as gay. This suggests that the erotic attraction people feel for each other in reunion can be as much an emotional need to be intimate as a sexual one. The first time John spoke with his sister on the phone, he thought, "I know her voice. I've met her."

"Searching for my mother satisfied my curiosity—I wasn't a lost boy anymore," he says. "But my sister was different. She provided what searching could not. A sense of completion. I've always felt like an alien, even though I look human. She was like the twin I always longed for, my missing piece. She makes me feel I belong to this world. I was born again. I feel alive."

This is the first time that John, who is married with five children, has been untrue to his wife with a woman. His sister was equally attracted to him, he suspects, because he looks like a younger version of their father, before he lost his hair and put on weight. "If I ever had a child, I would want the father to be just like you," she told John. He says he wasn't physically attracted to her, but wanted to give her what she wanted. They slept together one night, and he knew that she was pregnant. She was—with twins.

One baby died in utero, and the other was born with cerebral palsy, an affliction not uncommon in incest. After that, his sister broke off their relationship and refused to let him see the baby. John felt himself doomed and falling apart, as if everything was a retribution for his sin, but he was still obsessed with his sister. He persuaded his wife to move across the country with their children so that he could be near the baby—but they both knew it was to be near his sister. When I last spoke with him, he was fighting her in court for joint custody.

KEEPING A NATURAL ATTRACTION NATURAL

We have seen that some of the obsessive need for kin that emerges during search can take a sexual turn, and that lust can become part of the fierceness of reconnection. Still, not everyone who has a reunion feels genetic sexual attraction. And not everyone who does, acts on it.

One birth mother, who is married with two sons, spoke of how similar her newfound thirty-nine-year-old daughter is to her in appearance, body structure, aptitude, and psychological traits. For the past two years they have both been working to keep the attraction they feel for each other within safe boundaries.

"There was no doubt that I was 'in love' with her—just as I was with my sons when they were born," she said. "But with the help of my therapist and hers we were able to see this attraction as the natural one that a mother and newborn infant have for each other. From the beginning I was able to put my feelings into a perspective that made it safe for both of us. It was clear to me that I was her mother, and I was the one who needed to set limits. I did not have my usual drinks before dinner when I was with her, because I wanted to be completely clearheaded and in control. At one point my therapist asked me if I had fantasized what it would be like to be sexual with my daughter, and I said, 'You know, I tried to, and I couldn't even imagine it.' He said, 'Good! Your sexual taboos are working just right.' And so I had no difficulty saying to my daughter, 'I am the mother and I will keep this safe.' In that way we were able to spend as much time as we needed being close physically without being sexual. "

The daughter described the same feelings of wanting to connect and merge with her mother: "At first she held me all the time and I wouldn't let her go. Then I began to feel sexual towards her, and often had sensations of wanting to crawl back inside of her womb. Fortunately, she was an adult and a parent, and we both had good therapists who felt my feelings were okay, but I just couldn't act on them. It's been scary as hell. If I hadn't had the support I did, I probably would have turned away and considered myself a freak or a lesbian."

Nick, who is in his mid-twenties, became attracted to his sister, even though he felt "bonded" with his mother when they met. "I wanted to search from the time I was told I was adopted, at three. I found my mother six years ago when I was nineteen, and it turned out much like in my dreams, like the start of a new life. I never had to wonder again. I never had to search the crowds for a face that looked like mine. I could free up all that energy that went into wondering and hating the system that kept us apart."

Yet it was his sixteen-year-old-sister to whom Nick was drawn from the moment he saw her picture. "I was frightened by my romantic feelings for her," he admits. "I couldn't even have sex with my girlfriend before meeting her. I thought I must be some kind of pervert or something to feel this way about my sister. And when she stepped off the plane, my fears were confirmed. She was, indeed, beautiful and there was amazing chemistry between us. I was determined never to act on this feeling. During a private moment we had together, I told her I thought we had a very attractive family. She agreed, and mentioned that her friends found my picture very attractive—and she did, too. I said I felt the same about her picture. Once out in the open, it became funny and we both laughed at the humor of it or, I suspect, out of common relief that we felt the same way. With this thing acknowledged, it was no longer a source of stress, but rather a curious phenomenon that brought us closer together."

Battening Down the Hatches

As the possibility of experiencing genetic sexual attraction becomes known, adoptees, birth parents, and siblings are seeking practical ways to prepare themselves. It's not unlike bracing for an approaching hurricane—battening down the hatches. Those who are in the eye of the storm, or have been, feel safe enough to recount their experiences at support groups. Many seek counseling and the understanding of family members, read what is available on the subject, and weigh the social and psychological consequences of committing incest. Perhaps most reassuring for those hovering nervously on the brink is hearing from others that the strength of the attraction diminishes with time. The erotic feelings eventually fade as everyone moves out of the Ghost Kingdom and settles for acceptable roles within their extended family circles.

Yet I must confess that each time I hear someone's story, I am struck anew at the power of this attraction to transform seemingly normal people into tragic heroes out of Greek drama. At the same time, I know we must avoid sensationalizing it, but rather place it within the possibilities of human behavior.

"Is it incest?" I ask a psychoanalyst who specializes in sexual abuse cases.

"It's incest, but it is not what we usually mean by incest," he says. "It's not about a child being abused by an adult. We're talking here about someone growing up feeling his other half is missing. And then he enacts something as an adult that has been his childhood fantasy—not sex with the mother, but *union*. It's become sexualized, but it's about something totally else than sex. It's about feeling whole again."

"Then it's not sensational?" I ask, hoping that others will grasp it as he has.

"Sure, it's sensational," he admits. "I was blown away when I first heard about it. But then when I thought about it for a while, I thought, 'Oh, sure.'"[6]

Oh, sure, what?

As the data come in, we have to keep asking the questions: Does the unnaturalness of being separated from blood kin drive human beings to unnatural acts when they are reunited? Is our erotic arousal caused by our "selfish" genes seeking out their own kind, or by a psychological need for connection with our kin? Is it biology, memory, or fantasy that casts a spell over us? Are we in love with substance or shadow? Who will give us the answers: the scientists or the poets?

One way to understand this phenomenon is to accept the deep mystery in the attraction that family members who come together after a long separation feel for each other. And then to create a frame of reference to give meaning to the experience, as well as defensive strategies to keep it under control. This is possible if one is aware that:

- The adoptee meets the birth parent or sibling not in the legitimate world ruled by taboos but in the Ghost Kingdom, which is outside society's jurisdiction. The illicit features of the adoptee's birth, eroticized by society, become eroticized by mother and child.
- The attraction the adoptee feels is to the idealized parent rather than to the real person he or she finds. Freud said that in being in love with one's mother, one is never concerned with her as she is in the present, but with the youthful image carried over from one's childhood. The adoptee is concerned only with the idealized phantom he or she knew in the Ghost Kingdom.
- The parent or sibling, being part phantom, cannot give the adoptee the nurturance he needs. All is illusion. The adoptee is holding his own baby self, not the parent, in his arms.
- Incestuous feelings, consummated or not, are an attempt to undo the damage of rejection that the baby felt when it was sent into exile. Merging with either birth parent or a sibling is like returning home. It is not a sexual need, but a need to rebond, a need for reconnection.
- The consummated liaisons usually end up badly, with each side feeling betrayed. The adoptee may feel rejected again because the birth parent can be neither the lover nor the parent for whom he or she has yearned. Incest cannot satisfy an adoptee's insatiable need, because it

is not sex that the adoptee craves, but reconnection to undo the loneliness.

- If one feels attracted to a parent or sibling, one should avoid romantic situations and meet in family settings. One should demystify romantic feelings by speaking openly about them. One might even call a birth mother Mom and a birth father Dad as a reminder of the parental relationship.
- Whatever the adoptee's age, it is the birth parent's ultimate responsibility to behave like a parent and to set up proper boundaries that will protect everyone.

16

The Adoption Tie

Meeting my birth mother was a wonderful bonding catalyst
to the relationship with my adoptive parents. Now we can
truly claim each other.
—A MALE ADOPTEE

WHERE ARE THE ADOPTIVE PARENTS IN ALL THIS?
we must pause to ask. While the adoptees were growing up, the birth
parents were the invisible parents in their lives, but during search and
reunion it often seems that the adoptive parents become the invisible
ones. But visible or not, on stage or in the wings, the adoptive parents are
always there in the adoptee's psyche, and have an influence on the
reunion process.

The adoptee's search can be very threatening to adoptive parents
because it violates the unspoken rules of the closed adoption system on
which their parent-child relationship has been based. There are no rituals
for such a momentous event in their child's life, such as there are for bap-
tism, bar mitzvah, graduation, or marriage. No one knows how to react
when it happens. The adoptive parents are suddenly asked to accept an
alternate reality to the one in which they adopted; secrecy is to be
replaced by openness.

In searching for those once-invisible parents, the adoptee exposes the denial by which everyone has lived, as if in a gentleman's agreement. As everything is stripped away, the adoptive parents are catapulted back to their previous state of infertility and childlessness. It is a desolate time for them, even for those who gave birth to other children after adopting, as they are confronted with their earlier feelings of grief and loss around their infertility. No one—not the doctor, the lawyer, or the social worker—warned them that their children might need to seek out their origins. They tried to be good parents, and they thought that their adopted children were happy with them. I am reminded of the James Thurber cartoon in which a man says to his wife: "With you I have been happy, Lydia, and now you tell me you are going mad."

FEAR OF LOSING THE CHILD

When their reality slips like a rug out from under them, most adoptive parents are overwhelmed with fear of loss. They risk losing not only the child but the reality of their family and the continuity of their clan. They feel betrayed. The chosen baby, as one adoptee put it, "has fallen from grace." The parents may ask, "How can you do this to us?" or "Aren't we enough for you?" They may remind their child, "We're your real parents and don't you ever forget it." Some react with anger that covers over their fear and anguish. One father cut his two sons out of his will as a way of saying, "Either you are my sons or you aren't."

Still, I have noticed that no matter how distraught adoptive parents may be by the revelation of their adult child's search and ultimate reunion, they are usually able to retreat to some safety zone of their own. The eventual realization that their child has not disappeared from their lives, and still acts like their child, reassures them that blood is not necessarily thicker than water. They can still feel they are the "real" parents, if not the "exclusive" ones.

Some adoptive parents fall back on the old habit of denial that served them so well in the past, and try to go on with life as usual. They may behave as if the reunion never happened and never ask about the birth mother. Like ostriches with their heads in the sand, they want to believe that if they do not see or hear about her, she does not exist. They don't understand, as a male adoptee put it, that the purpose of searching is "to gain knowledge, not to lose or exchange people like melons after qualitative comparison."

Even adoptive parents who encouraged the reunion in the beginning may become threatened when the adoptee becomes friendly with the birth mother or father. "I thought she just needed to know some medical and family history," one adoptive mother said. "I didn't think she was going to form a relationship with her birth parents." They become doubly confused when the adoptee becomes sad and moody, not understanding why she seems unhappy now that she finally has what she thought she wanted.

Some adoptive parents find it safer to become part of the relationship than to fight it. One mother and father traveled with their daughter and her birth mother back to the town where their daughter was born, and they keep in contact with the birth mother. Others send holiday cards to the birth mother and her family, even if they have not met, and, if the adoptee approves, they may stop to introduce themselves when traveling near the birth mother's city.

FEAR OF LOSING THE PARENTS

Reunion is a two-edged sword. Just as adoptive parents fear losing their child, adoptees fear losing their adoptive parents. They may not tell their parents about their reunion, because they feel guilty about what they have done and don't want to hurt them. They also have the underlying fear that their parents will disinherit them, or even abandon them, just as their birth parents did.

One man, whose parents encouraged and paid for his search, worries because they *don't* seem threatened. Could it mean that they don't care enough about him to fear losing him? They are eager to meet the birth mother, but he has resisted bringing them together. He has also resisted getting too close to the birth mother, for fear that he will lose his fantasy of his adoptive parents as the real parents—another way of losing them.

BETWEEN TWO MOTHERS

Reunion could be described as a tale of two mothers. The birth mother originally relinquished her child to the adoptive mother, and now the adoptive mother feels that she is being asked to relinquish the child back to the original mother. Nancy Verrier writes from her perspective as an adoptive mother:

> It is not difficult to understand why many adoptive mothers are not overjoyed by the idea that their children want to search. After years of struggle and constant turmoil in the home, after the aching agony of witnessing their children relate more easily to everyone else's mothers than to them (it's safer!), they then see their children yearning to find that magical person with whom there is some undeniable, indefinable connection. It is mysterious, scary and makes many adoptive parents wonder why they subjected themselves to so much rejection and pain for this result.[1]

Verrier believes that every adoptive mother knows in her heart that her child's reuniting with her birth mother will change forever their relationship to each other. The adoptive mother may get in touch with her deeper fear—that she has never been able to replace that lost mother—and feel herself a failure. "It was an impossible goal in the first place," Verrier writes, "and she would be better off recognizing what she *did* do than regretting what she didn't, what she *couldn't* do."[2]

The adoption system is littered with regrets. The adoptive mother regrets that her child is not biologically related, and the birth mother regrets that she relinquished her child. The adoptive mother regrets that the birth mother has come back, and the birth mother regrets that she ever left. These two women, who have always been invisibly linked, try to cover up their feelings as they maneuver from their designated places on either side of the adoptee. "I bet you wish you never heard of me," a birth mother joked to the adoptive mother. "I expect you wish I didn't exist," the adoptive mother responded jocularly, knowing the uneasiness they each feel despite their friendship. "I know there are times she resents my closeness to our daughter," this adoptive mother explained to me. "And there are times I resent her being biologically related to our daughter."

Some adoptive mothers insist on meeting the birth mother, and some birth mothers insist on meeting the adoptive mother. The issue of status is at play here. The adoptive mother may feel a need to protect her role as mother, and the birth mother may feel a need to be acknowledged by the adoptive mother. Each needs the other to establish the authenticity of her slightly tarnished credentials, for, on some level, the adoptive mother does not feel she is entitled to claim the adoptee, just as the birth mother does not feel she is entitled to reclaim the adoptee. Each mother is threatened by the other. The adoptive mother worries that the birth mother will be critical of what she did or did not do for her child; the birth mother worries that the adoptive mother will be critical of her for giving up a child.

There is a lot of primitive energy going on between these two women, not unlike the kind that passes between women who love the same man.

One adoptive mother who admitted feeling "deep fear, anger, and resentment" for the birth mother could also admit to feeling a "spiritual closeness" bordering on love. "I've always felt a bond with you, that in many ways we were soul-sisters because we shared Michelle," she said. The birth mother felt secure enough to respond, "Now that I have found Michelle—seen her in life—I can let go of her. But I also have to say your joy and gain was only possible through my pain and loss."

Michelle and her adoptive father were struck by the connection between the two women. "Dad said that he thought you and my mother might form a relationship that is separate from me," Michelle wrote her birth mother. "I agree with him in the sense that there are emotions that you two share that are unique to motherhood. The rest of us can only try to understand these feelings." But after their second meeting, the relationship seems to have become too intense and threatening for Michelle's adoptive mother. She stopped writing to the birth mother, and shortly after that Michelle stopped too. The birth mother is left with the hope that the bond the adoptive mother shared with her is still there in some part, "only gone underground until she is able to trust me with Michelle."

Verrier believes that no matter how much the two mothers hurt inside, they must act in the relationship as mature adults in control of their actions. The mothers have to put the child's interests ahead of theirs, otherwise the adoptee is back in the chalk circle, being pulled apart by two mothers.

The author and adoptive parent Lois Melina points out that when an adoption opens as a child is growing up, the adoptive mother is not as threatened as when it happens later. The young child is still dependent on her for everything, and doesn't call out for his birth mother in the middle of the night. But when the adult adoptee has left his nest and nurturer behind, the adoptive mother wonders, What role do I have? Should the adoptee search for his birth mother, she may feel that her worst fears are coming true.[3]

TESTING THE
ALTERNATE REALITY

Adoptees are always relieved to find that their adoptive mother and father have survived the news of their search and reunion, especially when they were sure it would "kill" them. They need their parents to be there for them as they do their trapeze act of swinging out into the unknown as much as they did when they were little—if not more. They need their parents to accept their emotional ups and downs, their moods and crying spells, without taking them personally. They need the security of their adoptive bond to return to as they test the strength of their birth bond.

While it is important for adoptive parents to be part of the reunion process, however, it is also important for them to understand that the adoptee may have to make most, if not all, of the journey alone. It can be hard for adoptive mothers to stay on the sidelines. They want to go with the adoptee to meet the birth mother and are hurt if they are not included in the reunion plans. But just as the secrecy in the adoption system forced the adoptee to keep the birth mother split off in the Ghost Kingdom, so now it is hard for the adoptee to mend that split. Some adoptees feel possessive about the phantom mother who lived in their secret fantasies, and worry that the adoptive mother, like the wicked stepmother in fairy tales, will somehow try to banish her once again. Adoptive mothers have to be strong enough to understand that this is a phase the adoptee may go through in the reunion process.

Gail, an eighteen-year-old adoptee whose adoptive mother set up a meeting with the birth mother against her wishes, said: "I was furious because I didn't want her in that part of my life. For the first time I felt like I had something that was mine, totally mine, and I didn't want someone to take it away from me. My adoptive mother continued to call my birth mother occasionally after that, even though she knew it upset me greatly. My birth mother knew it too and asked her to stop."

Adoptees often go from struggling over who is the real mother to which is the real family. Some feel a need to dive into that alternate reality to find answers. This may mean disappearing into the birth mother or birth father's life, as if trying it on for size, as they experiment with what might have been. It may take months, or even years, before they can find a secure place between the realities that is theirs.

Gail moved in with her birth father's large family after her adoptive parents tried to maintain control by setting strict curfews. "I had a very strange sense of freedom and power over my life for the first time, and was not about to give that up," she recalled. The psychologist whom her adoptive parents insisted she see said that everyone needed to "stop grabbing for a piece of her." For the next six months, her adoptive parents had to remain on the sidelines while Gail's reunion drama played itself out. And Gail herself had to remain on the sidelines while her birth father and birth mother began a brief drama of their own—an affair that sometimes made them more involved with each other than with her. When her father became quarrelsome after drinking one night, Gail moved back to her adoptive home—"partly out of guilt and partly because of the tension." Though she continued to see her birth parents and their families, her adoptive parents refused to have any contact with them.

A MOTHER'S GIFT

Some adoptees see an adoptive mother who initiates or takes over her child's search as invading her child's boundaries and taking away his autonomy. But, in some cases, the adoptive mother is giving her child a gift by sanctioning what until then has been taboo. There are adoptees who would never dare to venture into that forbidden area of the self without the adoptive mother's guidance. As we saw with Paul, some adoptees may not object if the adoptive mother offers her help, but would never risk the journey alone.

When Joyce was twenty, her adoptive mother, with whom she had always been close, asked if she ever thought of searching for her birth mother. Joyce admitted it had crossed her mind that it would be nice, but she didn't think it would be possible. A week later her mother ran into the house screaming excitedly, "I found her!" She had called the birth mother before breaking the news to be sure that Joyce wouldn't be rejected. Joyce's birth mother had been very receptive to meeting the daughter she never expected to see again.

"It's been a fantastic reunion, even though it's had its ups and downs," says Joyce thirteen years later. "We talk on the phone every month. I argue with her like my own mother. I'm so like her, and it's good for me to see things in her that I have to fight in myself. My adoptive parents raised me like Mr. Rogers—they were ideal parents. I want to raise my kids the same way, which means not losing my temper and running hot and cold, like my birth mother does." Joyce is glad her adoptive mother searched. "I think it's the most unselfish act a person can do for their child. I don't have to carry guilt."

It is possible that the respect Joyce has always had from her adoptive parents makes her feel that none of her control has been taken away. When the communication lines are open, an adoptee can share the birth mother and father with her adoptive parents as in an extended family. But while this is the goal for future reunions, most adoptive parents are as yet too threatened to include the birth parents in their lives.

HOLIDAYS AND OTHER POTENTIAL STRESSORS

Weddings

"There should be a 'proper etiquette' book to help with difficult situations that come up after reunion," Gail said, referring to the crisis that erupted over her marriage plans. "My adoptive parents didn't handle things well in the beginning, and they were adamant that my birth parents not be at my wedding. My adoptive mother was still fuming that my birth mother had called herself my 'mother' when she left a phone message for me at their house. But I wanted my birth parents there. Since my birth father was one of the most important people in my life, and my birth mother paid for my wedding dress, I didn't think it was right that they couldn't see me walk down the aisle. My parents compromised with having them just come to the church, but not to the reception and dinner."

Gail is now living with her husband in another part of the country and is in touch with all of her families. "My adoptive parents are very loving when I am not living at home, but when we get together there is tension because of my continuing relationship with my birth parents. I feel I just have a bigger family. And I have an identity now—I feel like someone."

Weddings can also be an opportunity for adoptive parents and birth parents to meet for the first time in a festive way. Susan was thrilled when her adoptive parents suggested that her birth parents come from Europe with their families for her wedding. "I will have four mothers there," she said: "my adoptive mother, my birth mother, my stepmother, and my mother-in-law." She had not seen her birth mother since her trip to Paris, and had withdrawn from the relationship for some time afterward while resolving her feelings of grief and anger. Now she was ready to have all her families come together.

Alan's adoptive parents welcomed the idea of having his birth parents at his wedding, but the problem was that Hannah, his birth mother, refused to come if his birth father, Benny, was invited. Benny didn't mind Hannah being there, and expressed his wish to attend. Alan was caught in the middle of their unresolved issues, but felt he had to give in to his birth mother on this one.

Not all birth mothers feel entitled to take part in the wedding. One mother refused her daughter's request that she walk down the aisle with the whole wedding party saying, "Don't make me do that—don't ask me to make a spectacle of myself." It was as if she feared that the scarlet letter birth mothers wear emblazoned on their souls would be seen, as was Hester Prynne's, by "a thousand unrelenting eyes."

A birth father who felt that meeting his twenty-three-year-old daughter had helped him communicate more honestly with all the people he loved saw her wedding as an opportunity to sort out who he was in her life and who she was in his. "The event forced clarity. It was obvious to me that I was her birth father. But I was not her dad. I came to her wedding. But I did not go to the reception. I felt my place was not there—that part of the day belonged to her adoptive family."

Grandchildren

An unexpected time of tension that can test everyone's generosity of spirit is the arrival of a grandchild. One adoptive mother informed a birth mother, even before her daughter was pregnant: "The grandchild is *mine*." The birth mother responded: "I signed away my child, but *not* my grandchildren."

Even when the relationship between the two mothers has been going well, the arrival of a grandchild can ruffle it. Marcia, an adoptive mother, remembers having her grandchild taken out of her arms by the proud birth mother, who wanted to show him to her own parents, the birth grandparents. Watching the scene, Marcia realized that the room was filled with generations of the birth family, and that everyone, except her, was genetically connected to the baby. She left early, feeling that she was on the outside looking in, much as her daughter must have felt when surrounded by the adoptive clan on holidays. "My daughter shares something with me that her birth mother can't share," she says. "But the grandchild is new to both me and the birth mother; he is no more mine than hers."

Mother's Day

There are moments during reunion when adoptees would gladly have the word *mother* dropped from the English language. Many adoptees call their birth mother by her first name, but they may refer to her as "my mother." Adoptive mothers don't want to share the rank of "mother" with that "other mother" on most days, but especially on Mother's Day. Birth mothers try to be sensitive on the issue for the sake of the adoptee, but, in private, they assert that they are also the mother. Mother's Day can become a torment for everyone, as adoptees fret over whether they are expected to send the birth mother a card; the birth mother frets over whether she will receive one and whether she should send one; and the adoptive mother frets over whether the birth mother is going to get one.

I still remember how conflicted I felt when my birth mother sent me a Mother's Day card headed "To My Daughter" shortly after our meeting, as if even reading it were a betrayal to the mother who raised me. But as I watch adoptees struggle over these split loyalties on Mother's Day, I recognize it as a stage that some go through in the reunion process. I can even smile when I think of one teenager who was so tired of her adoptive mother and birth mother, who had become friends, colluding about everything, even her curfews, that she resolved the Mother's Day problem by not sending either of them a card.

BRINGING THE
PARENTS TOGETHER

While theoretically it sounds like a wonderful idea to bring all one's parents together, in reality it is difficult to do. Many adoptees keep putting it off for another day, or another year. Having kept their two sets of parents in separate psychic spheres, it is not easy to change that arrangement. They may want to preserve their own private world with their birth family until they have explored that relationship. And they may fear that the very parents who stood between them and their birth parents in the past will try to stand between them again. One woman admitted, "I felt almost as if my adoptive parents might take my birth mother away from me. This was definitely the child in me reacting, but it was a feeling I needed to work through."

Adoptees worry that the adoptive parents will silently judge the birth mother because of the taint attached to her unwed status during the pregnancy. They feel protective toward this mother, who is, after all, a part of their original self. But they also feel protective toward the adoptive parents, who are vulnerable in the presence of the woman who can pull the rank of blood on them.

The stigma, implicit in the secrecy around the adoptee's origins and the adoptive parents' infertility, arrives like an uninvited guest at a meeting between the parents and makes everyone ill at ease. No matter how high they have climbed in the world, the adoptive parents are once again the powerless, infertile couple who cannot produce their own child, and the birth mother is once again the confused, traumatized young woman who cannot provide for her own child.

When her birth mother came to town, Kaitlin actually encouraged her to meet her adoptive parents. She felt she had to deal with everyone's emotions in order to make her reunion work. She wanted them all to get along, to know that they had done "an okay job" so that everyone could live "happily ever after." Yet Kaitlin wasn't sure it was a good idea when she saw how difficult it was for her adoptive mother to see the woman who had given birth to her, and for her birth mother to see the house where she grew up. "I rushed the meeting," she said. "But I feel closer to my adoptive parents now. They've spoken about their infertility for the first time, what they went through. We had never talked about that. I got to know them on an adult level."

Sarah's adoptive mother refused to meet her birth mother, but she did agree to appear on a TV program with Sarah. "She was eager to show other adoptive parents that this is a workable situation and not something to be shunned or feared," Sarah explained. "However, ten years later when I told her I was having my birth mother over for a week, she absolutely flipped out. She reacted then as maybe she ought to have reacted when I first communicated with the 'other side.' She got over it and life went on, but I'll never forget her vehemence, her anger, and almost disbelief at what I was doing."

Some adoptive parents and birth parents manage to overcome whatever ambivalence and nervousness they feel for the sake of the adoptee. Some are even surprised at how much they have in common. The writer Jane O'Reilly, who was found by her thirty-two-year-old daughter, Emily, describes what it was like for her to meet the adoptive parents:

> We had lunch at Emily's parents' house. Her real parents. I can't think of an analogy to the experience. Perhaps meeting my son's future in-laws will be something like it, if he is marrying someone I like. I simply trusted that my daughter had not been given to people who were abusive or mad or mediocre. The worst scenario I allowed myself to consider was that she might grow up in a household where the people did not turn off the television set when company came. I never, in my wildest dreams, imagined the perfect parents she has, generous even to the point of encouraging her to look for me. It is enough to make me take seriously the idea of grace.
>
> The table was round, in front of glass doors, opening onto deep woods. I looked around the circle. The baby. Emily. Her parents. Me. The baby's father. Emily is not married to him. No one thinks they are living in sin.
>
> Isn't it interesting how once abortion was legalized, it was no longer a disgrace for a middle-class woman to have a baby out of wedlock? Emily, unlike me, had a choice. In a way I have spent my entire adult life fighting for her right to make that choice.
>
> "It is odd," I said to Emily's adoptive father, "how things turn out."
>
> "Very odd," he agreed.[4]

RECLAIMING THE ADOPTIVE PARENTS

We can see how complex it is for everyone when the seemingly immutable closed adoption system, which has shaped and distorted everyone's reality, collapses under its own weight. One has to search for new psychic quarters and, in the meantime, may try to camp out in the ruins of the old. The niceties of civility may be sacrificed for the certainties of survival, as adoptive parents try to hold on to an adoptee who may be equally disoriented.

One of the many paradoxes in search and reunion is that adoptees often find their adoptive parents when they find their birth parents. Once the barrier of secrecy has been lifted, they are able to see their adoptive parents in a new way. They can share their feelings with them and open up communication channels that had been clogged by secrecy. Janet observed, "Before, I thought all the bad things in me came from my narcissistic adoptive mother, and all the good things came from my perfect birth mother. By getting rid of my fantasy of a perfect birth mother, I can get rid of the bad adoptive mother I have inside me."

Mel felt his reunion affected his relationship with his adoptive mother in a positive way. "At first she was hurt by the knowledge that I had looked up my mother, and showed no interest in meeting her, but she became supportive in ways that surprised me later. When she saw I was disturbed at not hearing from my birth mother, she offered to check our hometown newspaper obituaries for news of her death."

Gail says, "Now that I have had some time to get to know my family of origin and have experienced the reality that they will not leave me again, I feel more comfortable with my adoptive parents. I can enjoy them and regard them as loving individuals who raised me and cared very much for me. I no longer have the same need to categorize them as 'real' or 'unreal' parents."

Sarah is relieved that her search has brought her closer to her formal, and often critical, adoptive mother. "It made me realize that I will never be the daughter she always wanted, but that I could respect her and even love her if I didn't always look at what I wasn't in her eyes. I was able to turn around and look at myself, and feel good about what was going on inside of me."

Alan remains close to his adoptive mother despite his ongoing relationship with his birth mother. "Nothing has changed," he says. "I'm emotionally like Hannah, but my psychological bond with my adoptive mother is beyond things like that. When something good happens to me, I want to call my mom and tell her."

An adoptee who used a "constant shadowy awareness of a birth mother out there somewhere" to distance her adoptive mother is now able to make her adoptive mother the real one. "And that's been really wonderful," she says, "because she's a very dear, sweet person in her late seventies. I think it's time I finally let her be my mother."

I like to think that in the future the reunion process will be easier for everyone, parents and adoptees alike. I'm hopeful when I listen to young adoptees setting out on the journey, such as the one who says that she wants all her friends, her former teachers, her adoptive family, and everyone important in her life to be present when she meets her birth mother for the first time. She even wants television cameras there!

What she is saying is that she wants to make it all *real*. By bringing everyone—all the inhabitants of the Ghost Kingdom and all the inhabitants of her adoptive life—together as witnesses, and having the meeting recorded on camera, she can bring her two worlds together into one.

PART III

The Self in Transformation

Man's real home is not a house,
but the Road, and life itself
is a journey to be walked on foot.
—BRUCE CHATWIN

17

Becoming Whole

> You see the one that I am, not the one that I was.
> But the one that I *was* is also still part of myself.
> —JEAN AMERY

A FEW YEARS AGO, WHILE I WAS DEVELOPING MY IDEAS on how the adoptee splits off a part of the self, I noticed a *New York Times* review of a photographic exhibit of a house that had been split in two. The artist, Gordon Matta-Clark, had literally cut a house in half and then shot it from different angles. I was intrigued that this form of conceptual art is known as "splitting," and could not resist a chance to see the split psyche of a house.[1] That afternoon I set out with my white Standard poodle, Basket, for a long stroll to the midtown gallery. I learned from the background material on the artist, who had died of cancer at thirty-five, that he was a twin and had been fascinated by women with large dogs.

The house that Matta-Clark split had been abandoned. He sawed it in two and photographed both halves, including the "negative space" between them. Formerly dark, concealed areas were now open to sunlight and fresh air, and took on a new appearance—we might even say a new identity. The review said that the show was exhilarating and haunting, charged by a high level of ambition and a sense of absence.

As I walked through the exhibit, I tried to imagine photographs of the split psyche of the adoptee, with its sense of absence. The Artificial half, seemingly there because of its material furnishings, on one side; and the Forbidden ghost half, the absent part, populated by absent people, on the other. And in between, the negative space, which is the abyss.

I saw how this negative space could have the same positive effect on the adoptee as it did on the house, lighting up dark corners of the psyche and revealing what was formerly unseen.

The similarity ends there. Matta-Clark's goal was to illuminate the dark unconscious of a house but leave it split. The adoptee's goal is to illuminate the dark unconscious of the self and make it whole.

MYTHIC RETURN

> So home drew Odysseus, who then set off again because it is not necessary to be in a specific place, in a house or town, to be one who has gone home.
> —A. BARTLETT GIAMATTI

In the course of this narrative, we have seen the adoptee as the divine child abandoned at birth; as the split self who lives an *as if* life; as the rebel who dares to break taboos; as the hero who goes on a journey through the primal depths of the Ghost Kingdom in order to be born again; and as the exile who tries to return home.

In myth, the hero does not complete the journey until he returns with the treasure he has won. Joseph Campbell tells us that this means he must "knit together" his two worlds.[2] In psychological terms, it means that reunion is not the end of the adoptee's journey, but just another station along the way.

Adoptees are often perplexed after reunion: they thought that just the sight of the birth mother or father, or a member of the birth family, would render them whole. Instead, they may feel more fragmented than before. They have lost the self that they started off with and have not yet found the self for which they searched. The high peaks of transformation still lie ahead. In order to scale them, adoptees must find a way to heal the split in the divided self. This means realigning the self, bringing together all the pieces to make it whole.

In order to achieve this:

Adoptees must weave a new self-narrative out of the fragments of what was, what might have been, and what is. This means they must integrate their two selves: the regressed baby who was abandoned and the adult that baby has become.

They must make the Artificial Self real, and allow the Forbidden Self to come out of hiding. They must integrate what is authentic in these two selves, and balance the power between them. It is during this period that the adoptee feels most vulnerable, because neither self is in charge.

They must integrate the internal and external birth mother (the fantasy and the actual one) into a composite birth mother. They must accept her for what she is, with her strengths and her weaknesses, and find forgiveness for the past.

They must integrate the internal and external adoptive mother (the one they resisted and the one they can now claim) into a composite adoptive mother. They must accept and forgive her, too.

They must integrate the birth father and the adoptive father in the same way.

They must accept that they cannot be fully the birth parents' child any more than they could be fully the adoptive parents' child. They must claim their own child, become their own person, and belong to themselves.

It is a formidable undertaking—and too late to turn back. At this stage of the journey, adoptees often feel they are not in control. They feel naked, exposed, and frightened, as if they were in a rowboat out on the high seas, lashed by overpowering waves of emotion rising out of the deep. One wrong move and they could be pitched overboard.

"How do we heal?" adoptees ask. Behind the question is the unspoken fear: "Can we heal?"

During a trip to Hawaii, I met a therapist who had been invited to work with a group of adoptees who were in various stages of search and reunion. The adoption experience was new to him, but he was no stranger to grief and loss and pain. He was an empathic man, and he seemed puzzled. He said that the adoptees in his group, and the ones he has begun to see in private practice, seemed traumatized. They do not shed their symptoms like his other patients. Their trauma seems deeper, as if it were very early—almost as if it were cellular.[3]

Trauma *is* earlier for adoptees than for most other people, I told him. It begins at birth, with separation from the mother. And it's more persistent because adoptees have no *pre-traumatic self*.[4] And then I explained what I meant by this.

We know that when adoptive parents have been traumatized by not being able to conceive a child, they already have adult selves that can absorb and work through the shock. So too, the birth mother may have been young when she was traumatized by her unwanted pregnancy, but she had a self to fall back on as she continued her life. But the adoptee, who experienced separation and loss early in life, usually at birth, has no previous self—no pre-traumatic self—from which to draw strength. And so we may well ask: How do adoptees heal?

HOW DO ADOPTEES HEAL?

The trauma specialist Judith Herman tells us that just as helplessness and isolation are the core experiences of psychological trauma, so are empowerment and reconnection the core experiences of recovery.[5] Adoptees must search for ways to find that empowerment and reconnection with the same energy they used in searching for their origins. There is no other way; for healing, like life, is a process. As we have seen, the path to healing is the search for the missing pieces of the self.

The Search

The very idea of search is empowering, no matter what the outcome. As one adoptee said, "It's not *what* you find, but *that* you find." For many adoptees, the healing begins when they take control of their lives by making the decision to search, and it continues imperceptibly with each victory along the way, each name or address or telephone number. Like the Old Man of Whitehaven, who danced a quadrille with a raven—"though they said it's absurd to encourage that bird"[6]—adoptees dance for the first time to their own tune.

"Acknowledging the need to search was like a declaration of independence," Lee said. "That alone was one of the biggest steps I have taken toward my own health and well-being." A man admitted, "I never enjoyed myself so much as when I did what they said I couldn't do. I followed a voice inside me that said, 'If you want to do it—do it.'"

Adoptees are empowered when they learn to confront very frightening emotions—such as the fear of being rejected by the birth mother—and find they are still alive after it. One man, whose birth mother not only refused to meet him but dismissed him on the telephone (saying, "If you want answers, see a psychiatrist; if you want a companion, get a dog"), expected to fall apart at any moment. In the past, he would have turned to alcohol and drugs. Now he was amazed at his own resilience, and began to realize that he had been made strong by confronting the challenges in the search itself. "For me, the healing in search is through the process, not the outcome," he said. "You give birth to yourself. You are your own midwife."

Another man, who found the search so threatening that he needed six months' sick leave from work, found such a responsive birth mother that he had to ask her not to call him every night. "I needed to risk rejection and abandonment and fear, and know it would be okay, that I would live," he said. "I feel healed. I can present myself as a whole unit."

Therapy

The search, then, is ultimately healing, but, as we have seen, it creates new problems in that it requires a reordering of the self. Some adoptees sail through this without outside help, but for others the journey is too difficult to make alone. A therapist can be an invaluable traveling companion if he or she is empathic to the quest. It is difficult, however, to find therapists who know the way. Many professionals are in the same denial as the rest of society about the adoptee's invisible connection to the invisible birth parents. I know adoptees who have gone through years of therapy, even psychoanalysis, without the subject of adoption ever coming up.

A perceptive therapist can help the adoptee who has been through search and reunion to integrate the Artificial and Forbidden selves, so that an authentic core self can take over. During this period, when it seems that no self is in charge, the adoptee may despair that the emotional chaos will never end. "I feel like a battle is going on between the outside me, who always tried to be congenial and never depressed, and the inside me, who is trying to change by expressing her feelings," says Robin. "The inside me feels trapped." Through therapy, she is learning that it is all right to express her anger. "I'm starting to let the storm exist outside of me so that it is not so intense on the inside. But the outside me says no, that will offend and push people away." The battle continues, but the intensity lessens as Robin learns that people don't disappear when she expresses her real feelings.

Gradually, the adoptee's core self will emerge—one that retains a sensibility for the needs of others that the Artificial Self so carefully honed, along with the ability to express one's own needs and to assert oneself. The goal for the adoptee is to feel that he has a right to exist, and to stake the claims that come with such entitlement.

It is not so much the kind of training as the sensibility of the therapist that is crucial. Some adoptees are helped by traditional psychotherapy. Others by bioenergetics, which places stress on work with the body as a way of releasing the frozen feelings within. One woman was grateful to primal therapy for making it possible for her to feel and reexperience her unfelt pains, rather than having to act on them.

I remember my amazement when an adoptee spoke of being cured by a hypnotherapist in *one* session. She'd had a breakdown after her birth mother ended their stormy six-year relationship rather than reveal the birth father's name. Three years of psychotherapy didn't lift her depression, and so Maggie decided to take a chance with the hypnotherapist.

"How did he do it?" I asked, ready to jump on the next plane and try it myself.

She described how the hypnotherapist took her back in time to the delivery room where she had just been born.

"The baby needs to give the mother something," he said.

"What?" she asked.

"A present. I have it here."

"What is it?"

"A small box wrapped in pretty paper."

"What's the mother going to do with it?"

"She is going to open it."

"What's inside?"

"Something bigger than she is."

"What's that?"

"The baby's pain," the hypnotherapist said. "You're giving it back to her. She has to open it every year on the baby's birthday."

Then the hypnotherapist said: "Now the mother has something to give the baby. It's another present."

"Does the baby open it?" she asked.

"Yes."

"What's inside?"

"A note."

"What does the note say?"

"It says: 'I'm sorry.'"

Even if this adoptee isn't completely cured, her depression has lifted. Her birth mother had not been able to recognize her pain, and to say that she was sorry. The hypnotherapist's exercise enabled the adoptee to hear that message, even if her birth mother could not deliver it.

Becoming Healers

Adoptees heal by becoming healers.

We could say that adoptees have always been healers. As babies, they healed the birth mother by going off to be raised by another clan. They healed the adoptive parents by sacrificing their own history and heritage so that the adoptive family line could be continued. By becoming replacement children for the child who never was or the child who died, they healed the adoptive parents' infertility.

Because as children they have to have empathy for their adoptive parents' needs, adoptees develop an enhanced sensitivity for the feelings of others. Some become mental health professionals, often working within the adoption system to change it. Others train to be teachers, physicians, or religious leaders.

Joining Adoption Support Groups

The Indians have a saying: Sorrow shared is halved, and joy shared is doubled. Adoptees find this to be true when they join one of the hundreds of adoption support groups that have sprung up across the country. There they come into contact with other adoptees who intuitively understand them. They have a lot in common, for, though they are not from the same family, they are from the same family system. They have experienced the same family dynamics and taboos. They are relieved to know that they are not crazy, that other people think and feel just as they do. Nothing is forbidden. They can express the anger that has been bottled up inside. And the grief. They are validated.

These meetings also give adoptees the chance to meet birth mothers who have searched or been found. They gain insight into the birth mother experience—the forces at play that caused her to give up her child and the years of emptiness and anguish that followed. By listening to these birth mothers, adoptees begin to glimpse the psychological complexities involved: a birth mother does not believe she is abandoning her child when she places it for adoption; she does not forget the child or forgive herself; she may not feel she is entitled to search for her child; and she worries about the feelings of the adoptive parents.

Adoptees also empower themselves by taking part in political and educational action organized by the support groups. This often involves working for open records in their state legislatures. One group organizes protest marches to Washington. Others participate in the annual "Open My Records Day" in their own communities. Local and national groups organize conferences with workshops on the psychological issues in adoption and the need for adoption reform. They go on radio and television to reach the public with their stories and message.

I have noticed that very few adoptive parents or professionals attend adoption support group meetings or conferences. Those who do often complain about the pain and anger adoptees and birth mothers express there. An adoptive mother who counsels new adoptive parents told me she would not advise them to attend such meetings because it would be too upsetting. Yet it is from those who have grown up adopted that adoptive parents can learn about the inner feelings of their own children who are just starting out on the journey. Rather than avoiding or denying the very real hurt that adoptees feel, but have not been able to express except at such gatherings, adoptive parents and professionals should open themselves up to what everyone has split off until now. It is time for everyone to come together in mutual healing.

One social worker found that the shock of attending an adoption conference had been a healing experience in that it woke her up to "the horror of my own complacent self-righteousness" about the work she had been doing. "I went home thinking that I wanted out of adoption," she said. "But then I realized that I had never really been in it before. So I decided to get in it, for real this time, and work for change."[7]

Not a few adoptees attend other kinds of support groups as well, for adoptive families are prone to the same addictions that other families have. Adoptees who were raised in alcoholic families, or who are themselves recovering alcoholics, attend meetings that address those problems. A few adoptee groups have designed their own twelve-step programs for the special needs of the adopted. Adoptees can also be found at such meetings as Alanon, Overeaters Anonymous, Narcotics Anonymous, and Children of Divorce.

Other Paths Toward Healing

"My guts twist for adoptees who can't have reunion," an adopted woman told me. "They don't have a chance to deal with reality." I thought of this a few years ago when I spoke at a psychiatric meeting in Ireland and was asked by a young doctor whether an adoptee must search in order to heal, or whether there were other ways.

It was a very good question, and one for which there is no definitive answer. "There are other ways to heal, of course," I replied. "But, if possible, finding one's heritage is the best, for it enables the adoptee to become grounded in biological and historical reality. The very difficulty of the search is a commitment to the transformation of the self." Yet I know there will always be adoptees who cannot risk the search. And there will be others who, for the various reasons discussed earlier, cannot reconnect. This does not mean they cannot heal.

Arthur, the writer who looks for love in the Ghost Kingdom, has still not been able to find his birth mother. He suspects that the name has been falsified. "I think adoption is so incredibly sad that we can only address it in parts," he tells me. "Perhaps when one severs the mother-child bond at birth, one creates a pain too intense to confront. I hope not." His way of coping with it has been to join the adoptee support group in his area and take part in adoption conferences. "At least I know I am not alone in this," he says. "There are five million of us, some of whom have awakened. Perhaps the pain is better endured when it is shared." Arthur has also found it healing to write a memoir of growing up adopted, which he published himself.

Alice Miller tells us that traumatic experiences that occur in early childhood and are repressed often find expression in the creative works of painters and poets. When she began painting as an adult, Miller found that the repressed feelings of her childhood—"the fear, despair, and utter loneliness"—emerged. She was able to see what lay "behind the dark curtain" concealing her forgotten past.[8]

Adoptees—searchers and nonsearchers alike—express their unique experience in literature, painting, theater, music, dance, and photography.

Art

In the art exhibits that adoptees hold at their conferences, one can find sculptures and canvases from the Ghost Kingdom: babies falling through space, pregnant women floating by without faces, children's heads that are splintered as if by shattered glass, bodies that are protected by guardians of sharp, steel spikes. One can also encounter gentler images of mothers and babies, whole or fragmented, but melded together. One exhibit by adolescent adoptees called "Faces of Adoption: Feelings We Wear Outside and Feelings We Hold Inside" revealed white plastic masks split in half by color or decorated with bright images on the outside and darker images on the inside.

Photography

Linda Kozloff has put together a book of photographic images, *Guided by Angels,* dedicated to her birth mother, who died of cancer at the age of forty-four. In her introduction, she writes:

> I wish to convey the message of union, family, love, and the some-times painful decisions and mistakes we make in our lives. I also wish to share this imagery and story with others who may be walk-ing a similar path. . . .

> My children were "angel guides" for me when I was weak and frus-trated and in so much pain from the darkness of not knowing who I was. Their lives spurred me on in hopes of making the connection to solve not only my mystery, but theirs as well.[9]

What strikes me about Linda's sepia photographs is their sensuality. She has given bodies to the disembodied fugitives from the Ghost Kingdom. The unashamed nakedness of mothers and fathers and chil-dren, partially draped in translucent gauze, reminds the viewer that this is the way we began, with that innocence and connectedness. Some-times the body of a woman or man lies alone, revealing his or her isolation and pain. Sometimes a body is intertwined with a baby or child.

Accompanying some pictures are excerpts from the letter Linda's birth mother wrote to the agency: "Life has been difficult to face, knowing the baby and I are so far apart." There are quotes from a letter her father sent Linda before they met: "I have a knot in my heart, not knowing how to ease the pain for you and me."

"This book is meant to bring peace and hope to others," Linda writes.

"I believe it is my duty to myself and all those on the path of adoption, the ultimate search for self."

Literature

The writer Harold Brodkey, an adoptee who is not involved in the adoption movement, once told me: "You use adoption as a form of freedom—it separates you from the norm." But he could have been talking about himself. In his long-awaited novel *The Runaway Soul,* and in many of his short stories, the protagonist is an adopted boy very much like himself who is unable (unwilling?) to break the connection he still feels with his dead mother:

> I have to imagine Ceil—I did not know her; I did not know my mother. I cannot imagine Ceil. She is the initial word. Everything in me having to do with knowing refers to her. The heart of the structures of my speech is my mother. It is not with my mother but with Ceil in her own life that my speech begins. . . . What I am is her twisted and bereaved and altered and ignorant heir. She died when I was two. I died as well, but I came to life again in another family, and no one was like her, everything was different.[10]

Brodkey says he decided to become a writer at the age of eight because he didn't know any way to find meaning except by writing things down. "Childhood trauma is not masterable," he declared. "Life is always a defense against grief. You're below sea level, like the Netherlands."

And yet with each story Brodkey writes about that adopted boy—that "genetic orphan," as he calls him—he is trying to master the trauma. He is trying to write his way into existence, as if he can materialize only through that motherless child. Every morning at his writing desk he seeks freedom from the burden of being adopted, but by late afternoon, as the shadows lengthen, he says he becomes depressed. The next morning, like Sisyphus, he is at his desk once more, trying "to recover the unrecoverable past," to escape what he calls "the literalness and finality of mother-loss."[11]

"Brodkey is all adoptees writ large, just like New York City is this country writ large," my husband comments. "There is more of everything. As an artist he can experience and explore relationships and images that other adoptees can't. He is fixed in his childhood. He lives with it and uses it. It is what you do, too. You create from it."

I have created from it, even when I didn't recognize the well from which I was drawing. Many of the folk creatures and animals in my children's books are orphans or far from home. All unknowingly, I sent them on the search for their roots as a rehearsal for my own.

Reclaiming One's Name

I woke from a dream one morning with a title for a book: *If I Had Known My Name.* I didn't know what it meant at first, but, of course, some part of me knew. As an adopted child, my birth name had been taken from me, and, therefore, according to the beliefs of many old cultures, I was vulnerable to all kinds of dangers. A name was considered a vital part of you, like your eyes or your teeth, and had to be kept secret so that an enemy could not harm you. I would have been given a second name to use in public, for anyone who possessed my secret name could have power over me. And, in a sense, this is what happened. By taking possession of my birth name, by sealing it away with the names of all adoptees, society took away my power and the power of all the adopted.

It is impossible to describe how adoptees feel when they learn that first or last name given them at birth. The birth name is a confirmation that you were born and that you exist. It is as integral a part of one today as it was in ancient times. As the poet Stanley Kunitz tells us: "Nothing is mine except my name / I only borrowed this dust."

Even when they cannot have a relationship with their birth parents, adoptees may reclaim their names as a way of reclaiming their original identities. They may use the first name, or take it or the surname (which, in most cases, is the birth mother's maiden name) as a middle name. In the short time I knew one man, a writer, he used three different first names: the one given him by his adoptive parents, the one given him by his birth mother, and the one he gave himself. "My adoptive mother objected to my signing articles with my birth name," he explained, "and my birth mother doesn't like my adoptive name. I hunted through books on names to find one to use as a byline, with no success. Finally, I took the name Hunter. Adoptees are hunters for their identity, and so I think it's appropriate."

Sometimes adoptees will use both their adoptive and their birth names, as if not sure which is the real one and which the impostor. "I am only equivocally Harold Brodkey," Brodkey once told me. "I knew my name was Aaron Weintraub at birth, not Harold Brodkey. I have to spend a certain amount of time just looking at my name in print, just to get it fixed in my mind."

I had a similar problem with my birth name: Blanche. In the past I had identified with Blanche DuBois in "A Streetcar Named Desire," especially with her famous line: "Whoever you are, I have always depended on the kindness of strangers." But even when I knew I was legitimately (or illegitimately?) Blanche, I could not comfortably take that name. Blanche was the baby I had left behind. She was the woman on a streetcar that never left the terminal. I had gone on without her. It was essential that I reclaim her, but I could not become her. Perhaps that's what my dream meant. If I had known my name, Blanche could have been an integral part of my life.

I am not alone in my inability to incorporate that once-forbidden name into my identity. "It takes more than a name to define yourself," an adoptee told me. "No name I give myself feels right. It's as if I cannot really have a name." Another adopted woman confessed: "I could never find a name I could say yes to."

Seeing Healing in Those Around You

As complex as reunion is for everyone, eventually some kind of healing is experienced by all the members of the triad. Once the denial and secrecy are lifted, everyone has a chance to be liberated.

It is healing for the adoptee to see the birth mother, freed from the burden of her guilt and shame, continue her life from where it stopped at surrender. She may begin a new career, end a loveless marriage that had been entered as a place to hide, and reconcile with her own mother, as she resolves the unfinished business between them. She may return to school. "Since I had a Ph.D., my mother figured she must be smart, so she went back to college," an adopted man told me.

A twenty-five-year-old man who made his birth mother wait four years to meet him feels healing taking place even though he now keeps an emotional distance. "I have begun to live the life that I had unconsciously put on hold all those years," he told me. "I am a completely different person than the one who started the search. And, in fact, I have even legally changed my first name to acknowledge that fact. Searching has empowered me, increased my self-esteem and confidence. Reunion has given me back the lost part of me I forfeited so many years ago. I am learning to connect again to people. I have learned to like myself. I can give and accept love. I am a worthwhile person. I am definitely *transformed*."

It is also healing to be able to share one's feelings with one's adoptive parents, after hiding them for so many years. To renegotiate the relationship as an adult child, and to be able to shed the old fear and guilt that one is being disloyal and ungrateful. Once they get over their initial shock and resistance, adoptive parents are often transformed, too. The lifting of secrecy frees them as well as the adoptee. I know of cases in which the fear of losing their child has motivated adoptive parents to give up the alcohol that had kept them stupefied over the years and to make an effort through therapy to put their lives and marriage back on course.

The same members in the triad who had been warned by society that they could be hurt by getting to know one another are now finding that they have been enhanced.

Staying in Process

We have seen that reunion is not any one moment, or month, or year, but a process. In order not to get stuck in any one place, or time, not to obsess over what is or might have been, the adoptee must keep integrating and growing and living in the present, dipping back now and then to recapitulate, before moving on to the next stage of the process.

Even a reunion that is going well can bring an unexpected cycle of depression in its wake because of the emotions it releases. An adoptee can still have occasional panic attacks and bouts of anger and grief, for issues are never completely resolved: they just get recycled and reappear when you least expect them.

I thought of this one morning at breakfast with my husband when I slipped into the old habit of reliving all the mistakes I have made over the years.

"Live forward," he said.

I marveled at his ability to let go of the past and to keep moving with the present into the future. It is still hard for me to do that, just as it is hard for other adoptees. The trauma, so early, so primal, is never completely resolved and must be played out, over and over again. Some part of it stays deeply embedded in our psychic structure.

"Organisms and people do what they can," my husband said with a smile.

I liked that.

We are, after all, part of the organic microcosm. We are limited in our abilities and, adopted or not, we try to go on. We do what we can.

Accepting Our Existential Fate

"To modify the past is not to modify a single fact," we are told by the writer Jorge Luis Borges. "It is to annul the consequences of that fact, which tend to be infinite."[12]

One impulse behind search and reunion is the adoptee's desire to modify the past. To deny the loss. To restore the mother. To rewrite the script that might have been. One learns, however, the wisdom in Borges's words. One cannot annul the fact that one was given up by one clan and taken in by another; one can only see the consequences of that fact in a new light that illuminates what happened in a healing way.

Part of the healing process takes place when adoptees are able to accept that what happened happened: it was their existential fate to be surrendered by one mother at birth and raised by another. To accept that, with all the relief of finding out who they are, there will always be the pain of that special history.

When, in the course of my research, I asked adoptees if they felt healed, I got a range of answers:

I'm not healed, but I function better.

I was completed rather than healed.

I have a past, a heritage, substance. I am whole.

I feel more in control of my life. I know now that I'm not some phantom person, but come from and am real flesh and blood.

I feel more like a normal person. I have more confidence, and feel more independent.

I was walking along the beach and fully realized that the little boy I was no longer had to wonder about his mother.

What would have happened if all the energy I expended on the search could have been directed into a career?

At least my four-year-old will never grow up feeling as disconnected as I did. One of the strangest sights I ever saw was my birth father, ex-husband, and son leaving together to go get a cup of coffee.

Adoptees may never completely heal, but after search and reunion at least they have a potential for growth. There is the chance to move from the traumatized self to the revitalized and transformed self.

Carol, an architect and divorcée who is in the early stages of an intense relationship with her widowed birth mother, who has no other children, is struggling to make sense of her life until now: "I think maybe I can be saved. I don't know when I'll know it, but I feel that search and reunion were my first tentative steps. What I look forward to most of all is the day when I'm no longer my birth mother's illegitimate daughter, or my adoptive parents' 'best thing that ever happened to them,' or what others view a 'youthful indiscretion.' I want to awaken one day free of the shadows of these good and terrible people. Can this ever be so for any of us, adopted or otherwise? In the meantime, I want to work for children like I was, and even more unfortunate ones, who have no voice, so that I can make my life and pain count for something."

After a lifetime of battling chronic depression and obesity, Lee feels better just knowing her mother's name, even though her mother died before she could locate her: "I am healthier—physically, mentally, spiritually—than I have ever been. I am confident, alive, willing to take risks, connected, *and* I am also afraid, hurting, and grieving. This does not feel like a split, but rather an integration of the ambiguities of life, an acceptance of things as they are. My life is no longer black and white, either/or. It is both/and."

The Eternal Search

Adoptees are often alarmed that they still want to go on searching for something after they have completed their search for mother, father, siblings, and extended family. They don't realize that to be searching is to be alive; that the most healing thing that happens to adoptees is that the search makes them into constant searchers. Having made their personal journey through time, space, and emotion, they are now ready to join others in the human condition on the Eternal Search to answer the great mysteries of life and death.

For some it will be a spiritual search in Native American traditions, New Age practices, or Eastern mystical religions—to take part, as the Buddhists say, in the joyful participation in the sorrows of the world.

Others, like Lee, seek the answers in divinity school. She can now see her former depression as "an essential period of dormancy that precedes great growth, like the seed sown in the frozen earth all winter which sprouts in the spring." She hopes to find her own voice and to use it: "Daring to be who I am with no apologies, to laugh, to cry, to be outrageous, to throw away conventional molds when they don't work—daring in any form—feels like the essential ingredient in my personal renaissance. My search is less urgent than it has been at times in the past. I have said yes. I am committed to making the journey as a creative person, a message bearer, a Christ in the world today, no matter what twists and turns I may encounter along the way. Finally, I am learning to appreciate the concept of 'quest' in the word 'question.' I am coming to know that life is not so much about arriving at some predetermined destination as it is about making the journey, not so much about finding the answers as it is about asking the questions."

Some adoptees search for a deeper meaning in history or in science. "If we do discover a complete theory of the universe, it should in time be understandable in broad principle to everyone," the astronomer Stephen Hawking writes at the end of *A Brief History of Time*. "Then we shall all be able to take part in the discussion of why it is that we and the universe exist."[13]

Until the ultimate secret is revealed to us, we will do well to live with the grace and dignity that Stanley Kunitz prescribes:[14]

Be what you are. Give
what is yours to give.
Have style. Dare.

The Best Interests of the Adopted Child

As I SAID AT THE BEGINNING OF OUR JOURNEY IN THIS book, we are Betwixt and Between change in the fragmented adoption field. The shortage of adoptable babies has created a system of supply and demand in which everyone in the triad is vulnerable to exploitation. Adoptive parents and birth parents alike are caught in the limbo between the open and closed adoption systems, with few guidelines to follow. But the child is the most vulnerable of all, because it cannot defend itself or speak up for its rights.

We live at a time when the term "best interests of the child" has come to mean whatever people want it to mean. When prospective adoptive parents and birth parents find themselves in adversarial roles, where their own best interests may conflict with the best interests of the child. When legal experts show more concern with limiting the time birth mothers and fathers have to revoke their consent than with the need for unbiased counseling of all parties before and after the baby is born.

Perhaps no one can write about the best interests of the child without bias, and so I want to state my bias clearly: the needs of the child must be put before those of the birth parents, the adoptive parents, and the legal agents involved.

The best interests of the adopted child can only be served:

When society recognizes the need for standards in the adoption field that protect the child: placing adoption practice in the hands of unbiased child welfare specialists, trained in the psychology of the adopted and without a profit motive. This would eliminate the need to advertise for babies and safeguard their interests.

When the child is seen as a real person—not a fantasy child, not an idealized child, not a special child, not a commodity—but a child with his own genetics, his own talents, and his own identity.

When the child is allowed to grow up in an open environment without secrets about who she is or where she comes from, including the right to an unamended birth certificate and to contact with her birth family.

When everyone recognizes the adopted child for what he is: a child with two sets of parents that give him a dual identity.

When the adoptive parents and the birth parents respect how they have filled each other's needs so that they can come together in some form of extended family for the sake of the child.

When everyone realizes that the best interests of the child are in the best interests of the adoptive family, the birth family, and society.

Resources

The Adoption
Reform Network

The adoption support groups listed here are made up of members of the adoption triad—adoptees, birth parents, and adoptive parents—as well as professionals in the mental health and legal fields. They are pro-adoption in that they are working for adoption reform—for a healthy adoption system that has open adoption and open records and that respects both the human and civil rights of the adopted child. The national umbrella groups, listed separately, include the names of many other groups across the country not listed here for reasons of space. Contact the support group in your community for help with search, for emotional support, for speakers, for referral to therapists familiar with adoption issues, and for agencies practicing open adoption.

UNITED STATES

Alabama

Orphan Voyage
304 Highway #53
Toneg, AL 35773

Arizona

Arizona Adoption Support Network
2238 South McClintock
Tempe, AZ 85282

Flagstaff Adoption Search and Support
    Group
P.O. Box 1031
Flagstaff, AZ 86002

Orphan Voyage
P.O. Box 8245
Scottsdale, AZ 85252

Search Triad, Inc.
P.O. Box 10181
Phoenix, AZ 85064-0181

Tracers, Ltd.
P.O. Box 18511
Tucson, AZ 85731

TRIAD
7155 East Freestone Drive
Tucson, AZ 85064-0181

Arkansas

Arkansas Adoption Triad
1912 Sanford Drive, #2
Little Rock, AR 72207

California

Adoptees Identity Discovery (AID)
P.O. Box 2159
Sunnyvale, CA 94087

Adoption Reality
2180 Clover Street
Simi Valley, CA 93065

Adoption with Truth
P.O. Box 20276
Oakland, CA 94611

California Searchin'
P.O. Box 553
Penngrove, CA 94951

Central Coast Adoption Support Group
P.O. Box 5165
Santa Maria, CA 93456

LA City Adoption Search Association
12440 Moorpark Street
Apartment A-179
Studio City, CA 91604

PACER of Marin
673 Redwood Avenue
Corte Madera, CA 94925

Post Adoption Center for Education
    Research (PACER)
P.O. Box 309
Orinda, CA 94563

Search Finders
P.O. Box 2374
Santa Clara, CA 95051

Search Finders of California
1537 Calle de Stuarda
San Jose, CA 95118

Truth Seekers of California
1053 Filbert
San Francisco, CA 94183

Colorado

Adoptees in Search
P.O. Box 24556
Denver, CO 80224

Adoptees in Search
Contract Station #27
P.O. Box 323
Lakewood, CO 80215

Lambs in Search
3578-D Parkmoor Village Drive
Colorado Springs, CO 80907

Orphan Voyage (nat'l. HQ)
2141 Road 2300
Cedaredge, CO 81413

Connecticut

Adoptees Search Connection (ASC)
1202 Hill Street
Suffield, CT 06078

Adoption Healing
288 Rowayton Avenue
Rowayton, CT 06853

Ties That Bind
P.O. Box 3119
Milford, CT 06460

Delaware

Finders Keepers
P.O. Box 748
Bear, DE 19701

District of Columbia

Adoptee-Birthparent Support Network
3421 M Street NW, #238
Washington, DC 20007

American Adoption Congress (nat'l. HQ)
1000 Connecticut Avenue NW, #9
Washington, DC 20002

Florida

The Musser Foundation
P.O. Box 1860
Cape Coral, FL 33910

OASIS (nat'l. HQ)
P.O. Box 630761
Miama Shores, FL 33153

Organized Adoption Search Informa-
    tion
P.O. Box 3874
Sarasota, FL 33578

Orphan Voyage
1533 Le Baron Avenue
Jacksonville, FL 32207

Orphan Voyage
13906 Pepperrell Drive
Tampa, FL 33624

Tallahassee Adoption Group
P.O. Box 3504
Tallahassee, FL 32315

Georgia

Adoptees' Search Network
3317 Spring Creek Drive
Conyers, GA 30208

Caring Heart
P.O. Box 88983
Atlanta, GA 30356

Hawaii

Adoption Circle of Hawaii
P.O. Box 61723
Honolulu, HI 96839

Adoption Support Group
P.O. Box 8377
Honolulu, HI 96815

Idaho

Adoption Support
P.O. Box 1435
Ketchum, ID 83340

Search Finders of ID
P.O. Box 794
Boise, ID 83707

Illinois

Adoption Triangle
P.O. Box 384
Park Forest, IL 60466

The Lost Connection
2210 North Illinois Street, #155
Belleville, IL 62221

Missing Pieces
P.O. Box 7541
Springfield, IL 62791

Truth Seekers in Adoption
P.O. Box 366
Prospect Heights, IL 60070

Indiana

As-I-Am
P.O. Box 1125
Muncie, IN 47308

Coping with Adoption
P.O. Box 1058
Peru, IN 46970

Full Circle
203 South German Church Road
Indianapolis, IN 46229

Indiana Adoption Coalition
P.O. Box 1292
Kokomo, IN 46901

Search for Tomorrow, Inc.
P.O. Box 441
New Haven, IN 46774

Iowa

Adoptees Quest
408 Buresh
Waterloo, IA 50703

The Adoption Experience
1105 Fremont
Des Moines, IA 50316

Kansas

Adoption Concerns Triangle (ACT)
2332 SE 37th Street
Topeka, KS 66605

Wichita Adult Adoptees
4551 South Osage
Wichita, KS 67217-4743

Kentucky

Adoption Connection
P.O. Box 1218
Nicholasville, KY 40356

Louisville Adoptee Awareness
P.O. Box 23219
Anchorage, KY 40223

Louisiana

Adoptees Birthright Committee
P.O. Box 7213
Metairie, LA 70010

Adoption Triad Network, Inc.
P.O. Box 3932
Lafayette, LA 70502

Lost and Found
1213 Bullrush Drive
Baton Rouge, LA 70810

Maine

Adoption Search Consultants of Maine
36 Grove Street
Bangor, ME 04401

Adoption Support
Taylors Point
Tenant's Harbor, ME 04860

Maryland

Adoptee Birthparent Support Network
5505 Emerson Street
Hyattsville, MD 20781

Adoptees in Search
P.O. Box 41016
Bethesda, MD 20814

Massachusetts

The Adoption Connection
11 Peabody Square, Room 6
Peabody, MA 01960

Adoption Healing
87 Chestnut Street
East Falmouth, MA 02536

Cape Cod Adoption Connection
P.O. Box 336
Brewster, MA 02631

Today Reunites Yesterday (TRY)
P.O. Box 898 / 214 State Street
Northampton, MA 01061-0989

Michigan

Adoptees Search for Knowledge
P.O. Box 762
East Lansing, MI 48823

Adoption Identity Movement (AIM)
P.O. Box 9265
Grand Rapids, MI 49509

Adoption Identity Movement (AIM)
P.O. Box 812
Hazel Park, MI 48030

Mid-Michigan Adoption Identity
  (AIM)
13636 Podunk Road
Cedar Springs, MI 49319

Missing in Adoption (MIA)
4198 East Cedar Lake Drive
Greenbush, MI 49838

Post-Adoption Support Services
1221 Minnesota Avenue
Gladstone, MI 49837

Retraced Roots
554 Peterson Road
North Muskegon, MI 49445

Society for Truth in Adoption (TRIAD)
8107 Webster Road
Mount Morris, MI 48458

Minnesota

CUB (Birthparents and Adoptees)
6429 Mendelssohn Lane
Edina, MN 55343-8424

Minnesota Reunion Registry
23247 Lofton Court North
North Scandia, MN 55073

Mississippi

Mississippi Adoption Network
P.O. Box 97462
Pearl, MS 39208

Missouri

Donor's Offspring
P.O. Box 37
Sarcoxie, MO 64862

Kansas City Adult Adoptees Organiza-
tion
P.O. Box 11828
Kansas City, MO 63119

Support Open Adoption Records
Search/Support Group
P.O. Box 190277
St. Louis, MO 63119

Montana

Search
P.O. Box 181
Big Timber, MT 59011

Nebraska

Midwest Adoption Triad
P.O. Box 37262
Omaha, NE 68137

New Hampshire

Living in Search of Answers
P.O. Box 215
Gilsum, NH 03448

New Jersey

Adoption Crossroads
85 Paramus Road
Paramus, NJ 07652

Adoption Reunion Coalition
15 Fir Place
Hazlet, NJ 07730

New Jersey Coalition for Openness in
Adoption
189 Cosman Avenue
Washington Township, NJ 07675

West Central Search and Support
Box 3604
Trenton, NJ 08629

New Mexico

Operation Identity
13101 Black Stone Road, N.E.
Albuquerque, NM 87111
(also provides search assistance to
German-born adoptees)

New York

Adoptee Liberty Movement Association
(ALMA) (nat'l. HQ)
P.O. Box 154
Washington Bridge Station
New York, NY 10033

Adoptees in Crisis
37 Ireland Place, Suite 165
Amityville, NY 11701

Adoption Crossroads (nat'l. HQ)
401 East 74th Street, #17D
New York, NY 10021
(also provides rap groups; recommended by author)

Adoption Group of Orange County
P.O. Box 385
Warwick, NY 10990

Adoption in Recovery
Rte. 1, Box 224A
Petersburg, NY 12158

Bloodroots
620 Central Chapel Road
Brocktondale, NY 14817

Jamestown Adoption Triad
Box 95
Falconer, NY 14733

Kinquest
Box 873 Bowling Green Station
New York, NY 10774

Triad Linking Center
Box 340
Vestal, NY 13851

Triangle of Truths
P.O. Box 2039
Liverpool, NY 13089

North Carolina

Adoption Information Exchange (AIE)
   (state HQ)
P.O. Box 1917
Matthews, NC 28106

Carolina Adoption Triangle Support
116 West Queen Street
Hillsborough, NC 27278

North Carolina Adoption Connections
P.O. Box 4153
Chapel Hill, NC 27515

Ohio

Adoptees Search Rights
P.O. Box 8713
Toledo, OH 43623

Adoption Network Cleveland
291 East 222 Street
Cleveland, OH 44123

Chosen Children
311 Springbrook Boulevard
Dayton, OH 45405
(serving southwest Ohio)

Insight to the Adoption Triad
Box 14217
Columbus, OH 43214

Reunite
Box 694
Reynoldsburg, OH 43068

Southeastern Ohio Searching (SOS)
4 Look Drive
Athens, OH 45701

Sunshine Reunions
1175 Virginia Avenue
Akron, OH 44306

Oklahoma

Adoptees as Adults
8220 N.W. 114th Street
Oklahoma City, OK 73132

Adoption Tree of Support
3703 Nogales Avenue
Tulsa, OK 74107

Oregon

A.N.S.R.S.
9203 S.W. Cree Circle
Tualatin, OR 97062

Family Ties
4001 Potter Avenue, #73
Eugene, OR 97062

Oregon Adoptive Rights Association
P.O. Box 882
Portland, OR 97207

Southern Oregon Adoptive Rights
(SOAR)
P.O. Box 202
Grants Pass, OR 97256

Pennsylvania

Adoption Forum
525 South Fourth Street, #3465
Philadelphia, PA 19147

Harrisburg Adoption Connection
P.O. Box 6634
Harrisburg, PA 17112

Pennsylvania Adoptee Search Team
(PAST)
1210 Taki Drive
Erie, PA 16505

Pittsburgh Adoption Connection
P.O. Box 4564
Pittsburgh, PA 15205

Pittsburgh Adoption Lifeline
P.O. Box 52
Gibsonia, PA 15044

Rhode Island

Parents and Adoptees Liberty Movement
861 Mitchell's Lane
Middletown, RI 02840

Yesterday's Children
77 Homer Street
Providence, RI 02882

South Carolina

Adoptees and Birthparents in Search
P.O. Box 5551
West Columbia, SC 29171

Adoption and Family Reunion Center /
ALMA
263 Lemonade Road
Pacolet, SC 29372

Searchers of Lost Heritage
P.O. Box 29
Clemson, SC 29633

TRIAD
P.O. Box 4778
Columbia, SC 29240

Tennessee

Group for Openness in Adoption
518 General G. Patton Road
Nashville, TN 37221

Rights of Origin
7110 Westway Circle
Knoxville, TN 37919

Tennessee's The Right to Know
5182 Oak Meadow Avenue
Memphis, TN 38134

Texas

Adoption Knowledge Affiliates
P.O. Box 402033
Austin, TX 78704

Love, Roots, Wings
10432 Achilles
El Paso, TX 79924

Orphan Voyage
5811 South Minster
Houston, TX 77035

The Right to Know
P.O. Box 1409
Grand Prairie, TX 75050

Searchline of Texas
1516 Old Orchard
Irving, TX 75061

Triangle Search
5730 Crest Grove
Corpus Christi, TX 78415

Utah

Utah Right to Know
3765 Alta Loma Drive
Salt Lake City, UT 84106

Vermont

Adoption Alliance of Vermont
91 Court Street
Middlebury, VT 05753

B & C Search Assistance of Vermont
P.O. Box 1451
St. Albans, VT 05478

Central Vermont Adoption Support
R.R. 1, Box 83
East Calais, VT 05650

Virginia

Adoptees and Natural Parents
949 Lancon Drive
Newport News, VA 23602

Adult Adoptees in Search
P.O. Box 203
Ferrum, VA 24088

Washington

Adoption Search and Reconciliation
14320 SE 170th
Renton, WA 98058

Washington Adoptees' Rights Movement
5950 Sixth Avenue South, #107
Seattle, WA 98108

West Virginia

Society's Triangle
411 Cabell Court
Huntington, WV 25703

Wisconsin

Adoption Information and Direction
(state HQ)
P.O. Box 1343
Milwaukee, WI 53201

Adoption Information and Direction
240 Terrace Court
Green Bay, WI 54301

Adoption Resource Network
Box 174
Coon Valley, WI 54623

Common Bonds
1217 Indigo Drive
Oshkosh, WI 54901

AUSTRALIA

Adoption Jigsaw (Victoria), Ltd.
G.P.O. Box 5260 BB
Melbourne, Victoria 3001

Adoption Jigsaw (W.A.), Inc.
P.O. Box 252, Hillarys
Perth, Western Australia 6025

CANADA

Adoption Connection
Box 20062
Brandon, Manitoba R7A 648

American Adoption Congress
Box 4853
Edmonton, Alberta T6E 507

Forget Me Not Family Society
Box 61526, Brookswood Post Office
Langley, B.C. U3A 8C6

Parent Finders (Edmonton)
P.O. Box 12031
Edmonton, Alberta T5J 3L2

Parent Finders (nat'l. capital region)
P.O. Box 5211
Station F
Ottawa, Ontario K2C 3H5

Society for Truth in Adoption
   (TRIAD)
P.O. Box 5114
Station A
Calgary, Alberta T2H 1X1

ENGLAND

NORCAP
No. 3 New High Street
Headington, Oxford OX37A5

Post Adoption Centre
5 Torriano Mews
Torriano Avenue
London NW5 2R2

FRANCE

Adoption Crossroads
15 Boulevard Saint Germain
Paris 75005

IRELAND

Adult Adoptees Association
Church Road
Greystones
County Wicklow

NEW ZEALAND

Adoption Jigsaw, Inc.
P.O. Box 28-037
Remuera, Auckland 5

Hutt Adoption Search and Support,
   68-7460
P.O. Box 38304
Petone

National Umbrella Network of the Adoption Reform Movement

Call these organizations for a chapter near you, conference schedules, speakers, and newsletters.

Adoptee Liberty Movement Association
   (ALMA)
P.O. Box 154
Washington Bridge Station
New York, NY 10033
Tel: (212) 581-1568

American Adoption Congress (AAC)
1000 Connecticut Avenue NW, #9
Washington, DC 20002
Tel: (800) 274-OPEN

Concerned United Birthparents (CUB)
200 Walker Street
Des Moines, IA 50317
Tel: (800) 822-2777

Council for Equal Rights in Adoption
   (CERA)
401 East 74th Street, Suite 17D
New York, NY 10021-3919
Tel: (212) 988-0110

Orphan Voyage
2141 Road 2300
Cedaredge, CO 81413
Tel: (303) 856-3937

Birth Parent Support Groups

CALIFORNIA

Bay Area Birthmothers Association
1546 Great Highway, #44
San Francisco, CA 94122

Birthparent Connection
P.O. Box 230643
Encinitas, CA 92023

COLORADO

Birthparents Adoption Trinity
P.O. Box 16512
Colorado Springs, CO 80935

CONNECTICUT

Birthparent Support Network
9 Whitney Road
Columbia, CT 06237

FLORIDA

National Organization for Birthfathers
and Adoption Reform (NOBAR)
P.O. Box 50
Punta Gorda, FL 33951

IOWA

Concerned United Birthparents (nat'l.
HQ)
2000 Walker Street
Des Moines, IA 50317

NEW JERSEY

Origins
P.O. Box 444
East Brunswick, NJ 08816

NEW YORK

Birthparent Support Network (BSN)
P.O. Box 120
North White Plains, NY 10603

Birthparent Support Network for Triad
93 Main Street
Queenbury, NY 12804

Manhattan Birthparent Group
Cherokee Station, Box 20137
New York, NY 10028

OHIO

Birthparent Support
3423 Bluerock Road
Cincinnati, OH 45239

Adoptive Parent Groups

The adoptive parent support groups listed here conduct pre-adoption and post-adoption workshops, hold annual conferences, publish newsletters, and work for legislative reform.

Adoptive Families of America
3333 Highway 100 North
Minneapolis, MN 55422
Tel: (612) 535-4829

The Adoptive Parents Committee
New York City Chapter
P.O. Box 3525
Church Street Station
New York NY 10008-3525
Tel: (212) 259-7921

Adoptive Parents for Open Records
Box 193
Long Valley, NJ 07853
Tel: (908) 850-1706

Families Adopting Children Every-
where (FACE) (nat'l. HQ)
P.O. Box 28058
Baltimore, MD 21239

New Jersey Coalition for Openness in
Adoption (nat'l. HQ) (includes
adoptees and birth parents)
189 Cosmar Avenue
Washington Township, NJ 07675
Tel: (201) 267-8988

The North American Council on
Adoptable Children (NACAC)
(nat'l. HQ)
1821 University Avenue
Suite N 498
St. Paul, MN 55104
Tel: (612) 644-3036

Open Door Society of Massachusetts
867 Boylston Street
Boston, MA 02116

Resolve, Inc.
1310 Broadway
Somerville, MA 02144
Tel: (617) 623-0744
(support organization on infertility; call
for chapter near you and referrals)

Resources for Adoptive Parents
4049 Brookside Avenue S.
Minneapolis, MN 55416
Tel: (612)-926-6959
(post-adoption services)

National and International Registries

ALMA
P.O. Box 154
Washington Bridge Station
New York, NY 10033
Tel: (212) 581-1568

Concerned United Birthparents (nat'l. HQ)
2000 Walker Street
Des Moines, IA 50317
Tel: (800) 822-2777

International Soundex Reunion Registry (ISRR)
P.O. Box 2312
Carson City, NV 89702
Tel: (702) 882-7755
(recommended by the American Adoption Congress; send SASE with request for registration form; no fee)

Periodicals

Adopted Child
P.O. Box 9362
Moscow, ID 83843

Adoption Therapist
House of Tomorrow Productions
c/o Hope Cottage
Financial Office
4209 McKinney Avenue, Suite 200
Dallas, TX 75205

AdoptNet Magazine
P.O. Box 50514
Palo Alto, CA 94303-0514

American Journal of Adoption
    Reform
Monthly Newsletter on Family Preser-
    vation
1139 Bal Harbor Boulevard
P.O. Box 184
Punta Gorda, FL 33950

Adoptalk
The Adoptive Parents Committee
80 Eighth Avenue, Ste. 303
New York, NY 10011

Birthparents Today Newsletter
3423 Blue Rock
Cincinnati, OH 45239

Chain of Life
Box 8081
Berkeley, CA 94707

CUB Communicator
Concerned United Birth Parents
2000 Walker Street
Des Moines, IA 50317

The Decree
American Adoption Congress
1000 Connecticut Avenue N.W. Ste. 9
Washington, DC 20036

Geborener Deutscher
805 Alvaredo Dr. N.E.
Albuquerque, NM 87108
(newsletter for German-born adoptees
    and their birth/adopted families)

OURS Magazine
Adoptive Families of America
3333 Highway #100 North
Minneapolis, MN 55422

People Searching News
P.O. Box 22611
Fort Lauderdale, FL 33335-2611

Roots and Wings
P.O. Box 638
Chester, NJ 07930

Resource/ Referral/ Counseling Organizations

This short list of referral organizations, open adoption agencies, and counseling centers represents just a few of the many such services that are springing up across the country. Check with the adoption support group in your community for further assistance.

REFERRAL SERVICES

American Genealogical Lending
  Library
P.O. Box 244
Department PF
Bountiful, UT 84010

Independent Search Consultants
P.O. Box 10192
Costa Mesa, CA 92627
(provides referrals in your area)

National Adoption Information Clear-
  inghouse
11426 Rockville Pike, Suite 410
Rockville, MD 20852
Tel: (301) 231-6512
(provides literature on adoption and
  referrals to therapists)

Tri-Adoption Library
P.O. Box 638
Westminster, CA 92663

OPEN ADOPTION AGEN-CIES AND CENTERS

Community, Family and Children Services

1000 Hastings Street
Traverse City, MI 49684
(one of the oldest open adoption agen-
  cies; call for referrals in other states)
Contact: James Gritter
Tel: (616) 947-8110

Friends in Adoption
44 South Street
Middletown Springs, VT 05757
(also provides counseling and referrals)
Contact: Dawn Smith-Pliner
Tel: (802) 235-2373

Hope Cottage
4209 McKinney Avenue
Suite 200
Dallas, TX 75202-4598
(also provides counseling, excellent lit-
  erature, and referrals)
Contact: Randolph Severson
Tel: (214) 526-8721

Independent Adoption Center
391 Taylor Boulevard
Suite 100
Pleasant Hill, CA 94523
(provides referral network)
Contact: Kathleen Silber
Tel: (510) 827-2229

COUNSELING SERVICES

Adoption and Custody Unit
Massachusetts General Hospital
Boston, MA 02114
Contact: Steven Nickman, M.D.
Tel: (617) 726-2724

Adoption Consultant Service
337 South Beverly Drive, Suite 103
Beverly Hills, CA 90212
Contact: Reuben Pannor
Tel: (310) 454-8141

Adoption Counseling Service
300 Central Park West, #7G
New York, NY 10024
(provides counseling to all members of
    triad, speaking engagements, and
    referrals)
Contact: Betty Jean Lifton, Ph.D.
Tel: (212) 874-0966

Adoption Teamwork Counseling
85444 Teague Loop
Eugene, OR 97405
Contact: Jeanne Etter
Tel: (503) 342-2692

Adoption Therapy
919 Village Center
Lafayette, CA 94549
Contact: Nancy Verrier, M.A.
Tel: (510) 284-5813

Birth Mother Grief Counseling
Massachusetts General Hospital
Boston, MA 02114
Contact: Phyllis Silverman
Tel: (617) 718-8018

Casey Family Services
7 Palmer Court
White River Junction, VT 05001-3323
Contact: Judith Bush
Tel: (802) 649-1400

Children's Home Society
Adoption Resource Center
P.O. Box 15190

Seattle, WA 98115
Contact: Randy Perin
Tel: (206) 524-6020

Deeg, Christopher F., Ph.D.
7 Dix Hills Court
Dix Hills, NY 11746
Tel: (516) 427-8403

Family Tree Adoption Counseling
    Center
448 Claremont Drive
Norman, OK 73069
Contact: Linda Babb
Tel: (405) 360-8134

Lopukhin, Michael
142 Amsterdam Avenue
Hawthorne, NY 10532
Tel: (914) 769-4777

Parenthesis Adopted Adolescent Project
P.O. Box 02265
Columbus, OH 43202
Contact: Betsy Keefer
Tel: (614) 237-6423

Parenting Resources
250 El Camino Real, Suite 216
Tustin, CA 92680
(provides counseling to all members of
    triad and referrals)
Tel: (714) 669-8100

Pre/Post Adoption Consulting Team
    (PACT)
385 Highland Avenue
Somerville, MA 02144
(provides counseling to all members of
    triad, professional training, lectur-
    ers, and referrals)
Contact: Joyce Pavao, E.D.
Tel: (617) 628-8815

Relate Counseling Center
15320 Minnetonka Boulevard, Suite
    200
Minnetonka, MN 55345
Contact Warren Watson
Tel: (612) 932-7277

Riedel, Claude
2239 Carter Avenue
St. Paul, MN 55108
Tel: (000) 000-0000

Scharf, Don, M.S.W., C.S.W.
788 Bonnie Drive
Baldwin, NY 11510
Tel: (516) 223-7002

South Shore Center for Psycho-
    therapy
215 Merrick Avenue
Merrick, NY 10532
Contact: David Kirschner
Tel: (516) 623-1190

Steed, C. Alan, Ph.D.
Loring Family Clinic
1730 Clifton Place, Suite 102
Minneapolis, MN 55403
Tel: (612) 872-9134

Strategic Health Services
12 Tennis Place
Forest Hills, NY 11375
Contact: Bernie Michael Gluntz,
    A.C.S.W.
Tel: (718) 575-3328

Tressler Lutheran Services
24 West Springettsburg Avenue
York, PA 17403
Tel: (717) 845-9113

Recommended Reading

Aigner, Hal. *Adoption in America, Coming of Age.* Larkspur, Calif.: Paradigm Press, 1992.

Allen, Elizabeth Cooper. *Mother, Can You Hear Me?* New York: Dodd, Mead, 1983.

Anderson, Robert. *Second Choice, Growing Up Adopted.* Chesterfield, Mo.: Badger Hill Press, 1992.

Arms, Suzanne. *To Love and Let Go.* New York: Knopf, 1983.

Baran, Annette, and Reuben Pannor. *Lethal Secrets: The Psychology of Donor Insemination.* New York: Amisted Press, 1993.

Bates, J. Douglas. *Gift Children, A Story of Race, Family, and Adoption in a Divided America.* New York: Ticknor and Fields, 1993.

Blau, Eric. *Stories of Adoption.* Portland, Oreg.: New Sage Press, 1993.

Boswell, J. *The Kindness of Strangers: The Abandonment of the Child in Western Europe from Late Antiquity to the Renaissance.* New York: Pantheon Books, 1988.

Brodzinsky, David M., and Marshall D. Schechter, eds. *The Psychology of Adoption.* New York: Oxford University Press, 1990.

Brodzinsky, David M., Marshall D. Schechter, and Robin Marantz Henig. *Being Adopted: The Lifelong Search for Self.* New York: Doubleday, 1992.

Chilstrom, Corinne. *Andrew, You Died Too Soon: A Family Experience of Grieving and Living Again.* Minneapolis: Augsburg, 1993.

Duprau, Jeanne. *Adoption: The Facts, Feelings, and Issues of a Double Heritage.* New York: Julian Messner, 1990. (Young adult.)

Dusky, Lorraine. *Birthmark.* New York: M. Evans, 1979.

Gediman, Judith S., and Linda P. Brown. *Birth Bond: Reunion Between Birthparents and Adoptees—What Happens After.* Far Hills, N.J.: New Horizon Press, 1989.

Gravelle, Karen, and Susan Fischer. *Where Are My Birth Parents? A Guide for Teenage Adoptees.* New York: Walker, 1993.

Gritter, James L., ed. *Adoption Without Fear.* San Antonio, Tex.: Corona, 1989.

Homes, A. M. *In a Country of Mothers.* New York: Knopf, 1993.

Imber-Black, Evan, ed. *Secrets in Families and Family Therapy.* New York: Norton, 1993.

Kirk, H. David. *Shared Fate.* Glencoe, Il.: Free Press, 1964.

———. *Adoptive Kinship: A Modern Institution Is in Need of Reform.* Toronto: Butterworth, 1981.

Kirschner, D. and L. S. Nagel, "Antisocial Behavior in Adoptees: Patterns and Dynamics." *Child and Adolescent Social Work* 5, no. 4 (1988), pp. 300–14.

———. "Understanding Adoptees Who Kill: Dissociation, Patricide and the Psychodynamics of Adoption." *International Journal of Offender Therapy and Comparative Criminology* 36, no. 4 (1992).

Krementz, Jill. *How It Feels to Be Adopted.* New York: Knopf, 1982. (Children's book.)

Lifton, B. J. *Twice Born, Memoirs of an Adopted Daughter.* New York: Penguin Books, 1977.

———. *I'm Still Me.* New York: Knopf, 1981. (Young adult novel.)

———. *The King of Children: A Biography of Janusz Korczak.* New York: Schocken Books, 1988.

———. *Lost and Found: The Adoption Experience.* New York: HarperCollins, 1988.

———. *Tell Me a Real Adoption Story.* New York: Knopf, 1994. (Children's book.)

Lindsay, J. W. *Open Adoption: A Caring Option.* Buena Park, Calif.: Morning Glory Press, 1987.

McColm, Michelle. *Adoption Reunions, A Book for Adoptees, Birth Parents and Adoptive Parents.* Toronto: Second Story Press, 1993.

Melina, Lois, and Sharon Kaplan Roszia. *The Open Adoption Experience.* New York: Harper Perennial, 1993.

Register, Cheri. *"Are Those Kids Yours?"* New York: Free Press, 1990.

Riben, Marsha. *Shedding Light on the Dark Side of Adoption.* Detroit: Harlo Press, 1988.

Rosenberg, Elinor B. *The Adoption Life Cycle: The Children and Their Families Through the Years.* New York: Free Press/Macmillan, 1992.

Schaefer, Carol. *The Other Mother: A Woman's Love for the Child She Gave Up for Adoption.* New York: Soho Press, 1991.

Schwartz-Salant, Nathan, and Murray Stein, eds. Abandonment issue. *Chiron (A Review of Jungian Analysis)* (1985).

Severson, Randolph W. *Adoption Philosophy and Experience.* Dallas: House of Tomorrow Productions, 1994.

Silber, Kathleen, and Patricia Martinez Dorner. *Children of Open Adoption.* San Antonio, Tex.: Corona, 1990.

Solinger, Rickie. *Wake Up Little Susie: Single Pregnancy and Race Before* Roe v. Wade. New York: Routledge, 1992.

Sorosky, Arthur D., Annette Baran, and Reuben Pannor. *The Adoption Triangle.* San Antonio, Tex.: Corona, 1989.

Stiffler, LaVonne Harper. *Synchronicity and Reunion, The Genetic Connection of Adoptees and Birthparents.* Hobe Sound, Fla.: FEA Publishing, 1992.

Strauss, Jean. *Birthright: A Guide to Search and Reunion for Adoptees, Birthparents and Adoptive Parents.* New York: Penguin, 1994.

van Gulden, Holly, and Lisa Bartels-Rabb. *Real Parents, Real Children.* New York: Crossroads, 1993.

Verny, Thomas, with J. Kelly. *The Secret Life of the Unborn Child.* New York: Delta, 1991.

Verrier, Nancy Newton. *The Primal Wound: Understanding the Adopted Child.* Baltimore: Gateway Press, 1993 (order from Nancy Verrier, 919 Village Center, Lafayette, CA 94549).

Watson, Kenneth W., and Miriam Reitz. *Adoption and the Family System.* New York: Guilford Press, 1992.

Acknowledgments

THE JOURNEY THAT I TOOK IN RESEARCHING AND WRIT-ing this book would not have been possible without the hundreds of adoptees who shared their individual journeys with me, in either interviews or written questionnaires. So, too, I was helped along the way by many birth parents and adoptive parents, who are so integral a part of the adoptees source and sustenance.

I want to thank members of our adoptee rap group, who were great traveling companions: Chelly Abitbol, Denise Bradbury, Clarissa Dane, Leslie Dann, Laurie Early, Sandra Fagin, Mary Beth Higgins, Diana Jones, Mary Ann Lewis, and Amy Lokken; and especially Nancy Naft, whose many talents include the design for the cover of this book.

My appreciation also to Don Scharf for conjuring up the image of the adoptee as warrior, Steven Whitney Hunter for sharing his poetry and art, as well as Robert Anderson and Alan Steed, all of whom, as clinicians, writers, and fellow adoptees, gave me insights into the psychology of the male adoptee.

During the course of this journey, there were many who helped in special ways with their friendship and encouragement and with their own inspiring work in the adoption field. I especially want to thank:

Annette Baran, always there with high spirits and high ideals, and Reuben Pannor, pioneers in the field of open adoption, who share a moral concern for the rights of the adopted child; Joyce Pavao, gifted clinician, who is training new generations of professionals in an under-

standing of the life cycle of the adoptive family; James Gritter, a pioneer
in creating open adoption communities; Randolph Severson, a family
therapist with zing, who sees both the spirituality and soul-deep trauma
in the field of adoption, and his colleague Carol Demuth, equally dedicated to healing and education in the field; Sharon Kaplan Roszia, one of
the first to guide adoptive parents into the open adoption experience; Pat
Dorner, another pioneer in opening up adoption; Linda Yellin, who is
creating a bridge between members of the triad; Mi Ok Bruining,
adoptee and poet, who is building dual bridges; and Stanley Schneider,
whose bridges stretch from Jerusalem to New York.

My appreciation to Lorraine Dusky, for her books and articles;
William Gage, for publishing *Geboren* for German-born adoptees; Lee
Campbell, for her healing workshops; Mary Ann Cohen, whose poetic
voice could not be stilled; and special thanks to Sally Fine for her Moses
baskets, which float through all of our psyches as well as through the
cover of this book.

My gratitude to the psychotherapists with whom I discussed my developing theories when working for my Ph.D. at the Union Institute: Joan
Ormont, for her encouragement and insights; Don Shapiro, for his
understanding of the importance of origins; Paul Wachtel, who could be
counted on to pose stimulating questions; Evelyn Lief, who gave me
insight into the psychology of the half-adoptee; and Maxine Theodoulou,
fellow adoptee, who provided insight on verbal abuse. And to Charles
Strozier, a generous friend, who unlocked, among so many other things,
the mysteries of Hans Kohut's writings on the self.

Once again my warm thanks and love to Erik Erikson for those wonderful years of dialogue on the adoptee's identity; Nathan Schwartz-
Salant, for numinous discussions of the mythical mother and mythical
child, and so much else; Michael Basch, for his invaluable work on dissociation, and Carol Basch, for her devoted work with adopted patients;
Lisa McCann, for wonderful talks and shared workshops; Don Hallock,
for his dedication to adoptees and birth mothers in Hawaii; Michael Perl-
man, for his deep concern for the fate of all family trees; and Florence
Falk, for her creative way of seeing and being.

And to three close spirit friends who did not live to celebrate this
book's publication: John Dominis Holt, writer and soul of Hawaiian culture; David Shainberg, psychoanalyst transformed into painter; and
Rabbi Marshall Meyer, who fought injustice with love.

Again thanks to fellow biographers with whom I have shared ideas over the years at the New York University Biography seminars, especially Gloria Erlich, for our talks on multiple mothers; Deirdre Bair, for discussions on the incestuous relationship of Anaïs Nin with her father; Sue Shapiro, for our conversations on the incest issues in genetic sexual attraction; and Shareen Brysac, for long lunches digesting our mutual existential condition.

My appreciation for some of the dedicated therapists who have been working over the years to help enlighten the public on the psychology of the adopted child: Harold Blum, Paul Brinich, David Brodzinsky, Calvin Colarusso, Christopher Deeg, Steven Nickman, and Marshall Schecter. For Robert Childs, who keeps the dream alive; Nancy Verrier, for speaking out as an adoptive mother as well as a clinician on the pain and loss that adopted children experience. And especially for David Kirschner, who with great integrity and courage has taken on the difficult task of educating the public on the psychodynamics of the deeply troubled adoptee.

And for Sam (Rollo) Ross and Myra Ross for creating a safe haven for children and animals at Green Chimneys, in Brewster, New York. And to Lourdes (Lulu) Balanon, for helping to make children safe in her country, the Philippines.

On the legal side, special thanks to Gertrud Mainzer and Leon Friedman for their friendship, for helping many adoptees through the judicial labyrinths, and for writing on the need for change in our antiquated adoption laws.

Warm appreciation to adoptees Joyce Aaron, Rick Adkins, Janine Baer, Joe Barry, Emily Bell, Leslie Bergman, Bill Bossert, Jan Brinn, Carey Brittenham, Susan Conboy, Chris Conway, Katie Crane, Connie Dawson, Wally Dixon, Meg Doyle, Todd Engel, Keith Epstein, Laura Flaherty, Roberta Fineberg, Betsy Forrest, Howdy Freeman, Kathleen Fritz, Ian Hageman, Arthur Hanson, Ann Henry, Craig Heyman, Hal Himmelstein, Ellen Jacobs, Marla Jacobson, Sophie Janney, Susan Kacerek, Darin Koltow, Linda Kozloff, Kathryn Kulpa, Morgan Light, Mandy McDevvit, David Mansfield, Karen Marchal, Elizabeth Mason, Richard Matteson, Joe Matz, Dennis Maxwell, Phil Millstein, Susan Moses, David Nast, Penny Partridge, David Perrin, John Pike, Caesara Pirrone, Shawn Ploen, Danny Quat, Mary Jo Rillera, Jennifer Segal, Bob Shaffer, Eve Sher, David Sills, Nancy Slump, Michael Spille, Meg Sprouse, Pam Stello, Patricia Storace, Linda Traum, David Zoffoli, and so many other adoptees, for sharing with me the torturous and exhilarating process of search and reunion.

And also to the stalwart adoptees of Cape Cod—Laurie Anderson, Carolyn Canfield, Jamie Haley, and Alison Lebaron—who have become healers as they developed a healing program.

And appreciation to birth mothers Barbara Kari Anderson, Joyce Bahr, Vicky Camp, Ann Francis, Barbara Gonyo, Deborah Johansen, Charleen Justice, Lynn Lape, Laura Lewis, Sherry Luce, Roberta Piper, Felicia Pirrone, Carol Schaefer, and LaVonne Stiffler. And to Ginny Peterson, who unlocked nature's secrets in Hawaii.

Cheers to the committed leaders of support groups in the adoption reform movement: Carol Gustavson and Jane Nast of Adoptive Parents for Open Records, for understanding their children's needs; Jean Paton of Orphan Voyage, who still nurtures everyone from her mountaintop in Colorado; Joe Soll of CERA, for organizing national conferences and marches on Washington in behalf of adoptee rights; Jon Ryan, founder of NOBAR, for protecting the rights of birth fathers; Janet Fenton and Carol Anderson and the members of the birth mother movement CUB; and Kate Burke and Ken Watson and the members of the AAC—all part of a truly grass-roots movement that has worked with passion and skill to open the minds and hearts and adoption records of this country. And a special hurrah to birth mother Sandra Musser, who stepped into adoption legend when she became the first to go to prison for committing civil disobedience against the unjust adoption laws.

Many thanks to my brilliant editor Jo Ann Miller, whose enthusiasm and invaluable suggestions have helped shape this book; and to Linda Carbone, whose rigorous editorial guidance helped me surrender the manuscript into her capable hands. And to my agent, Berenice Hoffman, who, as always, has been supportive throughout.

To my daughter and son, who have given me the joy of being a mother watching her children grow into vital and caring people, deeply involved in healing: Natasha Karen Lifton as a sensitive psychologist, and Kenneth Jay Lifton as a leader in the organ transplant movement. To my daughter-in-law, Michelle, also a healer, on the cutting edge of medical science. To Katsura Hori, an integral member of our family and a talented fashion designer. And to Penelope Foran, a true live wire, who trained my computer to put up with my ways.

And, always, to my protean husband, Robert Jay Lifton, who with his wry humor threatens to form the Adoptee Husband Liberation Front (AHLF), but in the meantime is his usual source of love, sustenance, wisdom, and inspiration.

Notes

Chapter 1: Betwixt and Between

1. Betty Jean Lifton, *Twice Born: Memoirs of an Adopted Daughter* (New York: Penguin Books, 1977[1975]).
2. Betty Jean Lifton, *Lost and Found, the Adoption Experience* (New York: HarperCollins, 1988[1979]).
3. Janusz Korczak, *How to Love a Child* (*Jak kochac dzieci*) Part I: Warsaw, 1919; Part II: Warsaw, 1920. English version in *Selected Works of Janusz Korczak,* ed. Martin Wollins, trans. Jerzy Backrach (Springfield, Va.: Department of Agriculture, 1967).
4. Alice Miller, *Prisoners of Childhood* (New York: Basic Books, 1979), p. 5.
5. Betty Jean Lifton, *The King of Children, A Biography of Janusz Korczak* (New York: Shocken Books, 1989).
6. Karen Horney, *Neurosis and Human Growth: The Struggle Toward Self-Realization* (New York: Norton, 1950).
7. See Robert Jay Lifton, *The Broken Connection* (New York: Basic Books, 1979); *Death in Life: Survivors of Hiroshima* (Chapel Hill: University of North Carolina Press, 1991[1968]; *Home from the War: Learning from Vietnam Veterans* (Boston: Beacon Press, 1992[1973]).
8. The extreme polarization of the adoption field began with and continues to be fostered by the National Council for Adoption (originally the National Committee for Adoption). It was founded in 1980 by the Edna Gladney Home and other traditional adoption agencies for the purpose of keeping adoption records sealed. It succeeded in getting proposals in the 1980 Model State Adoption Act for both open records and open adoption deleted from the final document. (See the

Federal Register, October 8, 1981, and my book *Lost and Found,* pp. 265–67.) After convincing some state legislatures to set up passive registries that are virtually reunion-proof, the NCFA has busied itself trying to prevent the passage of open-records statutes by any of the states.

Adoption records remain sealed in all but two states (Kansas and Alaska), but the gradual opening of adoption practice in this country has sent the NCFA on the offense again. Part of its backlash strategy is to polarize birth parents, adoptive parents, and adoptees by labeling groups working for adoption reform as "anti-adoption" while representing itself as pro-adoption. Mary Beth Seader, vice president of NCFA, used the tragic two-year court battle between the birth parents and would-be adoptive parents of two-year-old Baby Jessica to label the members of Concerned United Birthparents (CUB) "predators" and to accuse those who support them of infiltrating the child-welfare system, creating an anti-adoption attitude" (Lucinda Franks, "The War for Baby Clausen," *The New Yorker,* March 22, 1993). The escalation of language is part of the backlash tactics, so that words like *war* become the norm and terms like *family preservation* are called "Orwellian." (See "The War on Adoption: New Battlefront," *National Review,* June 7, 1993.)

The most recent battle has been an attempt to prevent the adoption search movement from facilitating reunions. In what was obviously a sting operation, two professional searchers—birth mothers Sandra Musser of the Musser Foundation of Florida and Barbara Moskowitz of Cleveland—were indicted and then convicted by a federal grand jury in the spring of 1993 in Akron, Ohio, for conspiring fraudulently to obtain confidential information from the Social Security Administration. Moskowitz, who plea-bargained, was let off with two months in a halfway house, two years' probation, and a $1,600 fine. Musser, who pleaded not guilty, was sentenced to four months in a federal prison in Florida, two months in house arrest with an electronic device, and three years of probation during which she was not to conduct any searches. Musser based her defense on civil disobedience against unjust and illegal laws that sealed adoption records.

Two other birth mothers, Rita Stapf and Barbara Lewis, were also indicted and convicted in upstate New York with the charge of obtaining confidential information through the state's computer system. They were sentenced to five years' probation and ordered not to conduct searches for six months.

A statement issued in defense of the searchers by adoption therapists and social workers at the Fourth National Conference on Openness in Adoption (Traverse City, Michigan, April 30, 1993) read: "We believe that what should be indicted is the system that led to the need to search secretly. Today adoption agencies no longer guarantee secrecy and anonymity. The adoptions of all the yesterdays deserve the same attention and consideration. Opening sealed birth records is the right of all who have been affected by this in this century. We believe that Musser and Moskowitz's actions need to be viewed from this vantage point and understood as acts of civil disobedience rather than criminality."

9. Many of the reformers in the field are adult adoptees who have become mental health professionals and lawyers. Having grown up in the closed system, they hope to spare future generations of adopted children the psychological stress that they have experienced, and to gain the same civil rights for adopted people as others have. They have been joined in this struggle by birth mothers who hope to spare future generations of women the psychological pain of not knowing what became of their children, and by a growing number of adoptive parents who understand their children's need to know their origins. The adoption reform movement is also made up of a large number of social workers, psychologists, and lawyers who are aware of the need for legislative reform. (See the list of adoption reform groups at the back of this book.)

10. E. H. Erikson, *Identity and the Life Cycle* (New York: Norton, 1980).

Chapter 2: The Mothered/Motherless Self

1. Quoted by Frobenius in *Der Kopf als Schicksal*. From the chapter "Kore," by C. Kerenyi in *Essays on a Science of Mythology,* co-authored with C. G. Jung (Princeton, N.J.: Princeton University Press, 1971), Bollingen Series, p. 102.

2. Jerzy Ficowski, *The Reading of Ashes* (London: Menard Press, 1984).

3. Kerenyi, *Essays on a Science of Mythology,* p. 36.

4. Nathan Schwartz-Salant, personal communication, 1991.

5. John Boswell, *The Kindness of Strangers: The Abandonment of the Child in Western Europe from Late Antiquity to the Renaissance* (New York: Pantheon, 1988). This encyclopedic book gives us an in-depth history of the unwanted child and shows how adoption has been historically linked to abandonment.

Chapter 3: The Conspiracy of Silence

1. In the earliest versions of the myth, the legendary material, Oedipus does not blind himself. In Homer's *Odyssey* (XL, 271ff.) he continues on the throne; in the *Iliad* (XXIII, 679) he dies in battle. See Jean-

Pierre Vernant and Pierre Vidal-Naquet, *Myth and Tragedy in Ancient Greece* (New York: Zone Books, 1990), pp. 90, 364.

It is clear that Sophocles was not adopted, or he would have known that, rather than being blinded by the truth, adopted people, like Oedipus, see better. Vernant and Vidal-Naquet point out that since Freud was not a scholar of myth, Sophocles' version would have been the only one he knew.

2. Mark A. Karpel, "Family Secrets," *Family Process* 19 (1980): 295–306.
3. Annette Baran, personal communication, 1992. See Arthur Sorosky, Annette Baran, and Reuben Pannor, *The Adoption Triangle* (San Antonio, Tex.: Corona Publishing, 1989), pp. 207–14.
4. Ann Hartman, "Secrecy in Adoption," in *Secrets in Families and Family Therapy,* ed. Evan Imber-Black (New York: Norton, 1993), p. 88.
5. Elizabeth Bartholet, *Family Bonds: Adoption and the Politics of Parenting* (Boston: Houghton Mifflin, 1993), p. 55.
6. Paul Brinich, "Psychoanalytic Psychotherapy with Adoptees," paper presented at the 36th Annual Meeting of the American Academy of Child and Adolescent Psychiatry, New York, 1989.
7. Barbara Shulgold and Lynne Sipiora, *Dear Barbara, Dear Lynne: The True Story of Two Women in Search of Motherhood* (Reading, Mass.: Addison-Wesley, 1992), p. 116. This book gives a vivid and honest picture of the struggles of two women to conceive, their overwhelming emotional need for motherhood, their ambivalence about adopting, the difficulties they experienced in trying to adopt, and their eventual happiness as adoptive mothers.
8. Quoted in Susan Chira, "Adoption Is Getting Some Harder Looks," *New York Times,* April 25, 1993.
9. See Bartholet, *Family Bonds.* She targets mental health professionals and adoption reformers as primarily responsible for the "adoption stigma" that she sees everywhere (pp. 171–86). In *Talking with Young Children About Adoption* (New Haven, Conn.: Yale University Press, 1993), Mary Watkins and Susan Fisher dismiss the "bad news" in adoption research and cite what is "more comforting to adoptive parents" (pp. 25–56).
10. Helene Deutsch, *The Psychology of Women, Motherhood,* vol. 2 (New York: Grune and Stratton, 1945), pp. 428–29.
11. John Boswell, *The Kindness of Strangers: The Abandonment of the Child in Western Europe from Late Antiquity to the Renaissance* (New York: Pantheon, 1988).
12. *Infertility* is defined as having tried to conceive unsuccessfully for a period of one year. One in six couples now experiences infertility. See Linda Forrest and Mary S. Gilbert, "Infertility: An Unanticipated and

Prolonged Life Crisis," *Journal of Mental Health Counseling* 14, no. 1 (January 1992): 42–58.

13. Ibid. Also personal communication with Sharon Kaplan Roszia, 1992.
14. Phyllis Lowinger, Resolve newsletter, Ohio, June 1993.

Chapter 4: The Hidden Relationship

1. Daniel Stern, *The Interpersonal World of the Infant: A View from Psychoanalysis and Developmental Psychology* (New York: Basic Books, 1985). All of Stern's quotes in this chapter are from this book.
2. Betty Jean Lifton, "A Web, a Thread, a String of a Teabag," presented at Provincetown Playhouse on the Wharf, 1964.
3. Thomas Verny with John Kelly, *The Secret Life of the Unborn Child* (New York: Delta, 1981). A growing number of professionals believe that there is now enough subjective and scientific evidence to validate the existence of prenatal memory. See M. Irving, "Natalism as Pre- and Perinatal Metaphor," *Pre- and Peri-Natal Psychology Journal* 4, no. 2 (Winter 1989); D. B. Chamberlain, "Babies Remember Pain," *Pre- and Peri-Natal Psychology Journal* 3, no. 2 (1989); Joseph Chilton Pearce, *Magical Child* (New York: Bantam Books, 1986).
4. Christopher F. Deeg, "On the Adoptee's Cathexis of the Lost Object," *Psychoanalysis and Psychotherapy* 7, no. 2 (New York: Brunner/Mazel, 1989), pp. 152–61; "Defensive Functions of the Adoptee's Cathexes of the Lost Object," *Psychoanalysis and Psychotherapy* 8, no. 2 (Fall/Winter 1990) New York: Brunner/Mazel, 1990, pp. 35–46.
5. Florence Clothier, "The Psychology of the Adopted Child," *Mental Hygiene* 27 (April 1943): 223.
6. Ibid.
7. Nancy Newton Verrier, *The Primal Wound: Understanding the Adopted Child* (Baltimore: Gateway Press, 1993). To order this invaluable book, write Nancy Verrier, 919 Village Center, Lafayette, CA 94549.
8. John Bowlby, *Separation: Anxiety and Anger* (New York: Basic Books, 1973).
9. Harry Guntrip, *Schizoid Phenomena, Object Relations and the Self* (New York: International Universities Press, 1969).
10. Deeg, "On the Adoptee's Cathexis."
11. D. W. Winnicott, "The Theory of the Parent-Infant Relationship," *The Maturational Process and the Facilitating Environment* (New York: International Universities Press, 1965), p. 39n.
12. Deeg, "On the Adoptee's Cathexis."

13. Paul Brinich, "Psychoanalytic Psychotherapy with Adoptees," paper presented at the 36th Annual Meeting of the American Academy of Child and Adolescent Psychiatry, New York, 1989.

14. Leslie M. Singer, David M. Brodzinsky, Douglas Ramsay, et al., "Mother-Infant Attachment in Adoptive Families," *Child Development* (1985): 1543–51.

15. David Brodzinsky, a child psychologist at Rutgers University, has found that as a group adopted children show a higher incidence of behavioral, emotional, and academic problems than their nonadopted peers. He concluded that the increased vulnerability of adopted children is restricted primarily to individuals in the middle childhood and adolescent years. See his "Adjustment to Adoption: A Psychosocial Perspective," *Clinical Psychology Review* 7 (1987): 25–47.

Chapter 5: The Broken Narrative

1. Sigmund Freud, "Analysis of a Phobia in a Five-Year-Old Boy," in *Collected Papers,* vol. 3, p. 149; and *The Standard Edition* (London: Hogarth Press, 1909).

2. Elizabeth Stone, *Black Sheep and Kissing Cousins: How Our Family Stories Shape Us* (New York: Viking Penguin, 1989).

3. Don Shapiro, personal communication, 1993.

4. A. M. Homes, *In a Country of Mothers* (New York: Knopf, 1993), p. 68.

5. V. P. Wasson, *The Chosen Baby* (New York: Carrick and Evans, 1939).

6. Betty Jean Lifton, *Tell Me a Real Adoption Story* (New York: Knopf, 1994).

7. Mary Watkins and Susan Fisher, *Talking with Young Children About Adoption* (New Haven, Conn.: Yale University Press, 1993). The sections of this book where the children talk to the parents are wonderful, but the authors talk to us in the defensive tone of a genre that attacks psychological literature that reports on the difficulties adopted children experience. The literature, according to the authors, reflects a "conviction that biological ties represent greater reality than social connections." It is the old nature-versus-nurture argument in new clothes. The authors accuse "the experts" of confirming "what everyone else has been intimating or telling us outright—that our families are defective, our children doomed to psychological pathology, and that genes will 'win out' over nurture." Unfortunately, the authors put down the very professionals who value the adoptive family enough to voice their concern for what is troubling the child. The inner feelings

that the children express in this book validate the professional findings, but, unfortunately, for the most part, the authors seem unable to
hear what the children are trying to tell them.

8. Ibid., pp. 178–83. One of the strengths of this book is that the authors
include a successful open adoption story that illustrates the comfort
both children and adoptive parents feel when there are no secrets.

9. Personal communication, 1991.

10. Charles Simic, *The World Doesn't End: Prose Poems* (New York:
Harcourt Brace Jovanovich, 1989).

11. Bennett Simon, *Tragic Drama and the Family* (New Haven, Conn.:
Yale University Press, 1988), pp. 195–96.

12. Daniel Stern, *The Interpersonal World of the Infant: A View from
Psychoanalysis and Developmental Psychology* (New York: Basic
Books, 1985), p. 262.

Chapter 6: Artificial Self, Forbidden Self

1. See Bessel A. van der Kolk, *Psychological Trauma* (Washington, D.C.:
American Psychiatric Press, 1987); Judith Lewis Herman, *Trauma and
Recovery* (New York: Basic Books, 1992); I. Lisa McCann and Laurie
Anne Pearlman, *Psychological Trauma and the Adult Survivor* (New
York: Brunner/Mazel, 1990).

2. Harold Blum, "A Psychoanalytic View of *Who's Afraid of Virginia
Woolf?*," *Journal of the American Psychoanalytic Association* 17
(1969): 888–903.

3. Harry Guntrip, *Schizoid Phenomena, Object Relations and the Self*
(New York: International Universities Press), 1969.

4. E. T. de Bianchedi et al., "Truth and Lies, Generational Transmission," colloquy, "Patrimonie génétique et droits de l'humanité,"
October 25, 1989. This team of Argentine psychiatrists has been
studying the children who "disappeared" between 1976 and 1983
when their parents were seized and killed by the Argentine military
junta. A group known as the Grandmothers of the Plaza de Mayo
Association was formed in 1977 to find the children who had been
"adopted" by military families and return them to their blood relatives. As of this writing, 53 children have been identified with the
help of molecular geneticists, and it is believed that 150 are still missing.

5. Karen Horney, *Neurosis and Human Growth: The Struggle Toward
Self-Realization* (New York: Norton, 1950).

6. D. W. Winnicott, "Ego Distortion in Terms of True and False Self,"
The Maturational Process and the Facilitating Environment (New

York: International Universities Press, 1965), pp. 140–52; R. D. Laing, *The Divided Self: An Existential Study in Sanity and Madness* (London: Penguin Books, 1965), pp. 73, 94–105.

7. H. D. Kirk, *Shared Fate: A Theory of Adoption and Mental Health* (New York: Free Press, 1981).

8. Laing, *The Divided Self*, pp. 94–95.

9. In F. Wickes, *The Inner World of Childhood* (London: Coventure, 1977).

10. Max Frisk, "Identity Problems and Confused Conception of the Generic Ego in Adopted Children During Adolescence," in *Acta Paediatrica* 21 (1964): 6–11.

11. "Time tunnel" is a term used by Judith Kestenberg to describe overlapping time schemes, the "phenomenon of an artificially actualized second reality." Quoted by Anita Eckstaedt in "A Victim of the Other Side," in Martin S. Bergmann with Milton Jucovy, *Generations of the Holocaust* (New York: Basic Books, 1982), p. 225; "pretend parent" is from Harold Blum, "Adoptive Parents: Generative Conflict and Generational Continuity," *Psychoanalytic Study of the Child* 38 (1983): 141–63.

12. Steven Barreto and Eric Bermann, "Ghosts as Transitional Objects: The Impact of Cultural Belief Systems Upon Childhood Mourning," paper presented at the sixty-ninth annual meeting of the American Orthopsychiatric Association, New York City, May 1992.

13. Blum, "Adoptive Parents."

14. Ibid. Blum is quoting here from "A Psychoanalytic View."

15. Personal communication, 1992.

Chapter 7: Stuck in the Life Cycle

1. Erik Erikson, *Identity and the Life Cycle* (New York: Norton, 1958); and *Identity: Youth and Crisis* (New York: Norton, 1968).

2. Personal communication, 1992.

3. D. W. Winnicott, "Adopted Children in Adolescence," report of the Residential Conference held at Roehampton, July 13–15, 1955 (London: Standing Committee of Societies Registered for Adoption), pp. 33–41.

4. Erikson, *Identity and the Life Cycle*.

5. H. J. Sants, "Genealogical Bewilderment in Children with Substitute Parents," *British Journal of Medical Psychology* 37 (1964): 133–41.

6. Ernst Kris, "The Recovery of Childhood Memories," paper presented at the Midwinter meeting of the American Psychoanalytic Association, December 4, 1955, New York City.

7. C. Murray Parkes, "Separation Anxiety: An Aspect of the Search for a Lost Object," reprinted from *The British Journal of Psychiatry*, special publication no. 3: 87–92.

8. Patricia Storace, "Illegitimacy," in *Heredity* (Boston: Beacon Press, 1987).

9. Kurt Vonnegut, *Fates Worse Than Death* (New York: Putnam, 1950).

10. Wallace Stegner, "Letter—Much Too Late," in *Family Portraits, Remembrances of Twenty Distinguished Writers*, ed. Carol Anthony (New York: Doubleday, 1989).

11. Erikson, *Identity and the Life Cycle*, p. 148.

12. Stanley Schneider, personal communication, 1991.

13. See Eleanora M. Woloy, *The Symbol of the Dog in the Human Psyche: A Study of the Human-Dog Bond* (Wilmette, Ill.: Chiron Publications, 1990), p. 15.

14. Green Chimneys was founded in 1947 by Sam ("Rollo") Ross as a boarding school where young children could learn about animals, and evolved over the years into a residential treatment center. Children go to school on the grounds and see a therapist at least once a week, but Green Chimneys is unique in that it has incorporated animals into its treatment process. The goal is to help children nurture creatures smaller and more helpless than they are, and to learn in the process to nurture themselves and others.

15. Marjorie Margolies and Ruth Gruber, *They Came to Stay* (New York: Coward, McCann and Geoghegan, 1976). At this writing, Marjorie Margolies-Mezvinsky is a Democratic Congresswoman from Pennsylvania.

16. Jane Marks, "How We Adopted Me," *New York Times Magazine*, May 23, 1993.

17. Elizabeth Bartholet, *Family Bonds: Adoption and the Politics of Parenting* (Boston: Houghton Mifflin, 1993). Bartholet's is one of the most vocal of the "kill-the-messenger" genre of books being produced as part of the backlash caused by increasing openness in adoption practice. She erroneously interprets psychological reports of the effects of the closed adoption system on the child as an attack on the validity of the adoptive family, and advocates *not* opening adoption records until they can be seen as "not of necessary and central importance to an adoptee's personhood or to parenting relationships." Bartholet dismisses the literature on identity theory and interprets the recent societal interest in the importance of roots as a denigration of adoptive ties. Overly defensive as an adoptive parent, she is not able to empathize with the needs of the adopted child, to which the psychological literature is speaking and for which adoption reformers are working. From atop the nature-versus-nurture barricades, she declares

with largess, "I do not think we should jettison the biologic model of parenting," but the reader is left with the feeling that if she could do it, she would.

18. See UN Commission on Human Rights, *Rights of the Child*, "Sale of Children" report submitted by Vitit Muntarbhorn, 48th sess., January 22, 1992, article 62, p. 12.

19. For a fine critique on the issues for American families with children from overseas, see Sallie Tisdale, "One Mother's Gain," *Vogue*, December 1991; Cheri Register, *Are Those Kids Yours?* (New York: Free Press, 1990).

20. Personal communication, 1993.

21. Personal communication, 1993. Dr. Pavao is founder of the Pre and Post Adoption Counseling Team (PACT), Somerville, Mass.

Chapter 8: The Antisocial Tendency

1. D. W. Winnicott, "The Antisocial Tendency" (orig. published 1956), in *Through Paediatrics to Psycho-analysis* (New York: Basic Books, 1975), pp. 306–15.

2. Quoted in Harry Guntrip, *Psychoanalytic Theory, Therapy, and the Self: A Basic Guide to the Human Personality in Freud, Erikson, Klein, Sullivan, Fairbairn, Hartman, Jacobson, and Winnicott* (New York: Basic Books, 1973), p. 152.

3. Winnicott, "The Antisocial Tendency."

4. Stanley Schneider and E. Rimmer, "Adoptive Parents' Hostility Toward Their Adopted Children," *Children and Youth Services Review* 6 (1984): 345–52.

5. H. J. Sants, "Genealogical Bewilderment in Children with Substitute Parents," *British Journal of Medical Psychology* 37 (1964): 133–41. See also Erik Wellisch, "Children Without Genealogy—A Problem of Adoption," correspondence, *Mental Health* 13 (1952): 41–42.

6. Adoption therapist Annette Baran suggests that the multilayered problems related to feelings of rejection, abandonment, and identity confusion due to the secrecy in the closed adoption system can, and often do, produce personality disorder. Personal communication, 1993.

7. Mary Watkins and Susan Fisher, *Talking with Young Children About Adoption* (New Haven, Conn.: Yale University Press, 1993), p. 25.

8. Luis Feder, "Adoption Trauma: Oedipus Myth/Clinical Reality," *International Journal of Psychoanalysis* 55 (1974): 491–93.

9. David Kirschner, "Antisocial Behavior in Adoptees: Patterns and Dynamics," *Child and Adolescent Social Life* 5, no. 4 (Winter 1988): 300–314; see also idem, "The Adopted Child Syndrome: Considera-

tions for Psychotherapy," *Psychotherapy in Private Practice* 8 (1990): 93–100.

10. See David Brodzinsky and Marshall Schecter, *Being Adopted, The Lifelong Search for Self* (New York: Doubleday, 1992), p. 10. The authors acknowledge that adoption is a "risk factor for having certain psychological problems, especially low self-esteem, academic problems, a range of rebellious activities known as 'acting out' behaviors: aggression, stealing, lying, hyperactivity, oppositional behavior and running away," but though they describe the same cluster of symptoms as Kirschner, they stop short of calling it a syndrome.

11. See Francine Klagsbrun, "Debunking the 'Adopted Child Syndrome,'" *Ms.,* October 1986.

12. Steven N. Nickman, "Adoptive Losses and Character Formation," *Psychoanalytic Study of the Child* 40 (1985).

13. Winnicott, "The Antisocial Tendency," pp. 310–11.

14. Ibid.

15. R. D. Laing, *The Divided Self: An Existential Study in Sanity and Madness* (London: Penguin Books, 1965).

16. "Roaming phenomenon" is from P. W. Toussieng, "Thoughts Regarding the Etiology of Psychological Difficulties in Adopted Children," *Child Welfare* 41 (1962): 59–65; "symbolic search" is from Max Frisk, "Identity Problems and Confused Conception of the Generic Ego in Adopted Children During Adolescence," *Acta Paediatrica Psychiatricia* 21 (1964):6–11.

17. Steven Greer, "Parental Loss and Attempted Suicide: A Further Report," *British Journal of Psychiatry* 112 (1966): 465–70.

18. Mi Ok Bruining, "Save a Place for Me," for Peter Young Sip Kim, Who Did Not Survive After All (June 5, 1991), in *A Chain of Life,* ed. Janine Baer (newsletter) (Berkeley, Calif., July/August 1991).

19. "Profiles of Student Life: Attitudes and Behaviors," from a study of 50,000 sixth- to twelfth-graders. Published monograph (*The Troubled Journey* [Minneapolis: Search Institute, 1990]) by Peter L. Benson, president of the Search Institute. Based on a sample of youth in primarily small towns and cities in the Midwest, this study found that teenagers who were adopted as infants are more at risk than nonadopted youth in the categories: sexually active, suicide, daily cigarette use, driving and drinking, group fighting, vandalism, and trouble with the police.

20. Edwin Shneidman, *Definition of Suicide* (New York: Wiley, 1988).

21. E. Corinne Chilstrom, *Grieving and Living Again: A Family's Experience of Tragic Loss* (Minneapolis: Augsburg Fortress, 1993).

22. Personal communication. The psychiatrist Dorothy Lewis points out that the literature on murder by juveniles is sparse. She believes chil-

dren who cross over the line to kill are different from those who commit suicide. Her research suggests that children who kill have suffered extreme abuse or a head injury in early childhood, or have a genetic inheritance that gives them a neuropsychiatric vulnerability. See Dorothy Otnow Lewis, "From Abuse to Violence: Psychophysiological Consequences of Maltreatment," *J. Am. Acad. Child Adolesc. Psychiatry* 31, no. 3 (May 1992).

23. Personal communication, 1993. See Jack Levin and James Alan Fox, *Mass Murder, America's Growing Menace* (New York: Plenum Press, 1985).

24. There are no national statistics on the number of adoptees who are serial killers, nor are such killers always identified as adopted. Adoptee serial killers, who are almost always men, invariably choose women as their victims. In addition to David Berkowitz ("Son of Sam") and Joel Rifkin ("The Ripper"), there are Joseph Kallinger ("The Philadelphia Shoemaker"), who is serving a life sentence for the 1974 murder of a nurse, his fourteen-year-old son, and a young boy; Kenneth Bianchi ("The Hillside Strangler"), who raped and strangled ten young women in the Los Angeles area over a four-month period in 1977–78; Gerald Eugene Stano, who confessed to killing forty-two women in Florida over a seven-year period, 1973–80, but was only tried for fourteen; Steve Caitlin, who is on death row in California for poisoning two of his wives and his adoptive mother in 1976–84; and Charles Albright ("the most depraved killer in Dallas history," according to the May 1993 issue of *Texas Monthly*), who was convicted in 1993 of murdering and mutilating three prostitutes, although he was suspected of killing many more.

25. David Abrahamsen, *Confessions of Son of Sam* (New York: Columbia University Press, 1985).

26. Personal communication, 1977. During the past few decades there has been a swing back to a stress on genetics over psychological or environmental influences as regards the adopted child. See Michael Bohman et al., "Predisposition to Petty Criminality in Swedish Adoptees," *Archives of General Psychiatry* 339 (November 1982); R. J. Cadoret et al., "Studies of Adoptees from Psychiatrically Disturbed Biological Parents: III. Medical Symptoms and Illnesses in Childhood and Adolescence," *American Journal of Psychiatry* 133 (1976): 1316–18; J. M. Horn, The Texas Adoption Project: "Adopted Children and Their Intellectual Resemblance to Biological and Adoptive Parents," *Child Development* 54 (1983): 268–75. It is difficult to study genetic linkage in this country because the adoption records are sealed, but the suspicion of "bad seed" is not far from public consciousness. (See cover of *New York* magazine: "The Bad Seed, Serial

Killer Joel Rifkin's Twisted World," by Jeanie Russell Kasindorf, August 9, 1993.)

27. Abrahamsen, *Confessions of Son of Sam.*

28. Leslie Walker, *Sudden Fury: A True Story of Adoption and Murder* (New York: St. Martin's Press, 1989).

29. Personal communication, 1993. See Paul Mones, *When a Child Kills, Abused Children Who Kill Their Parents* (New York: Pocket Star Books, 1991). The criminologist and psychologist Candace Skrapec points out that while adoptees do not seem to make up a significant proportion of the two hundred known serial killers, they seem to be more highly represented among those who kill their parents. Personal communication, 1993.

30. Betty Jean Lifton, "How the Adoption System Ignites a Fire," *New York Times,* March 1, 1986. DeGelleke was convicted of second-degree murder and arson. The testimony on the Adopted Child Syndrome by Kirschner and Sorosky helped him receive a minimum prison sentence.

31. See Klagsbrun, "Debunking the 'Adopted Child Syndrome,'" and William Feigelman, "Don't Stigmatize the Adopted," letter to the editor, *New York Times,* March 11, 1986. In 1988, an officer of the then National Committee for Adoption (now the National Council) cited the op-ed piece as "inflammatory." In 1993, Elizabeth Bartholet cited it in refuting the concept of a syndrome (see her *Family Bonds: Adoption and the Politics of Parenting* [Boston: Houghton Mifflin, 1993]).

32. The following list of adopted males who killed both parents came to my attention in East Coast newspapers over the past decade: Peter Zimmer, 15, Mineral Point, IA, 1983; Roger Scott Helm, Jr., 15, Glendale, AZ, 1984; Patrick DeGelleke, 14, Marion, NY, 1984; Patrick Campbell, 18, Darien, CT, 1988; Martin Tankleff, 18, Belle Terre, NY, 1991; Matthew Heikkila, 20, Basking Ridge, NJ, 1991; Daniel Kasten, 19, Lake Ronkonkoma, NY, 1990; Keith Chul Weaver, 14, Landisville, PA, 1991; Thomas Camerlengo, 26, Staten Island, NY, 1990; Steven Holmes, 19, Indianapolis, 1992; Ronald Janes, 37, Toledo, IL, 1991. In some cases, the victims included a sibling or grandparent.

It should be noted that adoptees who murder their parents are younger than the serial killers. Unlisted are a lesser number of adoptees, some female, who kill one parent, usually the adopted mother. Research studies on the influence of adoption trauma, genetics, and family environment are needed.

33. Emanuel Tanay, "Adolescents Who Kill Parents—Reactive Parricide," *Australia and New Zealand Journal of Psychiatry* 7 (1973): 263.

34. Campbell went unsentenced for two years from the time he pleaded

guilty in September 1988 to two counts of murder in exchange for a forty-five-year sentence.

35. Laing, *The Divided Self*, p. 7.

36. David Kirschner, "Understanding Adoptees Who Kill: Dissociation, Patricide and the Psychodynamics of Adoption," *International Journal of Offender Therapy and Comparative Criminology* 36, no. 4 (1992).

37. Quoted in Carolyn Colwell, *Newsday*, July 19, 1990. Tankleff was convicted of killing both his parents in their home in Belle Terre, NY. Though he pleaded not guilty after confessing to the police, he was sentenced to forty-five years.

38. Judge Michael R. Imbriani said that although the Adopted Child Syndrome is a "novel scientific theory," he would allow Kirschner's testimony because he feared a reversal by the State Supreme Court, which allows a wide latitude in death penalty cases. He said he would permit the testimony to support the defense theory that Heikkila suffered from severe emotional distress when he killed his parents, a mitigating factor that could convince the jury to spare him a death sentence. The prosecution argued that Heikkila's real motive was to steal his parents' credit cards and car to take his girlfriend out to dinner. (See *The Star-Ledger* [Newark, N.J.], January 12, 1993).

Chapter 9: The Adult Child

1. C. Alan Steed, "Children of Adoption: Are They at Greater Psychological Risk? A Critical Review of the Literature," paper, University of Minnesota Counseling and Student Personnel Program, 1989.

2. Paul Brinich, "Adoption from the Inside Out: A Psychoanalytic Perspective," in *The Psychology of Adoption*, ed. D. Brodzinsky and D. Schecter (New York: Oxford University Press, 1990), pp. 42–61.

3. Steven L. Nickman, "Adoptive Losses and Character Formation," *Psychoanalytic Study of the Child* 40 (1985).

4. Harry Guntrip, *Schizoid Phenomena, Object Relations, and the Self* (New York: International Universities Press, 1969).

5. C. G. Jung, *Essays on a Science of Mythology* (Princeton, N.J.: Princeton University Press, 1963), p. 87.

6. Gilda Frantz, "Birth's Cruel Secret / O I Am My Own Lost Mother / To My Own Sad Child," *Chiron: A Review of Jungian Analysis* (1985): 157–72. This entire issue of *Chiron* is devoted to essays on abandonment.

7. Harriet Gordon Machtiger, "Perilous Beginnings: Loss, Abandonment, and Transformation," in ibid., pp. 101–29.

8. "20/20," ABC-TV, January 1, 1987.

9. See Richard Isay, *On Being Homosexual* (New York: Farrar, Straus and Giroux, 1989); J. Michael Bailey and Richard Pillard, "A Genetic Study of Male Sexual Orientation," *Archives of General Psychiatry* 48 (1991): 1089–96 Darrell Yates Rist, "Are Homosexuals Born That Way?" *The Nation,* October 19, 1992, pp. 424–29; "The Lesbian Issue," *Essays from Signs,* ed. Estelle B. Freedman et al. (Chicago: University of Chicago Press, 1985).

10. Jung, *Essays on a Science of Mythology.*

11. Personal communication.

Chapter 10: The Call to Self

1. Jean Amery, *At the Mind's Limits* (New York: Schocken Books, 1986), p. 46.

2. A. Bartlett Giamatti, *Take Time for Paradise: Americans and Their Games* (New York: Summit Books, 1991).

3. Judith Herman, *Trauma and Recovery* (New York: Basic Books, 1992).

4. E. T. de Bianchedi et al., "Truth and Lies, Generational Transmission," colloquy, "Patrimonie génétique et droits de l'humanité," October 25, 1989. Reports from Argentina in 1993 indicate that while the younger children have adjusted quickly, some of the older teenagers have been reluctant to leave the only parents they have known. There is intense psychological pain after they are returned to their relatives, and they have difficulty coping with the destruction of the false world created by their "kidnappers." Many say they sensed there were deep unspoken secrets. Raised in tight-knit army and police communities, some of the children have strong military sympathies and are overwhelmed when they are told that their real parents were arrested and killed by the police. One psychiatrist said: "Restitution has to be painful, and the first reaction is always rejection of the biological family. But the most therapeutic thing is reality. These kids always had a sense that something was wrong in the past, and when they hear the truth they begin to make more sense of their history." One "disappeared" child, found at age twelve, said: "It was hard coming home but I've adjusted." See Nathaniel C. Nash, "Stolen Childhoods," *New York Times,* May 11, 1993.

5. Bianchedi et al., "Truth and Lies."

6. Sigmund Freud, *Moses and Monotheism,* 2d ed., vol. 23 (London: Hogarth Press), p. 20.

7. Joseph Campbell, *The Hero with a Thousand Faces* (Princeton, N.J.: Princeton University Press, 1973), Bollingen Series, p. 49.

8. Mircea Eliade, *L'Epreuve du labyrinthe* in "Narrative Time," trans.

Paul Ricoeur (Paris, 1978), p.109. (See *On Narrative,* ed. W. J. T. Mitchell [Chicago: University of Chicago Press, 1981], p. 181.)

9. Frank R. Stockton, "The Lady or the Tiger?" *Century Magazine* (1882).

10. M. Swan, *Henry James* (London: Arthur Barker, 1952), pp. 27–28.

Chapter 11: Alternate Reality

1. The term *reunioning pairs* is used by Judith Gediman and birth mother Linda Brown in their book *Birth Bond,* which is an intriguing look at reunion from the point of view of thirty birth mothers whom they interviewed (Far Hills, N.J.: New Horizon Press, 1989). See also Phyllis R. Silverman et al., "Reunions Between Adoptees and Birth Parents: The Birth Parents' Experience," *Social Work* 33, no. 6 (November–December 1988); and Lee Campbell et al., "Reunions Between Adoptees and Birth Parents: The Adoptee's Experience," *Social Work* 36, no. 4 (July 1991).

2. Clarissa Pinkola Estés, *Women Who Run with the Wolves, Myths and Stories of the Wild Woman Archetype* (New York: Ballantine Books, 1992), p. 374.

3. Jean-Paul Sartre, *Saint Genet: Actor and Martyr* (New York: Pantheon, 1963).

4. Lorraine Dusky, "The Daughter I Gave Away," *Newsweek,* March 30, 1992. See also Dusky's memoir, *Birthmark* (New York: Evans, 1979).

5. Dusky, "The Daughter I Gave Away."

Chapter 12: The Painted Bird

1. Muriel Rukeyser, personal communication, 1978. Muriel and I were also going to form the Orphanings club, open to all who wanted to join, because there are many ways to be an orphan.

2. Muriel Rukeyser, "The Speed of Darkness," *The Speed of Darkness* (New York: Random House, 1968).

3. Testimony during custody trial between Mia Farrow and Woody Allen for their biological son and two adopted children, in the State Supreme Court, *New York Newsday,* April 20, 1993.

4. Patricia Storace, "Illegitimacy," in *Heredity* (Boston: Beacon Press, 1987).

5. Luis Feder, "Adoption Trauma: Oedipus Myth/Clinical Reality," *International Journal of Psychoanalysis* 55 (1974): 491–93.

6. Mary Ann Cohen, "Patterson, April 9, 1968," unpublished manu-
    script.
7. Jerzy Kosinski, *The Painted Bird* (Boston: Houghton Mifflin, 1965).
8. See Randolph Severson, "The Primal Wound?" in his collected essays
    Adoption Philosophy and Experience (Dallas: House of Tomorrow
    Productions, 1994).

Chapter 13: The Fathered/Fatherless Self

1. Stanley Kunitz, "The Poet's Quest for the Father," *New York Times
    Book Review,* February 22, 1987.
2. Robert Bly, *Iron John, a Book About Men* (Reading, Mass.: Addison-
    Wesley, 1990), p. 121.
3. Ibid.

Chapter 14: The Found Adoptee

1. For an understanding of the birth mother experience, see Leverett
    Millen and Samuel Roll, "Solomon's Mothers: A Special Case of
    Pathological Bereavement," *American Journal of Orthopsychiatry 55,*
    no. 3 (July 1985): 411–18; Rickie Solinger, *Wake Up Little Susie, Sin-
    gle Pregnancy and Race Before* Roe v. Wade (New York: Routledge,
    1992).
2. For further exploration of this myth, see Nor Hall, *Mothers and
    Daughters, Reflections on the Archetypal Feminine* (Minneapolis:
    Rusoff Books, 1976); and C. G. Jung and C. Kerenyi, "Kore"
    (Kerenyi), in *Essays on a Science of Mythology* (Princeton, N.J.:
    Princeton University Press, 1969), Bollingen Series, pp. 101–55.
3. D. W. Winnicott, "Communicating and Not Communicating Leading
    to a Study of Certain Opposites," in *The Maturational Processes and
    the Facilitating Environment* (Madison, Wis.: International Universi-
    ties Press, 1965), p. 190.
4. Calvin A. Colarusso, "Mother, Is That You?" *Psychoanalytic Study
    of the Child* 42 (1987): 223–37.

Chapter 15: The Mark of Oedipus

1. It is possible that fathers and sons belong in this list, but I have not
    personally come across such cases.
2. It is not known where the term *genetic sexual attraction* originated.

Barbara Gonyo, a birth mother, mystified by the attraction she felt to the twenty-six-year-old son she found in 1979, first called attention to her experience in adoption circles. See her article "Genetic Sexual Attraction," *The Decree,* a quarterly of the American Adoption Congress, 4, no. 2 (1987).

3. Alexander Lowen, "The Will to Live and the Wish to Die," Monograph, The International Institute of Bioenergetic analysis, New York City (1982).

4. Carl Jung, *Symbols of Transformation, Collected Works,* vol. 5 (London: Routledge and Kegan Paul, 1956), para. 332. See also Robert Stein, *Incest and Human Love* (Dallas: Spring Publications, 1988).

5. Personal communication, 1985.

6. Richard Gardner, personal communication, 1993.

Chapter 16: The Adoption Tie

1. Nancy Newton Verrier, *The Primal Wound: Understanding the Adopted Child* (Baltimore: Gateway Press, 1993).

2. Ibid.

3. Lois Melina, personal communication, 1993. Melina is the editor of *Adopted Child,* a monthly newsletter dealing with adoption issues.

4. Jane O'Reilly, "Love, Emily," *Mirabella,* October 1991.

Chapter 17: Becoming Whole

1. "Cross Section of a House," by Gordon Matta-Clark, at the Holly Solomon Gallery. Review in the *New York Times,* December 14, 1990. Matta-Clark sawed through a vacant house in Englewood, N.J., in 1974. The reviewer pointed out that "splitting" was one of the "premier moments of a period in which anarchistic, architecturally oriented sculpture co-existed with conceptual art."

2. Joseph Campbell, *The Hero with a Thousand Faces* (Princeton, N.J.: Princeton University Press, 1949), p. 288.

3. Don Hallock, personal communication, March 1992.

4. I am grateful to my husband, Robert Jay Lifton, for coming up with the term *pre-traumatic self* when I was struggling to conceptualize the adoptee's difficulty in healing.

5. Judith Herman, *Trauma and Recovery* (New York: Basic Books, 1992).

6. Edward Lear, "The Old Man of Whitehaven," *Collected Works* (London: Gordon Press, 1973).

7. Quoted in Randolph Severson, *The Inaccessible Pinnacle, Further Essays* (Dallas: House of Tomorrow Productions, 1992), pp. 48–49.

8. Alice Miller, *Pictures of Childhood: Sixty-six Watercolors and an Essay* (New York: Farrar, Straus and Giroux, 1986).

9. Linda Kozloff, unpublished work.

10. Harold Brodkey, *The Runaway Soul* (New York: Farrar, Straus and Giroux, 1991).

11. Quotes are from personal communication with Brodkey, June 15, 1989, and from *New York Magazine,* September 19, 1988.

12. Jorge Luis Borges, *The Other Death,* quoted in Janette Turner Hospital, *Charade* (New York: Bantam, 1989).

13. Stephen W. Hawking, *A Brief History of Time, From the Big Bang to Black Holes* (New York: Bantam, 1988).

14. Stanley Kunitz, "Journal for My Daughter," *Poems of Stanley Kunitz, 1928–1978* (Boston: Little, Brown, 1979).

Index